The British Philosophy
of Administration

To my Mother and Harold

The British Philosophy of Administration

A comparison of British and American ideas
1900 – 1939

Rosamund M. Thomas, M.SOC.SC.,PH.D.

Longman
London and New York

Longman Group Limited London

Associated companies, branches and representatives throughout the world

Published in the United States of America by Longman Inc., New York

First published 1978

Library of Congress Cataloging in Publication Data
Thomas, Rosamund M
   The British philosophy of administration.

   Bibliography: p.
   Includes index.
   1. Public administration – Study and teaching –
Great Britain. 2. Public administration – Study
and teaching – United States. I. Title.
JF1338.A2T49 1977 350.000941 77 – 5938
ISBN 0-582-50124-5

Set in 10 point Garamond by Woolaston Parker Ltd, Leicester
and printed in Great Britain by Richard Clay (The Chaucer Press) Ltd, Bungay, Suffolk

Contents

v

List of Figures

List of Photographs

Preface

This book challenges the conventional wisdom surrounding the development of British administrative thought this century. The traditional wisdom is based heavily on American administrative doctrines, such as 'classical organisation theory' and 'human relations theory', which prove inadequate when compared with British administrative developments. Instead of progressing, first, from classical organisation theory and, second, to human relations theory, or from the science of administration to a preoccupation with human problems of administration, British administrative thinkers combined simultaneously these two developments into one *philosophy* of administration. This book identifies the alternative doctrines of the British Philosophy of Administration and the term 'philosophy' in this context means the unification of scientific principles with ethical ideals.

In Chapter 1, I portray the inadequacy of the conventional American doctrines in the light of the British Philosophy of Administration. In Chapter 2, I describe, in detail, the first doctrine of the British Philosophy of Administration – the fusion, as distinct from the separation, of politics and administration. In Chapter 3, I discuss the American scientific principles of POSDCORB and argue that the scientific principles underlying the British Philosophy of Administration are represented more accurately by the acronym SLOCUS than POSDCORB. Chapter 4 identifies the ethical ideals which compose the British Philosophy of Administration, including early British developments in human well-being in organisations. Chapter 5 outlines the problem of bureaucracy, which arose during this period and became entwined with the British doctrines. Finally, in Chapter 6, I draw some conclusions about the British Philosophy of Administration and illustrate the relevance of some of these administrative ideas in Britain today.

Rosamund M. Thomas
London, 1977

Acknowledgements

I should like to express my gratitude to the following persons for their support and interest in this study of British and American administrative thought. My warm thanks are extended to Mr Rod Rhodes of the University of Strathclyde and to Professor James Q. Wilson of the Department of Government, Harvard University, who provided constructive views on American administrative thought. My thanks are transmitted, also, to the United States – United Kingdom Educational Commission for the award of a Fulbright Travel Scholarship, which enabled me to visit Harvard for research purposes between 1972 and 1973.

It is with pleasure that I have corresponded with Lyndall Urwick, now living in Australia, regarding his contribution to British administrative thought and his recollections of working with Oliver Sheldon and B. Seebohm Rowntree at Rowntree and Co. Ltd, York. The highlights of our correspondence were the visits of Lt-Col. Urwick to London in 1975 and 1976, when we were able to meet personally. My further thanks are offered to Ms E. M. Mather, recently Staff Officer at Rowntree Mackintosh Ltd, York, for supplying information about Oliver Sheldon, whom she remembers from her long service with the Company, and Lyndall Urwick.

My appreciation extends to Professor Don K. Price of the John F. Kennedy School of Government, Harvard University, Dr Richard Chapman of the University of Durham, Professor David Murray of the Open University and Mr Ivor Shelley of the Royal Institute of Public Administration for their interest in the subject of this book. Finally, my thanks rest with Ms E. McCarthy who typed the manuscript and with the Institute of Local Government Studies, University of Birmingham for providing me with a base for my research activities.

We are grateful to the following for permission to reproduce copyright material: Author and Pitman Publishing Ltd. for a photograph from *Josiah Stamp: Public Servant* by J. H. Jones (Pitman Publishing Ltd.); author and Pitman Publishing Ltd. for a drawing from *The Philosophy of Management* by O. Sheldon (Pitman Publishing Ltd.); the author and Hodder and Stoughton Ltd. for a photograph from *Viscount Haldane: an autobiography* by Viscount Haldane (Hodder and Stoughton Ltd.). We regret that we have been unable to trace the copyright holder of the figure from *Red Tape*, January 1912; the figure from Gulick and Urwick (eds.), *Papers on the Science of Administration*; the photographs of William Henry Beveridge and Graham Wallas.

1

2

3

4

5   6

1. Lt. Col. Lyndall Urwick
2. Richard Burdon Haldane, Viscount Haldane
3. Professor Graham Wallas
4. William Henry Beveridge, Baron Beveridge
5. Josiah Charles Stamp, 1st Baron Stamp
6. Oliver Sheldon

Introduction

Traditionally, the Englishman has tended to think that there are many problems which are best solved by submitting them to the common-sense judgment of fair-minded laymen instead of assuming, as has been increasingly fashionable in the United States during the past thirty years or so, that most matters are better disposed of by experts. In fact, in America a whole school of thought has been developed around this latter viewpoint and it goes under the general rubric of the *computer-behavioral* school. The sticky problems of government and the economy are so complicated and tough, it is argued, that only a rigorous gathering of facts and their careful sifting into priorities and strategies has any chance of solving problems such as inflation – depression and organization at the top of government or business. If the democracies are not to be outmaneuvered by the totalitarians, it is held, we must find ways of governing the country by brains-trusters who are in a position to issue orders to administrators who as technicians will follow the script faithfully.

Those who have taken the British view, in contrast, have preferred to develop a philosophy which represents their view of a way of life. Theirs might be called the *cultural-humanistic* approach to reality. They hold that, although there is no general statement which it is possible to make without exception, there are certain overriding principles, or ideals, which can be ascertained from a study of history and in a careful appraisal of the common people's values and basic instincts. The success of this approach depends upon enough citizens and enough administrators having enough comprehension of principle, or ideal, to make their own syntheses and to act decisively when the chips are down. Theirs has been a liberal view. It has trusted the democracy and distrusted the expert. It has placed confidence in reserved power and not in concentrated power. It has believed in improvisation and self-reliance. It has trusted character and honor more than technique. In the eyes of the rigorous, this British view has been nothing more than 'muddling-through' – or the cult of the privileged and well-born – and hence is dated and likely to be outgrown as experts come to be appreciated more than gentlemanly codes.

From the standpoint of political philosophy in the historical-generic sense, the reconciliation of these two contrasting viewpoints takes this form: the citizen must be protected from arbitrary exertions of the awesome power of modern government, nor can the citizen survive and prosper unless the government is able to govern and govern well. Brains-trusting under any name is a form of privilege. But, governing by philosophical grasp is under the stern necessity to make government work and to be sufficiently successful to supply goods and services as effectively as in a more rigorously controlled system.

The case for public administration to be considered a branch of philosophy was strongly stated by Lord Haldane in the early years of the Royal Institute of Public Administration. In his opening speech, as reported in the *Journal of Public Administration*, Vol I, 1923, the Institute's first President argued that public administration is both a science and an art, that the main appeal of the public service career is performing service to the public, and the greatest challenge to the individual administrator is to act on the basis of a set of first principles but seek constantly to develop initiatives that will allow society to adjust to constantly changing problems and tensions. What must be sought is efficiency and economy, but these must be measured in terms of human consequences as well as of their effect upon the economy. Administration is a product of the development of civilization. We must act like the captains of industry, said Lord Haldane, but without relying solely or even mainly on the profit motive, as they do, because there are powerful incentives such as patriotism and honor which can be made to have an even greater appeal.

My appreciation of the men and issues Dr Thomas discusses is influenced primarily by a friendship I formed with Sir Henry Bunbury around 1931, when the Royal Institute of Public Administration was still in its infancy. Bunbury was Comptroller General of the British Post Office and one of the founders of the Institute. I was writing a book on British public utilities and especially the newly launched public corporation, such as the London Passenger Transport Board and the BBC, and this was Bunbury's field of expertise. In short, he introduced me to most of those whom Dr Thomas writes about because they were directly engaged in the field of my study. His testimony was that all of the men who had established the British public administration profession, particularly the practising administrators, were pretty much out of the same mould. They believed in first principles and derived them to a large extent from the moral philosophy tradition. Administrators are a part of culture and of leadership. Their distinctiveness comes from the fact that they are servants and yet they have a central position in holding the country together and helping it to find its desired place in the sun. They must be close to the economy, to labor, agriculture and all classes. But, they should never be out front in the political sense of that term and they should always be loyal. He said that most of these men were of liberal persuasion in the philosophical-historical meaning of that term, although they invariably chose to keep their own party preferences to themselves.

Bunbury's big problem at that time was to stop the losses of the telegraph service. I asked him who had given him the job and he replied that he had volunteered to undertake it. 'What did you do?', I asked. 'I began having lunch regularly with the head of the telephone service and the telegraph service', both of which were under the Post Office. 'Can you solve the problem?' 'Yes, I think so', he grinned, 'in fact we're about to tell the Postmaster General what we propose to do.' 'Will he do it?' 'Yes, I think so', said Sir Henry, 'because we've worked it out pretty thoroughly.' 'And you did all this at lunch?' 'Yes, the Liberal Club, every day.'

The first characteristic of these administrators was responsibility: they had initiative as well as accountability. The second was hard-headedness. Some of them, like Bunbury and Stamp, were primarily finance men. Bunbury, for example, was an avid reader of company reports. And what is more he knew the individuals who ran the large corporations exceedingly well. Once, for example – several years after my first acquaintance with him – I made a study, which Bunbury arranged, of Marks and Spencer, the mercantile chain store. Soon, I discovered he knew almost as much about what was going on in the company as top management did itself. Nothing ivory tower about these men.

Another characteristic was balance. This took many forms. The government should not overload itself and what it does it should do well. The way to control legal monopolies is not to regulate them to death because this will only kill their innovativeness and managerial spirit. Instead, the best way is to write the social controls into the charter itself, thus avoiding possible excesses and leaving the internal management to the paid executives.

Another characteristic was planning. Sir Henry wrote on this subject and traveled far afield to places such as Turkey and the United States to study planning. But all the time he was afraid of making it a fetish, something to be idolized, as an ideologue might. Most of these men were institutional economists and therefore thought of planning as only one among many elements of administration to be balanced into a working whole. Plan only what you need to plan, nothing more, Bunbury used to say. The better your managers, the more planning they will do for themselves; the poorer they are the more planning someone else will have to do – and the chances are it will not be done as well.

Another universal characteristic was a belief in people. Although an economist-financier, Bunbury's main interest was in people, not balance-sheets. These British career civil servants were all instinctively teachers. They studied people and were interested in them. They inspired people and learned from them. There was nothing stuffy or upstage about any of them. And yet they were hard-headed and businesslike at all times and never developed social affectations.

It is a mistake, I think, to characterize all of these top administrators as a social class, these Oxford and Cambridge men who ran the country through the Higher Civil Service during the period before and after the two world wars. They were not a class, unless one means by that that they had the code of the gentleman. But, like their counterparts in the United States and in other countries, this trait of character and personality has no essential tie to a particular class because it is found at all economic and social levels. They believed in first principles because they were tough-minded students. They preferred principle to dogma, which is the alternative, because they knew from reading history that dogma and good administration do not mix. Administration is cultural, philosophical. It is scientific only in the sense that, like many other things, it can be patiently studied in a cause-and-effect way to see what different things happen when different factors are emphasized or neglected.

Regrettably, academic philosophers seem to think that labels have to be attached to ideas before they are respectable. This is almost invariably a disservice. It is one thing to study the history of ideas, which is useful, and quite another to label a set of ideas which frequently has no other result than to damn it for a considerable number of people. This feeling about words and their improper use was strong among Bunbury, Haldane and their associates. They did not like to be called Utilitarians, for example, although they acknowledged their debt to the two Mills and to Jeremy Bentham. Some of them had a strong feeling for the Christian objectives of socialism and, yet, they resented being called Fabians. They were equally certain that they were not capitalists in the Ricardian connotation of that term, namely one who maximizes his profit opportunity so long as he stays within the law. All had a strong feeling for the organic nature of the economy and the fact that every event in one part of it is inevitably registered in every other part. The ideal was to encourage common citizens to govern themselves by learning as much as their leaders, and applying it in their daily pursuits.

It is no accident that education was Haldane's passion throughout life – that emphasis was central to his philosophy.

A clear difference between the British and American ideas of administration is reflected in the preference each country has given to its favored term. Most Americans feel that the term 'management' is preferable to 'administration'. They will tell you that 'management' is a dynamic-sounding word, whereas 'administration' is wooden. 'Management' stresses the total number of ingredients involved in getting a job done: 'administration' suggests the top layer only. Once when I was speaking to a meeting of businessmen in Puerto Rico I had a good chance to discover how strongly Americans feel about this issue. I was discussing my book, *Administrative Vitality* (a large part of which was written in England, incidentally), when the presiding officer said, 'It's too bad you didn't call your book "Management Vitality" – if you had I predict it would have become a best-seller.'

How Bunbury dealt with this issue is rather interesting. He admitted that administration does connote the top level of managers, like the Administrative Class of which he was a member, but he argued that the term 'administration' suggests principle and what executives do, whereas 'management' implies manipulation and concentration of authority. To him, management was something of an impersonal process, whereas administration respects the rights and initiatives of others. He was well aware of the fact that in American government, as contrasted with American business, the term 'administration' was used as consistently as in England, but he explained this on historical grounds. Woodrow Wilson, who opened up the field of public administration in the United States in 1882, was under the English influence. So was W. F. Willoughby, another early pioneer. And so likewise was Frank J. Goodnow, although for a different reason: he developed the field of administrative law, a term which was well established in Germany and France, the two countries where he studied. Later, when Charles A. Beard's influence on municipal government began to be felt, around 1906–08, and the municipal reform movement drew in a large number of scholars such as Luther Gulick, John Fairlie, Frederick Davenport, William Mosher and James Garner, the British connection was already established. The key word was 'administration'. It therefore fell to Frederick Taylor and his disciples, who came to be known as the scientific managers, to give currency to the term 'management' and its concepts which American business has relied upon ever since: Dr Thomas explains all of this very well in her opening chapter.

But to keep the record clear, it must be recognized that the divergences to which Dr Thomas calls attention and develops skilfully were a slightly later development and reached their apogee after the Second World War, when American scholarship in the public sector seemed determined to follow faithfully the precepts and methods of physical science, theoretical economics and behavioral psychology. Once this phase started, there was no room, it was held, for principles and philosophy, which were ridiculed as so many 'proverbs'. The behavioral crusade clearly added new dimensions to the study of administration, and for that we may be grateful, but it also resulted in an obfuscation of enduring realities in the administrative process which it has taken some time to rectify. In fact, the pendulum has swung so far back in the United States that some of the younger writers now seem to be content to define administration as sentiment and feeling, viewing hierarchy and organization as natural enemies to be captured and tamed.

The thing that always impressed me about Sir Henry Bunbury and his contemporaries was their sweet reasonableness. They were wise without being superior. 'Of course,' said Bunbury, 'the Germans are good administrators: how could they be otherwise when they are so systematic.' But system inevitably results in a rigid and unimaginative bureaucracy, and when this happens innovation and adjustment to change are an uphill fight. Equally, when the Americans become mad about science, simply because it has brought others prestige, they run the risk of sacrificing their role as shapers of policy. The more they depoliticize themselves, the less they know about the political process and the substantive fields of government and hence in effect they abdicate what is perhaps the most valuable part of their social responsibility. The nation suffers. And as the needed leadership of the career official is downgraded, the country tends to tear itself apart because of the ungoverned struggles of pressure groups, politicians and spellbinders.

Historically, the British and American traditions of administration have developed from some of the same sources, coming down through the ideas and writings of men like Plato, Aristotle, Cicero, Justinian, Rousseau, Locke, Hume and John Stuart Mill. The moral philosophy tradition has existed in both countries, being expressed by American writers like Jefferson, Emerson and Whitman and reflected in the lives of many public leaders in the two countries. Oliver Franks, Alexander Cairncross, or Adlai Stevenson in the United States, are recent examples of such leaders. Moreover, this tradition is also found strongly represented in certain giant corporations in the United States, the prime example being the world's largest and richest corporation, the American Telephone and Telegraph Company, which survived and prospered, its historians tell us, because it had a consciously held philosophy called that of 'New England gentlemen', who to all intents and purposes were as English as their forebears. This philosophy, as expounded by Walter Gifford and Arthur Page, held that power corrupts and that the antidote is service, that the justification of price is service and efficiency, that breach of trust is never forgotten by the public, and that a meritocracy is the only sure road to public confidence and the firm's survival. Having studied both, I see no essential difference between this tradition and that of the British leaders Dr Thomas deals with in her book.

But what of the future? Which view of administration is likely to win out? The view of those who define administration as intelligence-gathering and policy decision at high levels and foresee a universe divided into two classes: a small group of analysts surrounding the chief executive, supported by a larger number of managers whose forte is technique based upon technology. The first group must have the prescience of the computer, the latter the precision of a machine. The attempted justification for this solution is that life is increasingly complex: only those trained to handle such analyses and correlations can hope to deal successfully with them – and such experts are few in number. But, this so-called solution has two weaknesses that are likely to make it unworkable in the long run: a good administrator is not content to be treated like a machine without discretion, even when his income seemingly depends upon his acceptance of such a role. And, secondly, the human relations and values in such a system are abysmal. Ants are interesting creatures, but not many humans desire to emulate them.

The alternative is to perfect the ideas of the group of men about whom Dr Thomas writes, and I think this is more likely the way both countries will go. The thing that was so good about their ideas was that no important factor was neglected. They were not amateurs in skill: they were clearly professionals. But they were laymen in outlook and in personality and attitude. For example, as Messrs Schwartz and Wade point out in their book, *Legal Control of Government Administration* (1972), the British practice often is to use laymen to do the work that in the United States is done by judges, the reason being that laymen are assumed to have common sense and attitudes which the administrative process needs if it is to be both efficient and palatable to the public. In effect, this is diabolically clever. It prevents an enraged citizenry rising up at some time in the future and hanging bureaucrats from lamp posts. And, secondly, it does a great deal to educate the public concerning the difficulties of governmental administration that citizens characteristically grumble about.

Sir Henry Bunbury, Lord Haldane and their contemporaries subscribed to Leon Duguit's aphorism, 'The very purpose of administration is to get things done'. Believing this strongly, they looked upon their role as that of initiating and consummating. The dichotomy between ivory tower decision and low-grade execution did not appeal to them. It was not realistic. They knew that the only way to get motivated administrators is to give them a mandate allowing them to deliver a finished product. Too many levels of organization only add to problems of communication, teamwork and drive. The worst government is a stalemate. Sharply defined roles that are never synthesized are the means of assuring such stagnation.

Small wonder, then, that Sir Henry used to tell me, 'Frankly, I think that we have more administrators that you and I would call statesmanlike, than you do. But, equally, I believe that since you are a frontier people and the rough-and-ready type, you have a larger proportion of action-oriented line executives than we do.' What he meant, of course, was program directors, bureau chiefs, those who were called the Executive Class in Britain before that designation was folded into a larger category. Bunbury thought that the ideal administrator should do everything as part of a rounded jurisdiction – he should plan, organize, choose between rival means of accomplishment, and evaluate his own results before someone else had a crack at it. His administrator was a whole person. He had to be integrated in order to succeed in his challenge. And being an integrated person he felt challenged and satisfied at the same time.

We shall have computers, of course, and they will be useful so long as we do not worship them and then abdicate. Likewise, we shall have policy advisers and brains-trusters, and they are useful, too, if not allowed to lord it over those who have jobs to do. But what we need most is administrators, people who can do what Duguit suggested, deliver a finished product. Communists are learning that they need such persons as much as capitalists do. The key feature of a good administrator is wisdom combined with energy. Dr Thomas digs deeply into this question and sets forth her findings brilliantly and in good balance.

Marshall E. Dimock
Bethel, Vermont

Chapter 1

The British Philosophy
of Administration

*Lord Haldane ... his most abiding interests as a public man ... lay
in the fields of higher education and administration. These
interests were twin brothers born as the practical embodiment of
his philosophic mind.*[1]

Sir H. F. Heath

*... the term 'philosophy' has been introduced into the title of this
book ... It demands of us whether we are conducting our practice
according to any principles ... or merely snatching at the floating
straws which pass ... Have we linked all our new developments to
some fundamental conviction and reviewed them in the light of
some ultimate purpose?*[2]

O. Sheldon

For several decades, British administrative thinkers have accepted with
little challenge the relevance to their own administrative history of
certain American doctrines. Some of the conventional American
doctrines are associated more recognisably with *public* administration,
as in the case of the traditional politics –administration dichotomy
advocated by Woodrow Wilson while others derive to a large extent
from *business* administration, such as 'classical organisation theory'
and 'human relations theory'. Such doctrines are not relevant to an
understanding of the development of British administrative thought.
This book seeks to reinstate the distinctively British nature of the
development of administrative thought in this country.

Classical organisation theory was the name given by H. A. Simon to
traditional twentieth-century administrative theories and it usually
embraces the contributions of F. W. Taylor and the scientific
management school, Fayol, Mooney, Gulick and Urwick.[3] Henri Fayol
was French and Lyndall Urwick was British, but their names were

1. Sir H. F. Heath, 'Lord Haldane: his influence on higher education and on
administration', *Public Administration*, Vol. VI, 1928, 350.
2. O. Sheldon, *The Philosophy of Management* (London) 1923. Reprinted edn 1930, p.x.
3. The contributors included in classical organisation theory vary slightly according to
the author describing the theory. For example, V. Subramaniam excludes Max Weber,
but D. Katz and R. L. Kahn include Weber. See V. Subramaniam, 'The classical
organization theory and its critics', *Public Administration*, Vol. 44, Winter 1966,
435–46, and D. Katz and R. L. Kahn, *The Social Psychology of Organizations* (New
York) 1966, pp. 71–109.

linked with those of Americans under the title classical organisation theory because they were seen to promote points in common. Firstly, these men all tended to view the organisation as a machine, even though it consists of people, and they implied that just as a machine is built by given sets of specifications for accomplishing a task, so an organisation can be constructed according to a blueprint. Classical organisation theory, then, centres upon the formal structure of an organisation and because of this machine-like approach to the formal structure, it is known alternatively as 'machine theory' or 'formal organisation theory'. Secondly, the classical theorists all promoted scientific principles of administration. Although possessing this feature in common, they approached the search for principles in different ways. For example, Taylor undertook more measuring and experimentation in his quest for principles than Fayol or Gulick, who drew more directly on their experience of administration – and the specific principles they formulated differed. Even so, the acronym POSDCORB has been taken as the summary of the principles – namely, Planning, Organising, Staffing, Directing, Coordinating, Reporting and Budgeting.[4] There may be some variations in the literature on classical organisation theory but, despite these differences, there has been widespread acceptance in America and other countries of classical organisation theory as the foundation of twentieth-century administrative thought.

By the late 1920s, experiments had commenced in the United States into the *human* rather than the *machine* elements of the organisation, and the results led to the development of a theory of human relations. The experiments took place principally at the Hawthorne plant of the Western Electric Company, Chicago. The Hawthorne experiments, in addition to highlighting the human problems and needs of employees, showed that informal organisation, or the network of personal and social relations which arise spontaneously between work colleagues, exists within the formal organisation. Since human relations theory draws attention to the informal structure of organisation, it is often called 'informal organisation theory'. As with classical organisation theory, there are variants in the writing,[5] but these mild divergences

4. This acronym is commonly associated with L. Gulick's paper 'Notes on the theory of organization', in *Papers on the Science of Administration*, ed. by L. Gulick and L. Urwick (New York) 1937, pp. 13–15. Gulick prepared his paper originally in 1936 as a memorandum for the President's Committee on Administrative Management.
5. For example, F. J. Roethlisberger and W. J. Dickson have provided a chronological account of the Hawthorne experiments, whereas K. Davis has paid more attention to analysing the role of informal groups and informal leaders within organisations. See F. J. Roethlisberger and W. J. Dickson, *Management and the Worker* (Cambridge, Mass.) 1939. Reprinted edn 1964. See also K. Davis, *Human Relations at Work: The Dynamics of Organizational Behavior* (New York) 1957. Third edn 1967.

have not undermined the position of classical organisation theory and human relations theory as major developments in American administrative thought for the period 1900–39 – developments followed in the post-Second World War era by the emergence of 'decision-making theory' and 'systems theory'.[6]

More recently in the 1970s, British academics have argued that some of the historical American wisdom is now out of date or inadequate in the British context. They have sought to build up a definite body of British administrative thought, but the results have not been wholly satisfactory. Conventional American wisdom often reappears in their works as an important part of the history of British administrative thought. For example, R. J. S. Baker has retained the conventional categories of classical organisation theory and human relations theory as the basis for his discussion about the nature of British public administration. And, although he has included the work of the Haldane Committee and other British pioneers briefly in these two broad categories, his book claims to have found no adequate theory of public administration in Britain.[7] His claim is understandable, for certainly in the period 1900–39, no one 'theory' of British public or business administration existed, based – as the term 'theory' suggests – exclusively on identifiable and tested principles. Rather, there was a 'philosophy' of administration stemming from the combination of science *with* ethics and it is from this base that British administrative thought developed. Yet, in the absence of a British *theory* of public administration, Baker has provided no alternative *philosophy* of administration.[8]

Other academics in the 1970s have offered fresh insights into British administrative thought. P. Self has challenged certain American conventions, such as the politics –administration dichotomy and has set administrative theory in its political environment.[9] Another British scholar, M. J. Hill, has applied knowledge of modern sociology to public administration but, although the administrative theories he has

6. For a guide to 'decision-making theory' and 'systems theory', see R. A. W. Rhodes, *An Introduction to Organisation Theory* (London) 1972, pp. 30–47. See also F. E. Emery, ed., *Systems Thinking* (London) 1969.

7. R. J. S. Baker, *Administrative Theory and Public Administration* (London) 1972.

8. To an extent this science–ethics combination has been recognised in the past as the science–art combination; for example, see R. J. S. Baker, op. cit., pp. 188–93. However, the science–ethics base is more accurate, since the term 'ethics' was used more frequently than 'art' during the period 1900–39. Although Baker has drawn attention to the science–art combination, he did not go further in developing the British Philosophy of Administration.

9. P. Self, *Administrative Theories and Politics* (London) 1972, pp. 48–52 and 149–91.

adopted include references to British developments, he has constructed no satisfactory basis which permits a systematic challenge to conventional American doctrines.[10] Finally, A. Dunsire has supplied a thorough study of the term 'administration'. Yet, he still accepts certain American administrative developments, such as scientific management and the POSDCORB principles, without enquiring into the extent to which they genuinely apply to the history of British administrative thought.[11] Despite the usefulness of the foregoing contributions, no clear picture of British administrative thought emerges which enables a detailed challenge to be made to the importance of early twentieth-century American doctrines within the British context.

This book contests the conventional wisdom surrounding the development of British administrative thought, suggesting that the experience of the United States is less applicable to the history of British administrative thought than academic works purport. We argue that between 1900 and 1939 Britain was developing her own characteristic doctrines and the purpose of this study is to identify and describe the British Philosophy of Administration 1900–39. We concentrate on this period because conventional American wisdom is used most markedly for this era, in the absence of the British Philosophy of Administration. The term 'Philosophy' has been explained as the unification of science with ethics, but as an essential first step the word 'Administration' is defined. Many nuances of meaning have been attached to the word 'Administration' as Dunsire has noted,[12] but the one this study adopts is the 'central doctrines, or ideas, concerning the activity of conducting public and business affairs'. We restrict the doctrines to the Civil Service and industry because the British Philosophy of Administration focused particularly on these areas and we exclude, for example, local government and administration relating to the Dominions and Colonies. We identify the leading contributors to the British Philosophy of Administration as: (1) Richard Haldane (Viscount Haldane); (2) Graham Wallas; (3) William Beveridge (Baron Beveridge); (4) Oliver Sheldon; (5) Lyndall Urwick (Lt-Col.); and (6) Josiah Stamp (Baron Stamp) and they are introduced in further detail later in this chapter.[13] What is crucial about their

10. M. J. Hill, *The Sociology of Public Administration* (London,) 1972, pp. 15–60.
11. A. Dunsire, *Administration: The Word and the Science* (London) 1973, pp. 91–7.
12. Dunsire has distinguished fifteen meanings of the word 'administration', see A. Dunsire, op. cit., particularly pp. 228–9. However, none of his definitions accurately describes the doctrines composing the British Philosophy of Administration 1900–39, which emanated from *individual* pioneers and had not been welded together to form a positive *discipline* as, for example, his definition No. 15 suggests.
13. See also Appendix for details of these six administrative pioneers.

pioneering contribution is that it does not yield the two separate categories of classical organisation theory and human relations theory. Instead, these two developments which evolved *separately* in the United States developed *simultaneously* in Britain, so that the two categories in American administrative thought are replaced by the one British Philosophy of Administration. Although other doctrines existed in Britain between 1900 and 1939, we maintain that this Philosophy of Administration was the dominant theme of the period. This chapter sets out in more detail the central doctrines of American administrative thought and challenges their relevance to the understanding of British administrative thought. This negative task of challenge is followed by the positive task of establishing the doctrines found to underlie the British Philosophy of Administration. These alternative doctrines then form the basis for the ensuing chapters of this book.

1. The traditional American doctrines of administration

The British Philosophy of Administration 1900–39 developed from knowledge and thought about public and business administration and, therefore, it is convenient for discussion to amalgamate the main doctrines of American public and business administration for the same period. A basic framework containing the central doctrines of American *public* administration prior to 1940 has been supplied by D. Waldo.[14] To this framework, we add the *business* discoveries inherent in classical organisation theory and human relations theory. This amalgamation of doctrines not only provides a useful comparative device but it is also more accurate because scientific management and human relations, although originally developed in industry, strongly influenced the doctrines and practice of American public administration.[15]

Waldo has identified four central doctrines of American public administration prior to 1940 and he has incorporated the influence of scientific management within these doctrines. However, he excluded human relations theory, reserving it for the post-1940 era. Yet, the

14. D. Waldo, *The Study of Public Administration* (New York) 1955, pp. 40–2.
15. For reference to the influence of scientific management upon American public administration see, for example, L. D. White *Introduction to the Study of Public Administration* (New York) 1926, pp. 12–13.

American doctrine of human relations began to take shape from the late 1920s and, although it represents a definite move away from the science of administration to the study of human problems, it should be included in the earlier period. Accordingly, we place it as a fifth doctrine but recognise it as a separate development in American administrative thought. The essential American doctrines for the period 1900–39 can now be summarised as follows:

American doctrines

Development 1

1. Government consists of two separate processes; namely, politics and administration.

2. Administration can be made into a science. Indeed, the science of administration necessitates its independence from politics.

3. The scientific study of administration leads to the discovery of principles of administration analogous to the principles or laws of the physical sciences.

4. The principles of administration determine the way in which the goals of economy and efficiency can be realised.

Development 2

5. The human element in administration is as important as the science of administration.

The relevance of each of these traditional American doctrines to the emergence of the British Philosophy of Administration will now be challenged.

1.1. Government consists of two separate processes; namely, politics and administration

The assertion that politics and administration are separate processes did not figure prominently in the British Philosophy of Administration. Rather, politics and constitutional issues were regarded as being fused with administration instead of separate from it. The reasons for this tendency relate to the different governmental systems operating in Britain and the United States. Several contrasts are discernible between the systems of government in the two countries and four differences can be singled out as having shaped the evolution of the Civil Service and attitudes towards administration in both countries. Firstly, the constitution of the United

6

States, is *written* whereas the British constitution, although written down, is based on a set of *unwritten* conventions.[16] As a result, the British constitution has been interpreted as a more flexible and changing format for government than its counterpart in the United States. The British constitution slowly but continually *evolves* to suit the changing circumstances of government. Recognition of this fact between 1900 and 1939 accounts for why it was considered unrealistic to divorce political and constitutional factors from administration, since the former were seen to reverberate upon administration. For example, it was pointed out that the nature of the British constitution is not to circumscribe matters with rules but to rely upon the more elastic safeguard of taking advice. Ministers advise the Sovereign but they, in turn, are advised by senior civil servants – thus the latter acquire a constitutional as well as an administrative role in British government.[17] Because of the impingement of constitutional and political matters upon administration, contributors to the British Philosophy of Administration argued that the study of administration should include them.

Secondly, the governments of Britain and the United States had very different experiences in combating political corruption and influence. In Britain, the Northcote–Trevelyan Report of 1854, which was put into operation by Gladstone in 1870, made important strides towards replacing political appointments to the Civil Service by the system of competitive examination.[18] In addition, British civil servants adhered to the convention of political neutrality whereby they do not participate actively in party politics,[19] but serve their political –executive chiefs – the Ministers – with equal loyalty whether their policies represent Labour, Conservative or Liberal ideology. In the United States, the same results in freeing administration from political corruption and the same convention of political neutrality did not emerge. Although the Pendleton Act was passed in 1883, from which the present federal Civil

16. Finer suggests that it is more accurate today to refer to the British constitution as 'uncodified' rather than 'unwritten'. His reason is that the British constitution is written down in a variety of sources, but it is the set of usages (i.e. the conventions) which are neither written down nor codified. However, we have retained the old-fashioned word 'unwritten' because it was used widely during the period 1900–39. See S. E. Finer, *Comparative Government* (London) 1970, pp. 146–7.
17. See R. B. Haldane, 'The constitutional evolution of the Civil Service' *Journal of Public Administration*, Vol. II, 1924, 9–13. See also Ch. 2, section 1.
18. See H. J. Laski, 'Government', *Encylopaedia of the Social Sciences*, Vol. VII, 1932, 23. See also R. A. Chapman, *The Higher Civil Service in Britain* (London) 1970, pp. 8–36, for further details of the Northcote-Trevelyan proposals.
19. The convention of political neutrality grew up in Britain as a result of rules preventing the civil servant from combining a career in the Civil Service with a political career. See H. Finer, *The British Civil Service*, (London) 1937, pp. 201–2.

7

Service merit system has developed,[20] the political manipulation of offices continued on a greater scale in American government. Even as late as 1937, the number of political appointments to the federal Civil Service far exceeded those in the British Civil Service and it became the responsibility of the President's Committee on Administrative Management to suggest that more posts should be released from political loyalties and converted into merit appointments.[21] The fact that Britain faced less of a threat from the partisan spoils system and abided by the convention of political neutrality meant that there was less danger to administration from political influence and less need to seek to divorce administration from politics.

A third difference between the two governments lies in the British Cabinet system *vis-à-vis* the American Presidential system. Within the Cabinet system, a final statement of policy from the executive does not rest with the Prime Minister but with the Cabinet as a collective body. This is not the case in the American Presidential system, where Cabinet functioning is not a pooling of minds in the British sense. Instead the President obtains opinions in Cabinet discussions in order to clarify his own mind, rather than to seek a collective decision.[22] In Britain between 1900 and 1939, the effect on public administration of collective responsibility and concerted thought by the Cabinet was reflected in the recommendations to reform public administration. For example, the Haldane Committee (1918) referred to the Cabinet and its methods of making policy decisions and relaying them to the Civil Service in its proposals to reform the administrative machinery of government.[23] It was, then, partly because of the collective responsibility and concerted decision-making of the British Cabinet that British administrative thinkers linked administrative matters with political ones.

A final governmental distinction which has shaped the development

20. See F. C. Mosher et al., *Watergate: Implications for Responsible Government* (New York) 1974, p. 71.
21. *Administrative Management in the Government of the United States: Report of the President's Committee on Administrative Management* (Washington) 1937, pp. 7–13. This Committee was also known as 'the Brownlow Committee' after its Chairman, Louis Brownlow.
22. Differences between the British Cabinet system of government and the American Presidential system have been dealt with by H. J. Laski, *The American Presidency* (New York) 1940, pp. 70–110; and in 'The Price–Laski debate on the Presidential system', *Selected Readings for Government 1a* (Cambridge, Mass.) 1961, pp. 166–203. This spirited debate between D. K. Price and H. J. Laski was first published as 'The Parliamentary and Presidential systems', *Public Administration Review*, Vol. III, No. 4, Autumn 1943, 317–34 and Vol. IV, No. 4, Autumn 1944, 347–63.
23. Ministry of Reconstruction, *Report of the Machinery of Government Committee* (London) 1918, pp. 4–6. See also Ch. 3, p. 120.

of public administration is the fusion of executive and legislative institutions in Britain and their separation in the United States. Britain did not develop a separation of powers of the type conceived by Montesquieu whereby the three institutions of government – the executive, the legislature and the judiciary – are rigidly distinct.[24] By contrast, in the United States the separation of powers created distinct legislative and executive institutions, so that the leaders of the majority party in the legislature are not at the same time heads of the executive departments collectively responsible in the legislature for the conduct of government.[25] This interconnection of executive and legislative institutions in Britain has caused certain repercussions for public administration. British Ministers possess a dual political–executive responsibility which means that they are able to remain in power only as long as they obtain support from Parliament for their policies and administrative performance. This political–executive role of British Ministers has conditioned public administration in a manner unknown in the United States. For example, Ministers have to be prepared to answer questions in Parliament about the administration of their executive departments. Between 1900 and 1939, this risk of Parliamentary questions caused, and still causes today, civil servants to conduct their work with *caution* so as to avoid sensitive problem areas which might provoke embarrassing Parliamentary questions.[26] This caution can be overdeveloped as D. K. Price has warned, when pointing out that Americans for so long viewed the British Civil Service as an example of impartiality while reproaching themselves for partisan patronage that they tended to overlook this weakness in the British system.[27]

These four major differences between British and American

24. For a brief analysis of the theory of the separation of powers put forward by Montesquieu and the latter's misinterpretation of the British constitution, see *Committee on Ministers' Powers Report* (London) 1932. Reprinted edn 1972, pp. 8–9.

25. In the United States, the legislative and executive institutions are separate. The President and his Cabinet do not participate directly in the work of Congress; consequently, the President is never master of Congress. The situation is further complicated by the fact that the President (i.e. the Chief Executive) may not be of the same political party as that in control of one or both of the Houses of Congress. In Britain, by contrast, the executive and legislature work in harmony, since the same political party is always in control of both. H. J. Laski, *American Presidency*, pp. 111–16.

26. A personal account of the problems facing British Ministers on account of their dual political–executive responsibility in the period up to 1939 has been given by H. E. Dale, *The Higher Civil Service of Great Britain* (London) 1941, for example p. 115.

27. D. K. Price, 'Price–Laski debate', op. cit., 174–5.

government help to explain why contributors to the British Philosophy of Administration promoted alternative views to the politics – administration dichotomy readily accepted in the United States between 1900 and 1939. Progressing now from the politics–administration dichotomy, the second American doctrine is disembodied.

1.2. Administration can be made into a science. Indeed, the science of administration necessitates its independence from politics

The doctrine that administration can be made into a science was popular in the United States during the period 1900–39. In the sphere of public administration this doctrine gained impetus from Woodrow Wilson's essay (1887),[28] since he stressed that administration as a separate field of study should be treated as a science. So far, he argued, American writers had not contributed to the science of administration. It had developed principally in Europe in those countries which had experienced absolute rule – namely, Germany and France. Wilson briefly traced the effect of absolute rule in these two countries to illustrate how it had led to administrative reform. In Prussia, Frederick the Great, although a stern and masterful ruler, had sought to reorganise the public service for the benefit of the public. His no less absolute successor Frederick William III advanced this administrative work still further by planning some of the broader structural features which improved the form of Prussian administration. Even in France after the Revolution when Napoleon succeeded the monarchs of France, his power had been so unlimited that absolutism had been interrupted rather than destroyed and Napoleon was able to carry out immense administrative reforms with a view to perfecting the civil machinery.

The United States, by contrast, was a new country whose government had been based on liberal principles from the start and it is more difficult for democracy to organise administration than for monarchy, principally because in a democracy public opinion constitutes a 'multitudinous' monarch of differing opinions and administrative reform becomes a matter of slow compromise. A 'single' monarch, on the other hand, is able to decide upon a plan and carry it out according to his sole opinion, without compromise. Absolutism was not desirable for the sake of gaining administrative improvements, Wilson maintained, but nevertheless Britain and the United States had

---

28. W. Wilson, 'The study of administration' reprinted in *Public Administration and Policy*, ed. by P. Woll (New York) 1966, pp. 15–41.

suffered from the lack of administrative reform by a single head. He excluded Britain from the category of leader in administration on the grounds that Parliament had become King before an English monarch had devised a lasting form for the Civil Service of the State. On the basis of this thinking, Woodrow Wilson claimed that the time was overdue for the United States to contribute to the science of administration and recommended that his country should borrow the European science and *Americanize* it to suit the language and framework of American government – but first administration needed to be separated from politics, as advised by eminent German writers like Bluntschli.

Added to Woodrow Wilson's impetus to develop a science of administration in the United States was the enthusiasm of the scientific management movement to apply science to both business and public administration, and scientific management is discussed in connection with the third American doctrine. The net result in the United States between 1900 and 1939 was a stress on a science of administration which was seen as an end in itself worthy of systematic study and improvement. However, the emphasis in British administrative thought at this time was upon a philosophy of administration which sought primarily to unite scientific thinking with ethical thinking. According to the British philosophy, administration was not simply a science nor was it an end in itself. Rather, administration was a means of achieving a higher form of civilisation by, for example, upholding the ethic of service to the community. The British Philosophy of Administration, therefore, included a study of ethics which ranged from broad issues about the purpose and nature of civilisation to the narrower concern for individual emotions and satisfactions in work. Ethics were rated as important as science, so that many British administrative thinkers held the view that administration can be made into a philosophy on the basis of a study of ethics and science rather than science alone.[29]

M. E. Dimock, the American academic, noted the differing concepts of administration in Britain and the United States, and by the 1930s he was discontented with the American doctrine that administration can be made into a science and repeatedly suggested that Americans should

---

29. There were exceptions in Britain to the *philosophical* approach. For example, G. E. G. Catlin saw disadvantages in linking science with ethics in the field of politics and argued for a pure science of politics, free from ethics. However, Catlin's views did not predominate in Britain. See G. E. G. Catlin, *The Science and Method of Politics* (New York) 1927. Republished edn (Hamden, Conn.) 1964, pp. 297–300.

11

view it as a philosophy rather than a science.[30] In 1958 he drew up his own work, *A Philosophy of Administration*, in which he looked back to the period 1900-39 to comment on the British Philosophy of Administration. Although the doctrines of the British Philosophy of Administration were never assembled into a recognisable, cohesive body within this period, Dimock easily recognised the *philosophical* nature of British administrative thought and wrote:

> . . . in no country has moral philosophy been more consistently emphasized or with better effect.
>
> Lord Haldane was in this tradition and . . . many others . . .
>
> The thing that impresses me most about British moral philosophy is that it is so sincere, so woven into the warp of life that it is unostentatious and hence convincing. I am inclined to think that this moral philosophy . . . has more to do with Britain's institutional durability than many of the things that are more emphasized on this side of the water, such as their career civil service or their ruling aristocracy.
>
> I mention this for a specific reason. I think we need more of it – a great deal more of it – in the United States . . .[31]

Therefore, the second American doctrine that administration can be made into a science only partially represents developments in British administrative history. For, in this country during 1900–39, certain British administrative thinkers assumed that administration can be made into a philosophy.

1.3. The scientific study of administration leads to the discovery of principles of administration analogous to the principles or laws of the physical sciences.

The third American doctrine that the scientific study of administration leads to the discovery of principles is usually associated in the field of public administration with the POSDCORB principles and Luther Gulick's work for the President's Committee on Administrative Management (1936-37). Although the British Philosophy of Administration included the scientific study of administration alongside ethics, it yielded alternative scientific principles, which form not the acronym POSDCORB but SLOCUS. These British scientific principles are discussed in detail in Chapter 3.

In the case of American business administration, the scientific study

30. See M. E. Dimock, 'The criteria and objectives of public administration', in *The Frontiers of Public Administration*, ed. by J. M. Gaus et al. (Chicago) 1936, pp. 120-33, and M. E. Dimock, 'Scientific method and the future of political science', in *Essays in Political Science: In Honor of Westel Woodbury Willoughby*, ed. by J. M. Mathews and J. Hart (Baltimore) 1937, pp. 198-200.
31. M. E. Dimock, *A Philosophy of Administration* (New York) 1958, p. 59.

of principles was first attributed to F. W. Taylor[32] and other pioneers of American scientific management. However, because the British Philosophy of Administration was concerned with ethics as well as science, criticisms were manifest in Britain about American scientific management on account of its bias towards pure science. Indeed, four types of criticisms can be identified and they were voiced not only by contributors to the British Philosophy of Administration but also by spokesmen for the British government and by industrialists and their employees. In the first case, American scientific management was criticised for being preoccupied with mathematical calculations and the *speed* of work. Graham Wallas was one of the earliest British administrative thinkers this century to question the highly mathematical nature of scientific management and he pointed to the handicap of relying upon the slide-rule.[33] Another calculating device besides the slide-rule which was criticised was Taylor's stop-watch. A well-known British psychologist maintained that Taylor's use of the stop-watch was both inconsiderate and often unnecessary, because on occasions he entered factories with a sham notebook devised to contain a stop-watch inside it, for the purpose of timing workers' movements without their knowledge.[34]

Gilbreth invented more elaborate scientific apparatus than Taylor, since he paid greater attention to the *motions* of workers whereas Taylor had been concerned mainly with *time* study and rest pauses. Gilbreth's first studies involved the use of a stop-watch, but he proceeded to develop the cinematograph camera with a high-speed clock; the cyclegraph and the stereocyclegraph. From the latter, with further refinements, he set up wire models of movements. While his ingenuity was recognised in Britain, scepticism was expressed about the aim of this type of apparatus. For example, a British government report, *Time and Motion Study* (1923), criticised the speed factor underlying the inventions of both Taylor and Gilbreth, for it was feared that speed had become an end in itself rather than a means to the

32. F. W. Taylor, *The Principles of Scientific Management* (New York) 1911. Reprinted edn 1913.
33. The use of the slide-rule had been explained by Carl G. Barth in an American paper entitled 'Slide-rules for the machine shop as a part of the Taylor system of management'. See F. B. Gilbreth, *Primer of Scientific Management* (London) 1912, p. 33. Wallas, however, did not refer specifically to Barth but criticised generally the reliance on the slide-rule in American scientific management. G. Wallas, *The Great Society: A Psychological Analysis* (London) 1914, pp. 349–50.
34. C. S. Myers, *Mind and Work: The Psychological Factors in Industry and Commerce* (London) 1920, pp. 27–8.

work.[35]

The second type of criticism lodged in Britain against scientific management was that it utilised the wrong incentives. Graham Wallas again appears to have been one of the first in Britain to indicate weaknesses in the incentive schemes on which American scientific management was based. In 1914, he admonished Taylor for stressing economic incentives at the expense of other factors in human happiness, such as personal liberty. His objection was that possible adverse effects of scientific management, which might result from the uniformity of movements or the monotony of continually handling the same grade of material, had been subordinated in Taylor's thinking to an emphasis on wage increases.[36] Shortly after Wallas' warning, a Committee on the Health of Munition Workers was formed in Britain to pursue, among other matters, the question of incentives affecting the supply of munitions for the First World War. The Committee pointed out dangers in the use of economic incentives. One danger was that if the scheme was too complex, as in the case of the American premium bonus scheme, workers were likely to restrict output, either in the belief that they were being 'speeded-up' to produce greater output or due to a failure to understand the payment scheme. The Committee recommended, therefore, that economic incentives in Britain should be implemented with caution and in conjunction with other social and welfare incentives.[37]

Another criticism was that scientific management was only a set of mechanisms. By the 1920s, scientific management had come to be interpreted in Britain largely in terms of the *mechanisms* associated with it, like the timing devices, instruction cards and the use of functional foremen, while its *principles* had become obscured. Oliver Sheldon, a practising industrial manager with the Rowntree Co. Ltd at York, was aware that many British people held a distorted view of American scientific management because of this misinterpretation. Being more constructive in this matter than Graham Wallas, Sheldon was quick to see some virtue in the principles of scientific management if they could be disentangled from the concern with its mechanisms. Thus, in an interesting article of 1923, he took care to present what he believed to be Taylor's original intention. Taylor had himself argued that the best mechanism for applying general principles should not be

35. Report No. 14 of the Industrial Fatigue Research Board, *Time and Motion Study*, by E. Farmer (London) 1923, pp. 10–17.
36. G. Wallas, *Great Society*, pp. 350–4.
37. Ministry of Munitions Health of Munition Workers Committee, Interim Report, *Industrial Efficiency and Fatigue* (London) 1917, pp. 69–76.

confused with the principles themselves and Sheldon quoted Taylor's own words on scientific management. It is not a number of efficiency expedients or a particular system of paying men, but rather it involves 'a complete mental revolution, both on the part of the management and of the men'.[38] But, although Sheldon attempted to present a true understanding of scientific management, his article was published in the United States and it is doubtful whether he succeeded in reducing the British scepticism.[39]

A fourth criticism concerned the antagonism within the ranks of British labour. In the United States, keen opposition to Taylorism[40] had been expressed by organised labour, even though trade unions were less developed than in Britain. The reasons for this negative reaction were various, but they included the workers' dislike of being urged to work harder while at the same time being deprived of the traditional rewards of craftsmanship.[41] The scepticism demonstrated by British trade unions towards scientific management was not simply the product of rumours received from organised labour in the United States. It increased in unpopularity because Taylor's early writing had been prepared for the American Society of Mechanical Engineers and was addressed to

38. O. Sheldon, 'The art of management: from a British point of view', *Bulletin of the Taylor Society*, Vol. VIII, No. 6, December 1923, 209–10. Some years after Sheldon, D. Waldo distinguished clearly between the mechanism of scientific management and its principles, quoting Taylor's own words. His distinction closely resembles Sheldon's clarification but it is more detailed. For example, Waldo confirmed the *mechanism* of scientific management as time study, functional foremen, the 'differential rate', etc. On the other hand, he cited the four major *principles* of scientific management as: (1) the development of a true science; (2) the scientific selection of workmen; (3) the scientific education and development of workmen; and (4) intimate, friendly co-operation between the management and the men. D. Waldo, *The Administrative State* (New York) 1948, pp. 49–50.

39. See also O. Sheldon, 'Taylor the creative leader', *Bulletin of the Taylor Society*, Vol. IX, No. 1, Feb. 1924, 5–15. Following Sheldon, Urwick found it necessary to account for and correct Taylor's unpopular image in Britain in the following works: L. Urwick, *The Meaning of Rationalisation* (London) 1929; L. Urwick, *The Development of Scientific Management in Great Britain* (London) late 1930s; and L. Urwick and E. F. L. Brech, *The Making of Scientific Management*, Vols. I and II (London) 1945 and 1946. He pointed out in this literature that, although there was a brief active response to Taylorism in Britain prior to the First World War, British interest remained vague, cool and distant. In particular, see *Meaning of Rationalisation*, pp. 54–77.

40. In the early stages, Taylor's ideas were often referred to as the Taylor system or 'task and bonus management'. These earlier designations were largely superseded in the United States by the preferred term 'scientific management', following the hearings in 1910–11 before the Interstate Commerce Commission. See H. S. Person, 'Scientific management', *Encyclopaedia of the Social Sciences*, Vol. XIII, 1934, 603. For further details of these hearings, see S. Haber *Efficiency and Uplift* (Chicago) 1964, pp. 51–4.

41. See S. H. Slichter, 'Efficiency', *Encyclopaedia of the Social Sciences*, Vol. V, 1931, 438.

Fig. 1. The one-man Civil Service: A prophetic nightmare (from *Red-Tape*, January 1912).

businessmen on the subject of increased output rather than the treatment of labour. This disadvantage from labour's viewpoint caused British trade unions to look for issues to debate about this type of management instead of seeking to understand it.[42]

42. For example, one aspect singled out for criticism was Taylor's assumption that the man suitable to handle pig-iron should be 'ox-like'. See L. Urwick, *Meaning of Rationalisation*, pp. 67–8 and G. Wallas, *Great Society*, p. 361.

An influential memorandum on the industrial situation in Britain published in 1916 ascribed the cause of the dislike and distrust of American scientific management by British workers to the fear that they might become mindless automatons.[43] And clearly public employees shared the same fear as the cartoon(Fig.1), which appeared in the Civil Service trade union journal *Red-Tape*, suggests by depicting a 'speeded-up' British Civil Service manned by automatons.[44] In view of the antagonism expressed by organised labour, even the introduction of modified aspects of scientific management into Britain could not be carried out without first obtaining the full *co-operation* of British trade unions or by largely dissociating the experiments from any connection with F. W. Taylor or his followers.[45]

American scientific management was a certain attitude towards industrial problems involving the use of the scientific method to discover underlying principles or laws. In the British search for scientific principles, the scientific method was conceived less rigorously, being tempered by the simultaneous search for ethical ideals. The American doctrine, therefore, does not portray accurately the scientific study of principles within the British Philosophy of Administration.

1.4. The principles of administration determine the way in which the goals of economy and efficiency can be realised

Inextricably interwoven with American scientific management were the goals of economy and efficiency and these goals were treated as being almost synonymous. So great was the emphasis on efficiency in the United States that a veritable efficiency craze transpired, mainly as a result of Taylor's aim to maximise human effort with a view to making American industry more efficient.[46] By 1910, the efficiency craze had reached its zenith which lasted until America's entry into the First World War, when it began to recede.[47] In spite of this mild waning in the craze, the goals of economy and efficiency remained central to both American

---

43. A *Memorandum on the Industrial Situation After the War*, 1916. See L. Urwick, *Development of Scientific Management*, p. 37.
44. *Red-Tape* was commenced in 1911 to represent the views of the then existing Assistant Clerks Association. See B. Newman, *Yours for Action* (London) 1953, pp. 9, 139–42. Today, *Red-Tape* is the official journal of the Civil and Public Services Association, which represents the Clerical Grades and Machine Grades (e.g. typists) in the Civil Service.
45. See H. J. Welch and C. S. Myers *Ten Years of Industrial Psychology* (London) 1932, pp. 3–4.
46. See F. W. Taylor, *Principles of Scientific Management*, p. 7.
47. See S. Haber, *Efficiency and Uplift*, pp. 51–74.

business and public administration for the period 1900-39.[48]

Looking back to America's love of efficiency in this period, it has been described as 'nothing short of worshipful'.[49] Britain, on the other hand, had less of an obsession for efficiency, except by the Fabian Society, whose founders, particularly Sidney and Beatrice Webb, made efficiency one of its major goals.[50] But, on the whole, there was no efficiency craze in Britain akin to that in the United States, partly due to the scepticism manifest towards American scientific management. Even when contributors to the British Philosophy of Administration made proposals for efficient administration, their concept of efficiency was of a broader *qualitative* type extending beyond the *quantitative* approach of the scientific management movement in the United States. This qualitative concept which prevailed among British administrative thinkers embraced efficient human relations and was one of social as well as organisational efficiency. F. W. Taylor's concept had begun by including the desire to promote social efficiency in the sense of social harmony between management and men[51] but, under the pressure of the efficiency vogue, it appears to have become channelled into a narrower, quantitative and mechanical goal. Accordingly, not only was the efficiency craze a typically American phenomenon, but so was the quantitative concept of efficiency it represented. Dimock (1936) commented upon this peculiar American approach to efficiency:

> . . . the concept and implications of efficiency, as practiced in the United States, have a peculiar quality which is typically American. In this country the connotation of efficiency definitely conveys the mechanical, utilitarian meaning. Efficiency becomes tantamount to economy, penny-pinching, and profit-making. Let it not be thought that all of our business leaders, much less those in academic posts, subscribe to this mechanized view. We are simply anxious to drive home the point that this limited, 'hardboiled' interpretation of efficiency has been . . . one of the most dominant forces in the development of American ideology and institutions.

48. Dimock has pointed out that the goals of economy and efficiency came at a later time to American public administration than to American business administration. Nevertheless, they were the accepted goals in both types of administration for at least a generation. M. E. Dimock, 'Criteria and objectives', op. cit., pp. 116–17.
49. Ibid., p. 116.
50. See G. Wallas, 'Socialism and the Fabian Society', 1916. Reprinted posthumously in *Men and Ideas: Essays by Graham Wallas*, ed. by M. Wallas (London) 1940, pp. 104–5.
51. Haber has given four definitions of efficiency all of which were contained in the work of F. W. Taylor and he has included social efficiency as one of the four definitions. S. Haber, *Efficiency and Uplift*, pp. ix–x.

It must be admitted that at an earlier time there was a great deal of truth in the advice of a British official who, referring to American experiments in scientific management, counseled: 'It would be one of the greatest mistakes that could ever be made in this country. It is machine-like in concept and inhuman in its operation.'[52]

By the 1930s, American academics, including Dimock, began encouraging their countrymen to broaden the concept of administrative efficiency away from the quantitative conception determined by a slide-rule to a more expansive human and qualitative type. And, certain British administrative thinkers, such as Haldane, were cited as forerunners of this broader qualitative approach.[53]

With respect to the goal of economy, Taylor recognised that although American industry respected the need to conserve *material* resources, it was less aware of the need to prevent waste of *human* effort and his striving for increased output was to obtain economy of human labour.[54] The goals of economy and efficiency became translated into American government and are clearly discernible in the recommendations of the President's Committee on Administrative Management (1937) for the reform of public administration.[55] Economy was an integral part of British administrative thought and practice between 1900 and 1939 and was a necessary goal, for example, during the First World War when economies had to be introduced not only within the Civil Service but also by civil servants on behalf of the people, as in the case of the work of the Ministry of Food in food rationing.[56] However, the goal of efficiency, in particular, did not share the same spotlight in Britain that it did in America, for the reasons that a less quantitative approach to administration was taken and also because Britain faced an alternative pressing question – that of the derogatory charge of 'bureaucracy'. It is more relevant to suggest, therefore, that Britain had an alternative craze which reached its peak in the 1920s and 1930s in which the much-publicised word was not 'efficiency' but 'bureaucracy'.[57]

The first four traditional doctrines of American administrative

52. M. E. Dimock, 'Criteria and objectives', op. cit., pp. 117–18.
53. Ibid., pp. 116–33, and D. Waldo, *Study of Public Administration*, p. 43.
54. F. W. Taylor, *Principles of Scientific Management*, pp. 5–6.
55. *Report of the President's Committee on Administrative Management*, pp. 3–4.
56. See W. Beveridge, *Some Experiences of Economic Control in War-time* (London) 1940, pp. 17–27, and Sir H. P. Hamilton, 'Sir Warren Fisher and the public service', *Public Administration*, Vol. 29, 1951, 15–38. Sir Warren Fisher was Head of the British Civil Service from 1919 to 1939 and was closely associated with the goal of economy.
57. For full details of bureaucracy in Britain between 1900 and 1939, see Ch. 5.

thought for the period 1900–39 have been challenged in relation to the emergence of British administrative thought. The fifth doctrine of human relations, which formed a separate development in the United States, must be considered next.

1.5. The human element in administration is as important as the science of administration

In discussing the human relations movement, we do not wish to challenge the doctrine itself because it formed the very essence of the British Philosophy of Administration. Rather, the challenge is directed at the assumption that the human element was first discovered to be as important as the science of administration by the experiments of the Harvard Business School from 1927 onwards at the Hawthorne plant, Chicago. Certainly, significant and systematic experiments were undertaken in the United States into human relations, but discoveries had transpired earlier in Britain.

From the time of the First World War, British administrative thought and practice made progress in human relations as a result of the attention paid to ethics of administration, which were regarded as being of equal significance as the science of administration.[58] Britain, therefore, did not oscillate between the classical approach to administration, with its heavy emphasis on science, to the other extreme of human relations, but combined these two developments within the British Philosophy of Administration. These alternative doctrines are now discussed.

2. The alternative doctrines underlying the British Philosophy of Administration

Six British administrative pioneers have been identified on page 4 as having contributed to the British Philosophy of Administration. We have drawn their ideas together principally because they had in common a concern for ethics of administration as well as science. The British Philosophy of Administration was not amassed into a comprehensive form, but it was reflected none the less in the aims of

---

58. For full details of British discoveries in human relations, see Ch. 4.

the Institute of Public Administration,[59] formed in 1922, whose journal *Public Administration*[60] promoted this philosophy. Besides the common philosophical nature of their thought, there are subsidiary reasons for selecting these particular administrative pioneers, which relate to their services to administration. Graham Wallas, for example, was a highly original writer and teacher of administration who pioneered British ideas in human relations and also acted as a Commissioner for the Royal Commission on the Civil Service, 1912–15. Richard Haldane and Josiah Stamp gave enormous service to the Institute of Public Administration, both acting as President between 1922 and 1929 as well as contributing to British administrative thought and practice. Oliver Sheldon and Lyndall Urwick actively studied and practised business administration and their thought was particularly renowned in this field. Finally, William Beveridge introduced humour in the form of witty analogies into the British Philosophy of Administration which is a welcome change from some of today's rather turgid administrative writings.

By concentrating on the British Philosophy of Administration, we have had to exclude other British pioneers who offered worthwhile contributions to administration, but whose thought did not substantially diverge from or expand the doctrines of the British Philosophy of Administration – for example, W. G. S. Adams, Henry Bunbury, Stuart Bunning, Gwilym Gibbon, Stanley Leathes and Robert Morant.[61] There are three administrative thinkers, on the other hand, whose thought did differ on occasions from the British Philosophy of Administration and is too influential to overlook. These three pioneers

59. The aims of the Institute of Public Administration embodying a philosophy of administration in the sense of ethical ideals and scientific principles are quoted below:

'. . . the purpose of the Institute is–

(1) To maintain the high ideals and traditions of the Public Service . . .
(2) To promote the study of (a) vocational or professional practice of Public Administration; (b) the machinery necessary for the efficient day-by-day practice of Public Administration; and (c) the principles of historical, economic and political science with special reference to Public Administration and constitutional law and practice'.

H. G. Corner, 'The aims of the Institute of Public Administration', *Journal of Public Administration*, Vol. I, 1923, p. 50. Since 1954, the Institute has been known as the Royal Institute of Public Administration.
60. This publication was called the *Journal of Public Administration* until January 1926 when it was shortened to *Public Administration*.
61. With the exception of Robert Morant, all these administrative pioneers contributed to *Public Administration* between 1923 and 1939.

are Sidney and Beatrice Webb and Harold Laski and their views will be compared with the main doctrines of the British Philosophy of Administration, where relevant.

The central doctrines of the British Philosophy of Administration, which contrast with the two American developments, are set out below. Each doctrine is outlined briefly before being discussed in detail in the individual chapters of this book.

British doctrines

1. In the process of government, the two functions of politics and administration are fused rather than independent.

2. Administration cannot be reduced to a science alone. It is based on science *and* ethics and this combination constitutes a philosophy of administration.

3. The philosophical study of administration leads to the discovery not only of scientific principles but also of ethical ideals.

4. Being a matter of both science and ethics, the goal of efficiency assumes a qualitative rather than a quantitative nature. But even the qualitative goal of efficiency is overshadowed by the problem of bureaucracy. The twofold problem of bureaucracy is relevant to the philosophy of administration and becomes intertwined with it.

2.1. In the process of government, the two functions of politics and administration are fused rather than independent
It has been noted earlier that because Britain had made considerable progress by 1900 towards eliminating patronage from Civil Service appointments, there was less need to separate politics from administration. A corollary of this difference between British and American government was that there was less tendency within the British Philosophy of Administration to associate 'politics' with 'party loyalties', but rather politics was interpreted in the context of the British constitution. In this context, Ministers rely heavily on higher civil servants to advise them on policy and, therefore, politics was conceived principally as the activity of 'policy-making'. Haldane and Beveridge, for example, depicted the fusion of both policy-making and constitutional issues with administration by *describing* the civil servant's influential role in these processes.

Politics as the activity of 'policy-making' had implications for statesmen and administrators alike, and another contributor to the British Philosophy of Administration, Graham Wallas, extended this doctrine by *prescribing* methods to improve policy-making in British government. The British fusion of politics with administration was not applicable to public administration alone but was paralleled in the sphere of business administration by Oliver Sheldon, who provided prescriptions for improving industrial policy-making. We use the term 'fusion' here, however, not exclusively in the narrow sense of implying direct participation by administrators in policy-making but also in the broad sense of a *connection* between politics and administration as distinct from a *separation*.

This first doctrine of the British Philosophy of Administration indicating a fusion – or a need for fusion – between politics and administration was promoted soon after the First World War. It is associated primarily with Haldane, Beveridge, Wallas and Sheldon and is set out in Chapter 2 of this book. However, not all British administrative thinkers took the view that politics and administration were fused processes. Sidney and Beatrice Webb (1920) in a powerful but isolated treatise took a radical view of the whole question of the British constitution.[62] Their new concept of a socialist commonwealth of Great Britain was based on a completely fresh governmental structure which removed most of the existing executive and legislative institutions and created new Parliamentary and administrative organisations, in which politics and administration more closely resembled the American doctrine of a separation. Although the Webbs' proposal was radical, their thoroughness in discussing their concept and their detailed plan for the new institutions of British government renders their divergent views important in retrospect, if not at the time. For this reason their views are included in Chapter 2 with those of Harold Laski, in contrast to the first doctrine of the British Philosophy of Administration.

2.2. Administration cannot be reduced to a science alone. It is based on science *and* ethics and this combination constitutes a philosophy of administration

The second British doctrine forms the basis of this book and is not the subject of a separate chapter. It confirms that Britain did not espouse wholesale either the science of administration which emanated from

---

62. S. and B. Webb, *A Constitution for the Socialist Commonwealth of Great Britain* (London) 1920.

Germany and France or American scientific management. For these schools of thought failed to satisfy British administrative thinkers, who sought a more balanced *philosophy*. Their philosophy of administration entailed the enunciation of scientific principles, but it gave equal attention to ethical ideals and both are summarised under the next doctrine.

2.3. The philosophical study of administration leads to the discovery not only of scientific principles but also of ethical ideals

The scientific principles underlying the British Philosophy of Administration are important enough to warrant a whole chapter and they are identified and discussed in Chapter 3. An interesting point to note is that for decades the scientific principles of administration have been associated largely with the American POSDCORB principles of the 1930s and it is little realised that alternative scientific principles were promoted in Britain from the turn of the century. The chief British principles are Staff and Line, Organisation, Communication, and Span of control, which we have marshalled into the acronym SLOCUS. Various approaches to the SLOCUS principles were made by Wallas, Haldane, Sheldon and Urwick and each variant is exposed and analysed in turn. First, however, Chapter 3 begins with the less rigorous British definition of the term 'principle' followed by a review of the POSDCORB principles in the light of the British acronym SLOCUS.

Co-existing with the scientific principles of administration expounded by contributors to the British Philosophy of Administration was their commitment to ethical idealism. This idealism forms the content of Chapter 4, in which we reveal three specific ethical ideals. First, administration was viewed as a means of attaining a higher form of society, in which craftsmanship and creative expression play a significant role. The second ethical ideal was that administration should render a service to the community by supplying the public with quality goods and services at a reasonable cost and by stimulating social and educational organisation in the locality. The third ethical ideal was that administration should provide for the happiness and well-being of the worker through the supply of non-economic incentives instead of relying principally on economic incentives as in American scientific management.

These ethical ideals led to several important human relations discoveries within the British Philosophy of Administration. For example, the ideal of administration as a service to the community

24

focused upon the social needs of workers in their environment *outside* the organisation. Similarly, the ideal of the happiness of the worker illuminated the value of small group relations *within* the organisation and the importance of psychological as well as monetary incentives to increase output. In addition to these three ethical ideals promoted by *individual* contributors to the British Philosophy of Administration, Britain possessed several *corporate* bodies which put into practice similar ethical ideals. These corporate bodies realised actual experiments in human relations which predated the Hawthorne explorations of the late 1920s onwards. The British corporate experiments began as early as the First World War when the Ministry of Munitions carried out numerous investigations into the well-being of workers in munition factories, which resulted in a series of welfare reforms. Following these practical developments came the work of the British Industrial Fatigue Research Board and the National Institute of Industrial Psychology, which advanced the discoveries and implementation of human relations. We discuss both the individual and the corporate approaches to ethical idealism in Chapter 4 and draw comparisons with American human relations, notably the Hawthorne discoveries.

2.4. Being a matter of both science and ethics, the goal of efficiency assumes a qualitative rather than a quantitative nature. But even the qualitative goal of efficiency is overshadowed by the problem of bureaucracy. The twofold problem of bureaucracy is relevant to the philosophy of administration and becomes intertwined with it

The fusion of policy-making with administration was accepted by contributors to the British Philosophy of Administration as a useful means to effective government. Indeed, prescriptions were put forward to facilitate the public administrator's role in policy-making. However, critics of the British Civil Service questioned the administrator's role in the policy-making process, claiming that it was increasing the *power of officials* and leading to a dangerous form of bureaucracy. The power of officials was only one type of bureaucracy alleged to exist in the British Civil Service between 1900 and 1939. Criticisms of *rule of the bureau*, or red-tape, were voiced as loudly as those of the power of officials and, in both cases, critics conceived bureaucracy in its *dysfunctional* sense. They interpreted the growing power of officials as a threat to the sovereignty of Parliament and the liberty of British citizens. And the critics associated rule of the bureau with excess rules and regulations, a lack of initiative on behalf of public officials and delays in administration. Josiah Stamp replied to both charges of bureaucracy, by pointing out the *functional* reasons for its growth. Consequently, the doctrines of the philosophy of administration became intertwined with the problem of bureaucracy, which reached its peak in Britain during the 1920s. Chapter 5 of this book describes the bureaucracy debate and indicates the several ways in which it was relevant to the British Philosophy of Administration.[63]

Conclusion

The conventional American picture of the development of administrative thought is inadequate when compared with British administrative thought for the period 1900–39. But before the contrasting, alternative doctrines of the British Philosophy of Administration are presented in detail, some further characteristics should be noted about the strengths and weaknesses of the British doctrines. On the side of their strengths, they compose a forward-looking and human approach to administration and, by coupling together the science of administration with ethical ideals and human relations, British administrative thought preceded American developments in several respects. For example, the rigid politics–administration separation promoted in the United States between 1900 and 1939 was re-examined in the 1940s to give way to a more realistic concept along the British lines of an interrelation between politics and administration.[64] Other instances of the earlier British developments are the recognition of the SLOCUS scientific principles of administration well before the 1930s and the advanced progress in human relations prior to and during the 1920s.

The second strength of the British doctrines is the influence they gained in the United States during the period ending 1939. Currently, British administrative thought is based heavily on American doctrines so that the two-way traffic of administrative ideas during this era has been underestimated. Some examples of the movement of British administrative doctrines to the United States to influence American thinkers are, therefore, appropriate. In the case of the politics–administration fusion, it was Wallas' thought which penetrated most deeply into the United States. Wallas himself made several visits to North America, and during one visit he experimented in teaching by

63. Harold Laski also made a study of bureaucracy, but we exclude him from the main British Philosophy of Administration on account of his radical views. However, his approach to bureaucracy will be referred to in Ch. 5.
64. See D. Waldo, *Study of Public Administration*, p. 42.

discussing the ideas he later published in *The Great Society* (1914). In particular, he impressed the American student, Walter Lippmann, to the extent that Wallas made the following dedication in his preface to the book:

> Dear Walter Lippmann,
> This develops the material of that discussion-course ('Government 31') which you joined during my stay at Harvard in the spring of 1910 . . . I send it to you in the hope that it may be of some help when you write that sequel to your *Preface to Politics* for which all your friends are looking . . .[65]

L. D. White (1936) cited both Wallas and Haldane as great figures who in their day developed programmes of public administration[66] while in his earlier book (1926) it was the work of Haldane and Sheldon which motivated him most. White drew attention to Sheldon's *Philosophy of Management* and, in particular, referred to his ethics of administration, whereas in Haldane's case it was the scientific principles of administration which stimulated White to write about 'the remarkable report of the Haldane Committee'.[67] M. E. Dimock, as noted earlier, was greatly influenced by the philosophical nature of British administrative doctrines and thinkers and by the qualitative concept of efficiency, both of which he sought to introduce into American administrative thought. The Institute of Public Administration in Britain, which upheld the philosophy of administration, also extended its influence into the United States, arousing the interest of Luther Gulick, Don K. Price and D. C. Stone – to name a few.[68]

In view of the importance of the British Philosophy of Administration between 1900 and 1939, why has it not endured into current administrative thought and why is there reliance in Britain today on the conventional American wisdom? The answer to these questions lies in the weaknesses of the British Philosophy of Administration, of which four are apparent. The first weakness is that the British doctrines were never presented as a cohesive body of thought, but remained fragmented. This *fragmentation* was caused by the fact that the disciplines of public and business administration were only slowly

---

65. G. Wallas, *Great Society*, p. v.
66. L. D. White, 'The meaning of principles in public administration', in *The Frontiers of Public Administration*, pp. 21–2.
67. White quoted from Sheldon in *Introduction to Public Administration*, pp. 1, 206–38. In the same work, White referred to Haldane and the *Report of the Machinery of Government Committee* on pp. 16 and 50–68.
68. Both the Institute of Public Administration and its journal acquired real authority in the United States in their first ten years, see *Public Administration*, 1927–35.

emerging in Britain in this era and administrative thought was contained within other major disciplines – such as economics, history, engineering, sociology, philosophy and psychology. To portray the British Philosophy of Administration, therefore, it has been necessary to collect together and unify the disparate administrative ideas.[69] Owing to this fragmentation of administrative ideas, neither the administrative doctrines were accorded the merit they deserve nor did the individual pioneers receive their full acclaim. For example, it was noted of Wallas: 'Coming between the recognised areas of psychology, politics, philosophy, and history, he did not get the immediate recognition in any academic field . . . The central pundits of each field regarded him often mainly as the responsibility, pride and possession of the others'.[70]

One weakness, then, is that the British Philosophy of Administration was dispersed at the academic level between several disciplines of the social sciences. A second weakness is that it was also fragmented at the practical level of the administrative institutions interested in the subject. There was some natural overlap between public and business administration, since contributors to the British Philosophy of Administration did not limit their thought either to the Civil Service or industry. Josiah Stamp, for example, worked in both the British Civil Service and industry and was a member simultaneously of the Institute of Public Administration and the Institute of Industrial Administration.[71] Similarly, Wallas, Sheldon and Urwick wrote about or participated in both public and business administration. Despite this natural overlap, there was a lack of *common* administrative institutions with shared purposes and developments in Britain. Not only did the Institute of Public Administration run parallel to the Institute of Industrial Administration, but in the sphere of business administration the Institute of Industrial Administration by no means co-ordinated administrative developments. Instead, many small institutions grew up, each separately promoting interest in business administration, leading Sheldon in 1923 to complain:

> . . . each society or institute is ploughing its own lonely, rather narrow, furrow . . . There is comparatively little corporate organization, therefore little corporate research or corporate literature . . . It is high time that the dividing walls were razed to the ground, the shutters which hide us from

69. An exception to the fragmentation of administrative ideas was the Institute of Public Administration's journal, *Public Administration*.
70. J. Stamp, 'Graham Wallas', *Economica*, Vol. XII, Nos. 35–8, 1932, 402.
71. See J. Stamp, 'The contrast between the administration of business and public affairs', *Journal of Public Administration*, Vol. I, 1923, 158–9.

each other, taken down, and all our experiments, experiences, information, standards, practices and plans brought together for the good of the whole.[72]

A third weakness of the British Philosophy of Administration, still prevalent in British administrative thought today, is the reluctance to theorise. To an extent this reluctance was one of the strengths of the British Philosophy of Administration, for it provided the unostentatious and sincere quality admired in the United States.[73] Yet, this *simplicity* was also one of the very reasons why the British Philosophy of Administration has failed to last with the same impact as conventional American wisdom. The British doctrines remained essentially a philosophy and not a theory of administration, embodying description, subjective attitudes and explanations rather than rigorous, systematic analysis. This simplicity resulted from the practical backgrounds of the contributors to the British Philosophy of Administration, who interspersed their academic thought with practical insights based on experience. Graham Wallas, for example, was an academic thinker who believed in practising administration, as this tribute to him suggests:

Wallas was not . . . merely a teacher and a writer of books . . . He tried to make his books the expression of his very varied experience; and he knew, as few know, how difficult is the marriage of doctrine and practice. He had had long experience of the London School Board and the County Council. He had taken part in many an election. He was a valued member of the Royal Commission on the Civil Service 1914, where his fertility in suggestions is clearly discernible in the Report.[74]

The British practitioner-cum-academic approach to administration was reinforced by the fact that the doctrines were often presented as short, live addresses to members of various institutions, such as the Society of Civil Servants, the Institute of Public Administration and the British Association for the Advancement of Science, rather than as theoretical studies. The style and brevity of these addresses inhibited the development of methodology or theory and a case in point is bureaucracy. Much wisdom was set out in British administrative thought on this subject, yet due to the lack of any theoretical framework, as provided in Germany by M. Weber (1922) or in the United States by C. J. Friedrich and T. Cole (1932) or T. Parsons (1937), the British

---

72. O. Sheldon, 'Art of management', op. cit., 213. By 1935 there were signs of a grouping together of the fragmented institutions in the sphere of industrial administration. See L. Urwick, *Development of Scientific Management*, pp. 56–8.
73. See quotation from Dimock, this chapter, p. 12.
74. H. J. Laski, 'Graham Wallas', *The New Statesman and Nation*, 20 Aug. 1932, 199.

contribution to the understanding of bureaucracy has passed largely unnoticed.[75]

The United States possessed her practitioners-cum-academics in the field of administration between 1900 and 1939. F. W. Taylor, for example, drew richly on his practical experience, although he has been criticised for not presenting his ideas more systematically,[76] and Woodrow Wilson progressed from the academic study of administration to the role of President. But, in the United States more administrative thought came from pure academics and more attempts were made to theorise, with the result that many famous names and theories have continued to flow from the United States, associated with L. D. White (1926); W. F. Willoughby (1927); D. Waldo (1948 and 1955); H. A. Simon (1945); F. W. Riggs (1964); A. Downs (1967) and so on.[77] Accordingly, public and business administration gained greater and quicker academic acceptance in the United States, which is visible from the numerous professional schools of administration and academic departments created. In the field of public administration, the British academic F. F. Ridley has made known his discontent recently, contrasting the American developments with the paucity of British academic institutions or theories devoted to administration. He has demanded where the British equivalents of American grand theorists are and chastised British scholars for tending to scoff at American 'grand theory'. For, while such theories hold few practical lessons and often remain in the realms of pure theory, he argues that they nevertheless serve to advance administration from miscellaneous description to an integrated body of knowledge.[78] The British Philosophy of Administration, 1900–39, then, had the advantage over American administrative thought of not alternating between 'classical organisation theory' and 'human relations theory'. On the other hand, by tending towards miscellaneous description, the British doctrines rendered a lesser service to the progress of public and business

75. See Ch. 5, pp. 201–34 for the British views on bureaucracy compared with those of M. Weber, C. J. Friedrich and T. Cole, and T. Parsons.
76. See H. S. Person, 'The origin and nature of scientific management' in *Scientific Management in American Industry*, ed. by H. S. Person (New York) 1929, pp. 7–8.
77. L. D. White, *Introduction to Public Administration*; W. F. Willoughby *Principles of Public Administration* (Washington) 1927; D. Waldo, *Administrative State* and *Study of Public Administration*; H. A. Simon, *Administrative Behavior* (New York) 1945; F. W. Riggs, *Administration in Developing Countries: The Theory of Prismatic Society* (Boston) 1964; and A. Downs, *Inside Bureaucracy* (Boston) 1967.
78. F. F. Ridley, 'Public administration: cause for discontent', *Public Administration* Vol. 50, Spring 1972. 65–77. See also F. F. Ridley, *The Study of Government: Political Science and Public Administration* (London) 1975.

administration as academic subjects.

A final weakness in the sense of the long-term influence of the British Philosophy of Administration was the highly individualistic personalities of the contributors. During their lives, with the exception of Sheldon, the other five pioneers had many interests in common besides the philosophy of administration. For example, Wallas, Haldane and Beveridge moved in Fabian Society circles with Sidney and Beatrice Webb, although Haldane and Beveridge never became Fabians,[79] and Beatrice Webb was a member of the Machinery of Government Committee (1917–18) of which Haldane was Chairman.[80] Similarly, these contributors to the British Philosophy of Administration were associated closely with the Webbs in the development of the London School of Economics.[81] This School is one of the exceptions to the assertion that Britain has lacked schools specialising in administration. In 1895, Haldane supported Sidney and Beatrice Webb in the formation of the London School of Economics; Wallas became Lecturer and later Professor at the School; Beveridge was Director between 1919 and 1937 and Stamp was a student.[82] Yet, despite friendship and common interests between them, this small band of administrative pioneers retained highly individualistic views on life and on administration, which led to divergences in their thought. Wallas, for instance, left the Fabian Society in the early 1900s because of differences of opinion and Haldane disagreed with Fabian leaders Sidney and Beatrice Webb on some major issues.[83] This individuality did not help to cement the fragmented nature of the British Philosophy of Administration and may have added to its failure to endure as a cohesive body of doctrines, since the Webb's radical and diverging views served to diminish the impact of the main doctrines.

The weaknesses of the British Philosophy of Administration,

79. See J. Beveridge *An Epic of Clare Market: Birth and Early Days of the London School of Economics* (London) 1960, pp. 10–17. See also W. Beveridge, *Power and Influence: An Autobiography* (London) 1953, pp. 61–2.
80. See *Report of the Machinery of Government Committee*, p. 2.
81. See J. Beveridge, *Epic of Clare Market*, particularly p. 49. Lyndall Urwick was also introduced to the Webbs in 1913 and was persuaded by them to become an external doctoral student at the London School of Economics. However, he had to abandon this study in 1914 when he served in the British Army during the First World War. L. Urwick, Personal letter to the author dated 28 Feb. 1975
82. M. J. Wiener, *Between Two Worlds: The Political Thought of Graham Wallas* (London) 1971, pp. 30, 162; W. Beveridge, *The London School of Economics And Its Problems 1919–1937* (London) 1960; and J. H. Jones, *Josiah Stamp Public Servant: The Life of the First Baron Stamp of Shortlands* (London) 1964, pp. 86–7.
83. See M. J. Wiener, *Between Two Worlds*, pp. 51–6 and B. Webb, *Our Partnership*, ed. by B. Drake and M. I. Cole (London) 1948, pp. 429–31.

therefore, which have caused it to be overshadowed by American administrative doctrines, have been its fragmented nature at academic and practical levels, its lack of theorising and the individuality of its pioneers. However, a clear body of doctrines existed, albeit in fragmented form, and they carried considerable influence in the United States and the Dominions within the period 1900–39. The following chapters seek to restore the influence of the British Philosophy of Administration by describing these doctrines and bringing them back into focus.

Chapter 2

The fusion of politics
within the British Philosophy
of Administration

*'The study of politics is now in an unsatisfactory position... This
dissatisfaction has led to much study of political institutions; but
little attention has been recently given in works on politics to the
facts of human nature ... The neglect of the study of human
nature is likely, however, to prove only a temporary phase of
political thought ...'*[1]

G. Wallas

The British Philosophy of Administration promoted the doctrine that
politics and administration are fused processes, while the traditional
American doctrine concentrated on a separation between the two
processes. This chapter presents the views of contributors to the British
Philosophy of Administration which illustrate the doctrine of fusion.
However, before the British views are discussed, it is useful to define
what was meant by politics in the context of both the American and
British doctrines.

Four governmental differences have been cited in Chapter 1 as
having shaped the attitudes towards administration in both countries.[2]
In particular, two characteristics of government in the United States
influenced the growth of the American politics–administration
doctrine, so creating *two* dichotomies within the doctrine. Firstly, the
fact that the United States faced a substantial problem in freeing
administration from the spoils system led to the development of one
dichotomy based on the definition of politics as partisan domination or
'party influence'. This dichotomy was advanced by Woodrow Wilson in
his essay of 1887. His intention was to dissociate administration from
the dysfunctional consequences of the spoils system. Wilson believed
that if public administration could be separated from party domination
it could be made more businesslike, which in his view was a necessity
due to the increasing complexity of government tasks.[3]

1. G. Wallas, *Human Nature in Politics* (London) 1908. Republished edn (London) 1962,
   p. 15.
2. See Ch. 1, pp. 6–10.
3. W. Wilson, 'The study of administration', reprinted in *Public Administration and
   Policy*, ed. by P. Woll (New York) 1966, pp. 16–20.

L. D. White perpetuated this separation of politics from administration and drew attention to earlier examples of party domination in American public administration. He pointed out that when Jackson was inaugurated as President in 1829 he made wholesale removals and appointments in public administration, forgetting neither friend nor enemy. In 1926, White compared the extensive number of civil servants politically appointed in the United States after nearly fifty years of the merit system in the federal service, with the few political appointments in the British Civil Service. His comparison caused him to comment that the Jacksonian doctrine, 'To the victors belong the spoils', still dominated a large section of American public administration. Although White realised that there were functional consequences of the American spoils system,[4] like Wilson, he considered that party influence handicapped efficient administration.[5] The first separation of politics from administration, therefore, was based on the concept of politics as 'party influence'.

A second important characteristic of American government to shape the doctrine was the formal separation of powers on which the constitution was founded, which resulted in separate legislative and executive institutions. Because of this formal separation of powers, American students of government tended to enlarge the constitutional pattern in their theories, finding it natural to distinguish between legislative, executive and judicial processes. Appleby (1949) has identified the constitutional separation of powers in the United States as the main reason for the second separation of politics from administration, based on the definition of politics as 'policy-making'. He maintained:

> Most scholarly efforts in the field of government ... were long, and quite naturally, attempts to look at government from single, separate vantage points ... For a half-century or so while political science was developing as a distinct discipline, much of its literature tended to accept as substantially real a separation of powers which excluded from administration any – or at least any important – policy-making functions.[6]

4. It should not be overlooked that the spoils system still played a useful role in American government in the late nineteenth and early twentieth centuries. Merton is well known for having enunciated clearly the functional, albeit crude, role assumed by the spoils system in American society. See R. K. Merton, 'The latent functions of the machine', *Urban Government: A Reader in Administration and Politics*, ed. by E. C. Banfield (New York). Revised edn 1969, pp. 223–33.
5. L. D. White, *Introduction to the Study of Public Administration* (New York), 1926, pp. 41–5, 219–33.
6. P. Appleby, *Policy and Administration* (Alabama) 1949. Reprinted edn 1965, p. 3.

Thus, American literature involved a second dichotomy of a separation between policy-making and administration, which was a theoretical division retaining the constitutional pattern and putting a premium on the separate *institutions* of government rather than on the *reality* of policy-making.[7] American writers have sometimes discussed the politics–administration doctrine by stressing one or other of these two concepts of politics. For example, Goodnow (1900) paid more attention to the separation between 'policy-making' and administration[8] while White (1926) demonstrated more interest in separating 'party influence' from administration. Other American writers have combined the two separations and concepts of politics. Woodrow Wilson, for example, sought to separate administration from both 'party influence' and the function of 'policy-making' and, indeed, from constitutional matters in order that it might develop as a science in its own right.[9] Since the 1940s, the traditional American doctrine has been contested by numerous writers,[10] but what does not necessarily emerge from the later discussions is that the doctrine contained these two dichotomies based on different concepts of politics.

In the case of the British doctrine, it was the second definition only of politics as 'policy-making' which applied. With the problem of patronage largely behind them by 1900, contributors to the British Philosophy of Administration turned their attention to policy-making.[11] But, because the evolution of the British constitution had

7. Besides Appleby, op. cit., Easton has referred to the traditional *institutional* approach to political science in the United States during this period. See D. Easton, *The Political System: An Inquiry into the State of Political Science* (New York) 1953. Reprinted edn 1965, p. 151.

8. F. J. Goodnow, *Politics and Administration: A Study in Government* (New York) 1900, pp. 18–93.

9. W. Wilson, 'Study of administration', op. cit., pp. 15–41. It should be noted, however, that Wilson admired the British system of Parliamentary government. And, on other occasions, such as in his text *Congressional Government* (Boston) 1885, he recommended a form of Parliamentary government for the United States.

10. Minority spokesmen began to challenge this traditional American doctrine during the late 1930s; for example M. E. Dimock, 'The meaning and scope of public administration', in *The Frontiers of Public Administration* ed. by J. M. Gaus et al. (Chicago) 1936, pp. 3–4. However, the main contester is usually taken to be P. Appleby, *Policy and Administration*. Later challengers of the doctrine include H. Seidman, *Politics, Position, and Power: The Dynamics of Federal Organization* (New York) 1970, pp. vii–36, and P. Self, *Administrative Theories and Politics* (London) 1972, pp. 149–91.

11. Some British Civil Service posts were still subject to uncontrolled patronage in the early twentieth century, see *Royal Commission on the Civil Service, Fourth Report of the Commissioners* (London) Majority Report, 1914, pp. 24–43. Nevertheless, manifold progress had been made in the late nineteenth century with regard to the competitive examination system and patronage was considered no longer to be a major problem.

created fused legislative and executive institutions, these British pioneers did not follow the American pattern of dividing government into parts. Instead, they retained *in toto* the activities of government, reflecting upon constitutional and policy-making functions and their interaction with administration. Moreover, these British thinkers moved away from the study of formal governmental institutions to provide a realistic picture of policy-making, seeking consciously to dismantle the illusions and outdated beliefs which shrouded the processes of government. For example, as we shall see, Beveridge shattered the illusion that the Minister runs his department and pointed out that, in reality, it is the permanent and anonymous career civil servants who run the executive departments and not the Ministers themselves.

From the foregoing clarification of the term 'politics', two subsidiary contrasts can be drawn between the British and American doctrines, in addition to the obvious distinction of fusion versus separation. The first contrast is that the British doctrine contained only one definition of politics as 'policy-making' and not two definitions as in the American doctrine. The second contrast is that the British doctrine concentrated on the reality of policy-making instead of focusing on theories about the formal institutions of government. However, other British administrative thinkers in the period 1900–39 diverged from the British Philosophy of Administration. These dissenters were Sidney and Beatrice Webb and Harold Laski who were primarily radical reformers rather than realists and they displayed symptoms of the American zest for the formal, institutional study of politics. The views of the Webbs and Laski will be compared with the doctrine of the British Philosophy of Administration in the course of this chapter.

Although the British doctrine centred upon the one definition of politics as 'policy-making', it fell naturally into two strands. The first strand was a *descriptive* one, with contributors to the British Philosophy of Administration describing the fusion between policy-making and administration and, indeed, between constitutional matters and administration. The writings of Haldane and Beveridge form the main body of this first strand and the purpose of their descriptions, as suggested earlier, was to introduce reality into the understanding of British government. The second strand was a *prescriptive* one, dealing with methods for improving policy-making and its links with administration. Whereas the first doctrinal strand was confined to the processes of government, the second prescriptive strand encompassed both government and business and it emerged from the works of

Wallas and Sheldon. Wallas attempted to improve the study of human nature, which he believed would create a truer knowledge of human thought processes and, hence, of policy-making.[12] The fusion, or connection, between policy-making and administration is more subtle in this case. It stems from the fact that Wallas intended his improved methods of policy-making – or judgment – to apply to politicians and administrators alike. In other words, he did not limit his prescriptions to politicians, but acknowledged that public administrators are involved in policy decisions which affect the nation and they have a responsibility to improve their thought processes as much as politicians.

The first doctrine of the British Philosophy of Administration of a connection between policy-making and administration is now presented in detail from these descriptive and prescriptive viewpoints.

1. The administrator and policy-making: The descriptive strand

Both Haldane and Beveridge described the public administrator's involvement in policy-making *and* constitutional issues. Their views represent a direct antithesis to Woodrow Wilson's argument of 1887, in which he proposed that administration should be separated from both policy-making and constitutional matters. This descriptive strand of the doctrine includes constitutional issues, but this inclusion in no way alters the one basic definition of politics as 'policy-making' underlying the British Philosophy of Administration. Rather, these constitutional descriptions extend and reinforce the British doctrine that government is a matter of interwoven processes and not separate ones. In Haldane's writing, his references to the administrator's role in constitutional affairs are lengthier and more interesting than his views on the administrator's policy-making role and, for this reason, they are considered first.

Haldane's experience in British government was as a Minister rather than a civil servant but, in his capacity as War Minister at the

12. Towards the end of the period under study, Harold Lasswell in the United States recognised that policy-making was a process which required knowledge about human personality and he paid tribute to Wallas' earlier ideas. Lasswell, however, promoted a third definition of politics as 'the contest for power' by élite groups (whether or not *party* contest). See H. D. Lasswell, *Politics: Who Gets What, When, How,* (New York) 1936. Reprinted edn (New York) 1972, pp. 80–94, 216. By contrast, within the British Philosophy of Administration, power was discussed mainly under the heading of 'bureaucracy' rather than 'politics' and, accordingly, it forms part of Ch. 5 in this book.

beginning of this century, he was responsible for the administration of the War Office. Added to this administrative experience, he chaired the Ministry of Reconstruction's Committee on the Machinery of Government and in this position was called upon to investigate and make recommendations for the improvement of the Civil Service machine following the First World War.[13] His experience and interest in public administration gained him a reputation in the field, which led in 1922 to his appointment as first President of the new Institute of Public Administration. One of Haldane's early Presidential addresses to the Institute was on the subject of 'The constitutional evolution of the Civil Service' and in this address he drew the attention of civil servants to their constitutional role in British government.

He pointed out that the British constitution embodies not a concept of rules, but the more elastic safeguard of taking advice before acting and he traced the origin of the modern constitutional convention, whereby the Cabinet acts as an advisory body to the Sovereign, to the Norman Conquest. The Norman kings, although professing to act by legal power, in reality, took systematic advice from a body of councillors. This advice kept them informed of public opinion, Haldane argued, which all sovereigns need to have on their side, for public opinion is the real source of sovereignty. He proceeded to link the historical background of the British constitution to the modern advisory role of the Cabinet, assisted by the Civil Service. At the time of his address in 1923, there were six Secretaries of State in the Cabinet. These Cabinet Ministers, he explained, are direct and responsible advisers to the Sovereign – in this case the King. The Prime Minister, if he is dissatisfied with his Secretaries of State, has to make a formal request to the Sovereign to remove any one of them, since each has received seals from the Sovereign. Haldane cited an example from his personal experience as Secretary of State for War from 1905 to 1912 to illustrate how the advice of civil servants to these Cabinet Ministers affects the latters' role as advisers to the Sovereign.

Each Secretary of State has the full legal authority to undertake the work of any of the other Secretaries. Hence, as Secretary of State for War, Haldane was called upon to act, temporarily and additionally, as Secretary of State for Home Affairs while his colleague in the Home Office took a holiday. As Secretary of State for War, he had recently despatched a letter to the Home Office requesting some powers. In his own words:

13. See *Report of the Machinery of Government Committee* (London) 1918.

38

... I had just addressed a letter to the Home Office for some powers. I had written an official letter, as Secretary for War. But when I was at the Home Office one of the first things I was called upon to do was to refuse my own request, and I wrote a letter to myself saying 'No'.[14]

The inference from this example is that each Secretary of State is advised by a different set of civil servants and this advisory role of the Civil Service checks the Minister's power, making him reluctant to insist on his own preferred course of action. In other words, any arbitrary power of the Minister which could arise in Britain on account of her unwritten constitution is curtailed by the Civil Service. While the unwritten British constitution may not incur the use of arbitrary power, Haldane provided another example to show that its changing nature can give rise to obscurity. Drawing this time on his experience as Lord Chancellor from 1912 to 1915,[15] he made the following recollection.

About the third day of his arrival in this post, he received a warrant for £1,850 from the Treasury. It appeared that an ancient custom of the British constitution entitled Lord Chancellors to an emolument to purchase silver plate and the custom originated from the time when the Lord Chancellor, as the King's principal Minister, received funds for this purpose. Accordingly, the payment to Haldane did not appear on the Estimates but on the Civil List of payments. Under a Liberal Ministry, he decided that he was paid adequately and would return the majority of the payment to the Treasury. However, he suggested that some £300 of government money should be used to purchase from him an old State coach and some gold robes belonging to former Lord Chancellors and for which he had no use. Three weeks later, the evening paper announced:

Terrible scandal in connection with the financial arrangements of the Lord Chancellor's office . . .[16]

The Treasury had not mentioned the £1,850 which had been returned under the head of the Civil List, but had put in a supplementary estimate for over £300 for Haldane's coach and robes and the Public Accounts Committee had complained.

In a simple manner, Haldane's two examples indicate how the British Civil Service is involved in *constitutional* issues and the wide

14. R. B. Haldane, 'The constitutional evolution of the Civil Service', *Journal of Public Administration*, Vol. II, 1924, 15.
15. Haldane was Lord Chancellor again from 23 January to 7 November 1924, see Sir C. Schuster, 'Lord Haldane as Lord Chancellor', *Public Administration*, Vol. VI, 1928, 361-4.
16. R. B. Haldane, 'Constitutional evolution', op. cit., p. 18.

range of knowledge required by civil servants to fulfil their tasks. Regarding Haldane's descriptions of the public administrator's *policy-making* role, they are inherent, to an extent, in the foregoing constitutional examples. And, unlike Beveridge, he did not elaborate in depth upon the civil servant's policy-making role. Instead, Haldane took this fusion as an accepted fact; a conclusion which is clearly illustrated in the *Report of the Machinery of Government Committee*. The Haldane Committee's Report published in 1918 set out a category of recommendations under the heading of 'Formulation of policy' which suggested further structural arrangements in the Civil Service to assist public administrators in formulating policy. These arrangements are based on the scientific principles of 'staff' and 'line' and they include research and intelligence – or 'staff' – facilities to aid policy-making.[17] The description of the public administrator's involvement in policy-making is contained, therefore, in the Committee's blatant reference to policy formulation by civil servants and to its simple admission that 'the elaboration of policy cannot be . . . readily distinguished from the business of administration'.

The Committee believed that if the research or 'fact-finding' process could be developed further in the British Civil Service, along the lines of the newly constituted Department of Scientific and Industrial Research,[18] public administrators would be able to assume greater responsibility for policy-making activities. The Committee pointed out that:'A Cabinet with such knowledge at its disposal would, we believe, be in a position to devolve, with greater freedom and confidence than is at present the case, the duties of administration, and even of legislation.'[19]

Haldane confirmed his acceptance of the fusion of policy-making with administration in British government in 1920, when he addressed the Society of Civil Servants. In his address, he stated that it is impossible to draw a hard and fast line between policy and administration. He wanted a Minister to be able to go to Parliament armed with policy ideas, which had been thought out at length by civil servants and supported by factual knowledge. He was careful to stress he was not advocating that the expert administrator should *govern*, for

17. The scientific principles of 'staff' and 'line' are discussed in detail in Ch. 3, pp. 88–100
18. The Department of Scientific and Industrial Research was established under a Committee of the Privy Council in 1915–16 to meet an acknowledged need for scientific and technical progress. See D. N. Chester, ed., and F. M. G. Willson, *The Organization of British Central Government 1914–1964* (London) 1957. Second edn 1968, pp. 25, 249–73.
19. *Report of the Machinery of Government Committee*, pp. 6–7.

that would be bureaucracy, but beyond this passing reference to the power of the official, Haldane dismissed the danger.[20]

Turning now to Beveridge's descriptions, they are outlined in the same order beginning with the civil servant's involvement in constitutional matters and followed by his policy-making role. Beveridge served for many years as a practising public servant but in May 1919, when he was Permanent Secretary to the Ministry of Food, he was invited by Sidney Webb to leave the Civil Service and become Director of the London School of Economics. Beveridge accepted the new post as Director of the School which he held from 1919 to 1937, but he continued in his new capacity to encourage the development of public administration. In 1921, he was called upon to deliver a lecture to the Society of Civil Servants and he took advantage of being able to look back on his personal experience of public administration. On reflection, he considered the work to be demoralising in the sense that the civil servant is so close to the workings of government that he can hold no romantic illusions about it. He pointed out that the poet, professor or businessman may retain many illusions about the British constitution but civil servants are on the 'inside' and know too much about its reality. Indeed, civil servants are the 'seams' of the British constitution without which it would fall to pieces, but because of their involvement they are aware of the frauds of the constitution. Beveridge identified two frauds – or great illusions – of the British constitution to support his argument that civil servants are the 'seams' of the constitution since they uphold these illusions.

The first illusion is that the Minister really runs his department and knows all that it is doing. This illusion, Beveridge pointed out, is fostered by the mechanism of the Parliamentary question. During the process of Parliamentary questions, a Cabinet Minister demonstrates to the House of Commons his apparent omniscience about the administration of his department, even though it is the officials who prepare his answer. Sometimes, however, the illusion is shattered as Beveridge recalled by citing an incident which took place during the First World War. The official in charge, having supplied the answer to the Parliamentary question, attached to it a note for the guidance of the Minister, but the Minister regrettably read out before Parliament both the answer and the confidential note:

20. R. B. Haldane, 'The machinery of government', *The Civil Servant and His Profession* (London) 1920, p. 42. The Haldane Committee had commented upon the risks of power by officials but, again, the reference was only brief. See Ch. 5, pp. 214–5.

The answer to the first part of the question is in the negative; the remaining parts therefore do not arise.

This Member is being very tiresome; to give him any information only whets his appetite for more.[21]

The first illusion, then, is that the Minister is 'all-knowing' about the activities of his department and it is fostered by the Parliamentary question. The second illusion, closely interwoven with the first, is that the Minister is personally responsible for work, which in fact has been undertaken by civil servants and this illusion is encouraged by the convention of anonymity. In other words, the individual Minister assumes responsibility for work accomplished by civil servants in his department whose names remain unknown. Being a former civil servant, Beveridge was aware of these constitutional illusions which give the impression that the British Minister is 'all-knowing' and 'all-responsible' when, in reality, he depends upon civil servants for information and guidance. But Beveridge was content simply to draw attention to these illusions. He did not seek to change either the British constitution or the Civil Service's supporting role within it. However, he took the precaution of suggesting that the civil servant on entering the Service should continue to abide by the triple vow of poverty, anonymity and obedience, similar to the vow taken by members of the famous Order of St. Francis. By poverty, Beveridge did not mean destitution, but he did believe that the civil servant should not try to compete with the business world in income. He must accept a salary sufficient to permit him to raise and educate his family to a high standard, but beyond this he must not seek to parallel his income to that of the businessman.

The second element of the vow demonstrated Beveridge's accord with the long-standing convention of anonymity by public officials – at least to the extent that their names are not divulged. He insisted that he had no intention of disturbing the illusion of the British constitution by which the responsibility is the Minister's but the work that of the civil servant. The third element of the vow was obedience and, although he noted the fusion of constitutional and administrative issues in the form of the civil servant's role in advising the Minister, Beveridge was anxious that the official should not pass the boundaries of obedience to the extent of *dictating* policy which would create the worst form of bureaucracy. Like Haldane, therefore, he made brief reference to the power of officials but did not elaborate further on the risk.

21. W. Beveridge, 'The civil servant of the future', *The Development of the Civil Service* (London) 1922, pp. 229–30.

Concerning the civil servant's policy-making role, Beveridge (1920) was of the opinion that the constitutional illusions which directed attention to the Minister caused the extent of the public official's influence in policy-making to be overlooked. Although he favoured retaining the convention of anonymity in the sense that civil servants should not be named individually, he was aware that the 'silent' nature of the Civil Service meant the apparent business of the public administrator was taken to be the recording and communicating of Ministers' decisions rather than participating in policy-making. Therefore, as an ex-civil servant, Beveridge decided to present the inside or realistic point of view at a public lecture.[22] He likened the fusion of policy-making and administration in the Civil Service to a Victorian 'marriage' between the Minister and his senior civil servant – the Permanent Secretary or his equivalent. His lecture illustrated not only the official's contribution to the policy-making process but also the inverse situation of the Minister's intrusion into administration during the emergency circumstances of the First World War. Beveridge lamented the temporary breakdown in the Victorian marriage which had occurred during the war and he opened his lecture with an explanation of how in wartime, Ministers had actively assumed the work of *official* head of their department as well as *political* head. Normally, the official duties are undertaken by the Permanent Secretary in the Civil Service, but because Ministers had few Parliamentary duties and no Cabinet meetings during the war, they engaged more actively in administrative affairs, so upsetting the delicate marriage relationship.[23] Beveridge argued that since the war was over, politicians and administrators should return to their normal marital relationship. Although he described separately the roles of the Minister and the civil servant within the Victorian marriage, his analogy demonstrates clearly the influence which the official brings to bear on policy-making.

Describing first the Minister's role in the marriage, Beveridge likened him to the head of the Victorian household who undertakes in his name all public acts, including correspondence. He alone speaks and votes for the household and formally he makes all important decisions

22. W. Beveridge, *The Public Service in War and in Peace* (London) 1920, pp.1–63.
23. In 1916, the Prime Minister, Lloyd George, discarded the traditional Cabinet and formed a War Cabinet of five Ministers only. Most 'departmental' Ministers were excluded from Cabinet meetings until the full Cabinet resumed in 1919, and during this war period, they had extra time to devote to public administration. See also D. N. Chester, ed., and F. M. G. Willson, *Organization of British Central Government*, pp. 285–91.

in the same way that the Victorian husband decides where the family shall live and where the boys shall be educated. He makes these decisions, however, on advice which if disregarded would prove very uncomfortable for him. The Minister is the head of the household and yet he is not in regular charge of it. Indeed, the prosperity of the department depends on his outside achievements and if he is an active fighter in Parliament and in the Cabinet, he will succeed in increasing the powers of his department, as well as pay and promotion opportunities. If he is weak, his department can do nothing and he is powerless inside his department to restore the deficiency. In such cases, the Permanent Secretary may be seen to take an active, rather than a silent, part in Cabinet committees and in discussions with other departments, but he experiences the handicap of being a mere official just as a mere woman is handicapped when carrying out the work of a man. For, like men with women, Ministers with officials have an instinctive jealousy of those officials who appear at their intimate deliberations.

Beveridge described the business of the Permanent Secretary within the Victorian marriage as minding the house and keeping all the members of the household in order. His function includes making officials work, preventing them from quarrelling and seeing that the Minister leaves for his daily toil in Cabinet or Parliament equipped with all the requisite information. Metaphorically speaking, the Permanent Secretary has to ensure that the Minister has all his buttons on and his hat brushed for public appearance. Like the Victorian wife, the Permanent Secretary has no public life and is unknown outside the home; she exercises power by influence rather than directly.[24] The Minister, like the Victorian husband, is responsible for the acts and faults of the Permanent Secretary, and must stand up for him in public and shield him from attack. Beveridge continued:

> Like the Victorian wife also, the permanent secretary is all for monogamy; like men, ministers often have hankerings after polygamy, and want occasional change of society. This is a very remarkable relation, and it is strange that it has worked so well, particularly when it is remembered that the marriage is in all cases one of arrangement, not of affection. The permanent secretary has no voice in choosing the minister, and the minister none in choosing the permanent secretary.

24. Another book describing the fusion of policy-making with administration within the period 1900–39 was written by H. E. Dale, *The Higher Civil Service of Great Britain* (London) 1941. Dale, like Beveridge, was a former higher civil servant who, in describing his experiences, adopted a similar marital analogy to illustrate the Minister's reliance on his departmental civil servants. Ibid., pp.85–6.

Often the two never see one another till the day of the wedding. A divorce is as difficult as an Act of Parliament.[25]

The foregoing analogy by Beveridge confirmed a fusion – or connection – in the form of a relationship between policy-making and administration in which the public administrator takes a real but behind-the-scenes role in policy-making. These *realistic* descriptions by Haldane and Beveridge of the fusion of constitutional and policy-making issues with administration will now be contrasted with the more *radical reforms* for British government proposed by Sidney and Beatrice Webb and Harold Laski.

When indicating the civil servant's involvement in maintaining the illusions of the British constitution, Beveridge made it clear that he did not favour the Webbs' scheme of total constitutional reform for Britain.[26] Underlying the Webbs' scheme (1920)[27] was their belief in Fabian socialism which caused them to envisage a constitution for a new socialist commonwealth of Great Britain. Since the constitution of the socialist commonwealth would prosper socialism instead of capitalism, the Webbs considered that it would be necessary to make substantial modifications to the existing institutions of British government. Although they retained the monarch as the titular head of the socialist commonwealth, the Webbs could find no place for the House of Lords since they were against hereditary legislators, criticising them for being a narrow caste privileged by immense private riches. The House of Commons would be divided into two – to yield a 'Political' and a 'Social' Parliament both with their own executive branch. The Political Parliament and its Executive would be responsible for foreign affairs, the courts of justice, internal law and order while the Social Parliament and its Executive would direct national and social affairs, but the two Parliamentary assemblies would consult together, possibly by means of joint committees or conferences. Under the Webbs' scheme the principle of a bicameral legislature was retained, but it took the form not of the two Chambers of the Lords and Commons but of the Political Chamber and the Social Chamber.

The Social Parliament and its Executive would manage the nation's economic and social activities. This organ of government would have supreme control over national economic resources, including the power

25. W. Beveridge, *The Public Service*, pp.9–29. Quotation p. 22.
26. W. Beveridge, 'Civil servant of the future', op. cit., p. 231.
27. S. and B. Webb, *A Constitution for the Socialist Commonwealth of Great Britain* (London) 1920. It should be noted that in 1929 Sidney Webb received the title of Lord Passfield.

to tax normally vested in the Crown and Parliament, and the industries necessary to use these resources, so bringing the instruments of production under the ownership and control of the State. In the case of social activities, the Social Parliament and its Executive would be responsible for essential public services, such as health, education and transport.[28] However, the Social Parliament, the Webbs suggested, would not create a Cabinet of Ministers with collective responsibility, such as they proposed for the Political Parliament which would stand or fall on a vote of the Political Parliament in the traditional way. Instead, the work of the Social Parliament would be based on the model of the London County Council – that is, there would be a system of standing committees of the Social Parliament to correspond to each main department of work; each committee being responsible for overseeing its own commodity or service and advising the Social Parliament on issues that arise within that service.[29] Under this scheme, the *administrative* departments of the Social Executive would not be placed under individual *political* Ministers but policy-making and administration would be separate. Immediately a contrast is seen with the British Philosophy of Administration doctrine of a fusion between policy-making and administration, for the Webbs argued:

> The essential feature of our proposal is the *separation* of current administration on the one hand from the decision of policy on the other. In the whole sphere of policy – such as the quality and quantity of the service to be rendered, and how, when and where the commodity or service is to be made available for the needs of the community – the Social Parliament will be, through its standing committee, the supreme authority. But with the day-to-day administration in the widest sense, including appointments and promotions, purchases and sales, and the choice between this or that method or technical device of the service, the principle should be that there should be no more Parliamentary interference . . .[30]

A further check would be necessary on the executive departments, the Webbs conceded, besides the supervision by the standing committees of the Social Parliament. Since this responsibility would no

28. The Webbs proposed the nationalisation of industries and services, including railways, canals, the mining industry, afforestation, insurance and banking, while the nationalisation of other services would be left to experience to decide. S. and B. Webb, op. cit., p. 168.
29. Although the Haldane Committee (1917–18) did not discuss Parliamentary control at length, it did suggest standing committees of Parliament to oversee public administration. It is possible that Beatrice Webb, as a Committee member, put forward this suggestion. See *Report of the Machinery of Government Committee*, p. 15.
30. S. and B. Webb, *A Constitution*, p. 169 (author's italics).

longer fall on individual Ministers, they suggested that other executive departments should assume the task of control. Accordingly, they proposed *two* departments for each nationalised industry or service; the first to actually *administer* and the second to *control* the administration. Their plan, then, abandoned ministerial responsibility altogether in the case of the Social Parliament and its Executive.[31] Like Beveridge, the Webbs claimed that ministerial responsibility was 'illusory' and they condemned the procedure of Parliamentary questions and answers for merely increasing the work of the official rather than controlling public administration. But, whereas Beveridge sought only to point out the illusions of the constitution in order to reveal reality – and presumably to enhance the morale of civil servants by noting their important role in constitutional matters – the Webbs removed the convention of ministerial responsibility from the Second Chamber and its Executive. With this abandonment of the convention of ministerial responsibility went also the convention of anonymity, for without ministerial responsibility there could be no Ministers' robes behind which anonymous civil servants could conceal themselves, waiting to advise or to be protected.

The Webbs differed again from Haldane and Beveridge by being preoccupied with the risks of executive power, and their major constitutional reform was devised intentionally to minimise the risk of tyranny by the official. They claimed that their scheme, based on the division of powers and functions between two co-ordinate Parliaments controlling two distinct national executives, would afford the necessary safeguards for individual liberty. Indeed, they argued that the existing methods of Parliamentary control – in which the convention of ministerial responsibility was 'illusory' – created a bureaucratic conspiracy against Parliamentary control.[32] It will be seen in Chapter 5 that the Webbs were not alone in fearing a bureaucratic conspiracy against Parliament. But, it was not until 1929 that allegations against this form of bureaucracy became rife, following outspoken criticisms by Lord Hewart, then Lord Chief Justice of England. Although the Webbs' plan for the socialist commonwealth was a masterly treatise, contributors to the British Philosophy of Administration paid little serious attention to it because of its revolutionary nature. Beveridge and

31. The Webbs retained Cabinet government and full ministerial responsibility in the case of the Political Parliament, but augmented it by a system of standing committees for each Ministry, charged with continuous supervision of the work of the departments to ensure correct policy implementation. S. and B. Webb, op. cit., p. 117.
32. Ibid., pp. 108–76.

Haldane preferred to retain the existing constitution, but simply to indicate the realistic fusion between constitutional and policy-making issues and administration. And, even though Sidney and Beatrice Webb incorporated several of the recommendations of the Haldane Committee on the Machinery of Government into their constitutional reforms,[33] they were far more radical than Haldane on account of their Fabian socialism, as Beatrice noted:

> Haldane believed more than we did in the existing governing class: in the great personages of Court, Cabinet and City. We staked our hopes on the organised working-class, served and guided, it is true, by an élite of unassuming experts who would make no claim to superior social status, but would content themselves with exercising the power inherent in superior knowledge and longer administrative experience.[34]

If contributors to the British Philosophy of Administration did not take the Webbs' constitutional reforms seriously, Harold Laski (1925)[35] did. Being at this time a Fabian[36] and a *radical reformer*, he also put forward proposals to modify substantially the institutions of British government. Like the Webbs, he disapproved of the House of Lords as the Second Chamber in British Parliamentary government[37] and approached his reforms by studying other methods of two-chamber government, which directed him to the Webbs' scheme. Indeed, Laski had joined the staff of the London School of Economics in 1920 and he dedicated his reforms to the School and to Sidney and Beatrice Webb – its founders. But, although he gave serious attention to the Webbs' scheme and found it attractive, he pronounced it unworkable. He argued that because the Social Parliament had the taxing power, it would sooner or later draw essential control to itself. In addition, he criticised the fragmentation of policy which would arise from the Webbs' bicameral suggestion, maintaining that foreign policy cannot be separated from economic policy. A Social Parliament cannot pass

---

33. For example, the Webbs retained the Haldane Committee's proposal for the organisation of administrative departments according to major purpose. See Ch. 3, pp. 100–15.
34. B. Webb, *Our Partnership*, ed. by B. Drake and M. I. Cole (London) 1948, p.97.
35. H. J. Laski, *A Grammar of Politics* (London) 1925. Reprinted edn 1926.
36. Laski was a Fabian in 1925 when *A Grammar of Politics* was first published but he had become a Marxist by 1938 when he added a new Preface to the book, indicating his change in views. See K. Martin, *Harold Laski (1893-1950): A Biographical Memoir* (London) 1953, p. 74.
37. Laski disliked the House of Lords for reasons similar to the Webbs. He claimed '... it involves setting aside permanently a small class in the State and giving to it a special control over policy. That is a denial of equal citizenship ...' H. J. Laski, *Grammar of Politics*, pp.328–9.

measures raising money for a department of foreign affairs and then be persuaded not to criticise the conduct of foreign affairs.

Neither did Laski approve of the joint committees between the two Parliaments, for he believed that power would reside either in the committees or the legislatures would sit almost continually in joint session. Whichever the case, policy would not be policy at all but a series of statutes uninformed by any general principles. His conclusion was that the making of policy requires a *single* assembly charged with oversight over the whole field of administration rather than a bicameral legislature. His reforms, therefore, were based on a single and magnicompetent legislative assembly which could maintain a cohension of policy and would replace the existing Houses of Lords and Commons. This new single legislature would be elected for a period of some four years, as in the United States' model of government, but otherwise he retained the traditional form of Cabinet government, whereby the executive is composed of elected members of the legislative assembly.[38]

Earlier, Laski (1921)[39] had stated his reforms for the conventions of ministerial responsibility and anonymity in a lecture to the Society of Civil Servants. In a manner similar to Beveridge, he pointed out certain illusions, or what he called 'traditions', which had become attached to the conventions. Beveridge has described the illusions, but Laski went further by seeking to reform the conventions themselves. While he did not suggest removing ministerial responsibility and anonymity altogether, as the Webbs did in the context of the Social Parliament, his reforms were substantial. They included the proposal that Command and official papers should bear the name of the civil servants who write them rather than being the creation of a 'mindless somewhat' presented through the Minister to a Parliament which knows he has neither written nor read them.[40] Secondly, Laski proposed that Ministers should take their permanent officials to the committee stage on all Bills and allow them to participate openly in policy discussion rather than to hide behind the Ministers. He insisted that he was urging

38. Ibid., pp. 335–48.
39. H. J. Laski, 'The Civil Service and Parliament', in *The Development of the Civil Service* (London) 1922, pp. 20–36.
40. Laski proposed that civil servants should be named individually for their work, but Beveridge did not favour such identification as seen in this chapter, pp. 42–3. However, another contributor to the British Philosophy of Administration, Graham Wallas, was less emphatic than Beveridge and suggested that it would 'humanise' British public administration if, from time to time, an official report was published with the civil servant's signature. See G. Wallas, *The Great Society: A Psychological Analysis* (London) 1914, pp. 290–2.

only that the official should state publicly what he was known to whisper in the ministerial ear:

> I do not mean that the doctrine of ministerial responsibility ought to be destroyed, I do not even mean that the doctrine of quasi-anonymity is altogether harmful. I mean that it must be made possible for the private member, and therefore for the man in the street, to envisage what you do and who you are. It is, perhaps, a curious thing, but it is psychologically true, that one always suspects the working of an impersonal institution.[41]

Two schools of thought can be seen to have existed in Britain between 1900 and 1939: the main doctrine of the British Philosophy of Administration which stressed *realism*, and the other of a more *radical* nature. Of the latter school, the Webbs were more extreme than Laski in the 1920s since he appears to have integrated strains from both schools into his works, which is not surprising when he came into contact with both the realists and the Webbs at the London School of Economics.[42] For example, he outlined innovative reforms for the institutions of British government based on a single legislature to replace the Lords and the Commons, but he favoured keeping Cabinet government whereby the legislative–executive institutions are fused. Again, on other occasions, Laski promoted the British Philosophy of Administration doctrine of a fusion between policy-making and administration,[43] which the Webbs rejected. His reforms were also less drastic than the Webbs' in connection with the conventions of ministerial responsibility and anonymity which they abandoned altogether with respect to the Social Parliament and its Executive. Laski sought only to modify them.

The doctrines of the British Philosophy of Administration are the main subject of this book, but having identified both the realistic doctrine of the British Philosophy of Administration and the more radical reforms of the Webbs and Laski, both schools will be analysed briefly. The strength of the British Philosophy of Administration doctrine of a fusion between policy-making and administration, portrayed in the descriptions by Haldane and Beveridge, was that it

41. H. J. Laski, 'Civil Service and Parliament', op. cit., pp. 25–6.
42. For an interesting account of Laski at the London School of Economics in contact with Wallas, Haldane, Beveridge and the Webbs, see K. Martin, *Harold Laski*, pp. 44–75.
43. For other occasions when Laski promoted the doctrine of a fusion between policy-making and administration, see H. J. Laski, *An Introduction to Politics* (London) 1931, pp.79–80, and W. A. Robson, 'Harold Laski', *Public Administration*, Vol. 28, 1950, 219–20.

moved away from constitutional and political theory, which was often unrealistic, to describe the actual workings of British government. Unlike the American doctrine of a separation between policy-making and administration Haldane and Beveridge, by choosing examples based on their experience, conveyed the 'inside' and real picture of the civil servant's involvement in policy-making and constitutional matters. However, several weaknesses were inherent in their simplistic, subjective views. While the realistic approach was useful as a means of communication at live addresses, it provided little academic substance on which to found the British doctrine of fusion. Neither Haldane nor Beveridge added to their addresses at a later stage with a systematic account of the workings of the British constitution or the civil servant's role within it. Therefore, their addresses remained part of a miscellany of published ideas in British administrative thought between 1900 and 1939.

Further weaknesses in Beveridge's descriptions were that he did not spell out very clearly the constitutional illusions, but tended to overlap the conventions of ministerial responsibility and anonymity. As he was addressing a group of civil servants his descriptions were understood but, as a basis for the academic study of public administration, they are too summary and presume too much prior knowledge of the Civil Service to form an adequate realistic view of the workings of British government. Furthermore, Beveridge exacerbated the unsystematic nature of British administrative thought by introducing into the fusion of constitutional and administrative issues, the question of pay in the Civil Service. In connection with the vow of poverty, he expected the civil servant to abide by this vow and to display the same dedication to his profession as the monk gives to his religion. Although many civil servants at this time were prepared to serve the State – and the motto of the Society of Civil Servants which Beveridge was addressing was 'We Serve the State'[44] – he was asking a great deal of the official by suggesting he should agree to relative poverty compared with the business administrator – particularly when the public administrator's salary may *not* have permitted him to educate his family to the standard Beveridge envisaged.[45] However, his intention in referring to the vow of poverty

44. See Sir C. Harcourt-Smith, 'Opening address' to a series of lectures to the Society of Civil Servants, published in *The Civil Servant and His Profession* (London) 1920, p. 2.
45. For example, Josiah Stamp left the British Civil Service for a career in industry because he wished to accrue sufficient money to educate his children to university level. See J. H. Jones, *Josiah Stamp Public Servant: The Life of the First Baron Stamp of Shortlands* (London) 1964, pp. 100–1.

was to uphold the ethical ideal of service to the State, which is indicative of the ethical idealism within the British Philosophy of Administration discussed in Chapter 4.

Another point of weakness in the case of both Haldane and Beveridge is that they failed to discuss seriously the possible dangers which might result from the civil servant's increasing role in policy-making. Beveridge was of the opinion in 1920 that the public underestimated the civil servant's role in policy-making, which led him to stress the official's influence. A few years later, however, the country faced a major outbreak of criticism against the growing *power of officials*. In fact, in the early 1920s, comments were already building up in professional journals, such as *Public Administration*, about the legislative and judicial powers exercised by civil servants. Haldane and Beveridge, having confidence in the Civil Service, appeared unaware that critics, like constitutional lawyers, might fear the misuse of power by officials. Although the later allegations of bureaucracy – or the *power of officials* – proved on investigation to be potential rather than actual dangers, it was an omission on the part of Haldane and Beveridge not to have foreseen some of the future criticisms.

The second school of thought, in contrast to the British Philosophy of Administration, was intent on radical reforms rather than on describing realism. The Webbs were extreme in their reforms, concentrating on promoting Fabian socialism by means of an entirely different British constitution. Their reforms centred around a network of new political and administrative institutions and their approach can be likened to that of Jeremy Bentham, who, in the nineteenth century, devised an original code of reform for the administrative institutions of British government.[46] Beatrice even named Bentham as 'Sidney's intellectual god-father'.[47] The Webbs were both rational and efficient; they systematically traced the whole detailed scheme for their socialist commonwealth which they regarded as a feat in 'social engineering'. It is not surprising, then, that Beatrice referred to her husband as a 'social engineer' rather than a 'popular leader'![48] In retrospect, the Webbs' approach appears to have had a closer affinity with the American doctrine of a separation between policy-making and administration than with the British doctrine of fusion. This is evident from the fact that they based their reforms on a separation of powers which

46. J. Bentham, *Constitutional Code*, in *The Works of Jeremy Bentham*, Vol. IX, ed. by J. Bowring (Edinburgh) 1843.
47. B. Webb *Our Partnership*, p. 210.
48. Ibid., p. 6.

incorporated a system of checks and balance similar to that underlying the American constitution. Furthermore, their engineering approach embodied a mechanical attitude to efficiency more akin to that of Frederick Taylor than to the contributors of the British Philosophy of Administration.[49] The main strength of the Webbs' reforms was its systematic character which contrasts markedly with the descriptions of Haldane and Beveridge. However, the doctrine of the British Philosophy of Administration was the accepted wisdom.

Two criticisms of the Webbs' scheme, in addition to the weaknesses outlined by Laski, should be mentioned. Firstly, Sidney and Beatrice demonstrated an ambivalence towards the conventions of ministerial responsibility and anonymity. This ambivalence is revealed by their condemnation and abandonment of the conventions in connection with the Social Parliament, but their retention of full ministerial responsibility in the case of the Political Parliament. Accordingly, they weakened their argument against the conventions. The second criticism is that the Webbs relied on 'government by committees'. They proposed standing committees, committees to link the two Parliaments and advisory committees within their scheme, so introducing another element of American government (even though their plan was based partly on the London County Council model), for specialised committees of Congress have been a long-standing feature of Congressional government.[50] The Webbs anticipated the criticism of 'government by committees' in their book in these words:

49. The Webbs stressed efficiency as an aim in their constitutional reforms on several occasions; for example, they referred to the increased publicity they proposed for public administration as an 'efficiency torchlight'. S. and B. Webb, *A Constitution*, pp. 194–5.
50. Legislative committees were to a large extent inevitable in Congressional government because of the absence of effective executive leadership or responsibility to the legislators. In 1920 the House of Representatives had 60 legislative committees, and in 1921 the Senate reduced its committees from 73 to 33. These committees exert a no less effective control over the House than does the British Cabinet, and in the United States discussion of a pending matter is more real in committee than in the House itself. Moreover, by the 1920s, the committees' *inquisitional* power had become increasingly active, so that they exerted control over administrative departments through inquisitions. By contrast, although the British Parliament had used committees since 1340, the House of Commons was not segmented into legislative committees like the American Congress. Standing committees were only slowly expanded in the House of Commons, and in 1920 there were six such committees. There was some opposition to their growth by opponents, who argued that they struck at the convention of Cabinet responsibility to the whole House. However, the Webbs and Laski favoured the growth of committees within the British legislature. See L. Roberts, 'Committees, legislative', *Encyclopaedia of the Social Sciences*, Vol. IV (London) 1931, 40–4.

Those who declaim against the absurdity of 'government by committees' do not realise the extent to which every great industry is, even under Capitalism, already 'governed by committees' – by boards of directors (of which there are, in 1920, over 66,000 in Great Britain) ... The difference between what is now proposed and what already exists under Capitalism is not any increase in the complication of the machinery of administration, but its simplification and rationalisation on the one hand, and on the other the dragging of it into light. What we wish to substitute for the present chaos is systematic co-ordination. What we propose to end is not simplicity but secrecy.[51]

Although the Webbs argued against the criticism of 'government by committees', Chapter 3 of this book will show that there are serious weaknesses in over-utilising the committee as a method of communication and there is no doubt that their plan did embody this weakness of an over-reliance on committees.

Laski was also a radical reformer, publishing in his lifetime some twenty-two books on government[52] and, like the Webbs, he retained an institutional approach to the subject. He grew progressively more revolutionary[53] as he moved from Fabianism to Marxism but, in the 1920s, he was somewhat less provocative than the Webbs. As a result, his institutional reforms – and not those of the Webbs – found a place in the acknowledged textbooks on political science.[54] However, a main weakness in Laski's works was that, despite his radical claims, he maintained the traditional nineteenth-century approach of examining government from the viewpoint of constitutional and institutional theory and, in this respect, he was more old-fashioned than contributors to the British Philosophy of Administration.

The first strand of the British Philosophy of Administration doctrine of a fusion between policy-making and administration has concerned the *descriptive* views of Haldane and Beveridge. These realistic descriptions have been contrasted with the radical reforms of the Webbs and Laski. The second strand within the doctrine of the British Philosophy of Administration will now be detailed and it relates to the *prescriptive* views of Wallas and Sheldon.

51. S. and B. Webb *A Constitution*, p. 200.
52. See W. A. Robson, 'Harold Laski', op. cit., p. 219
53. The use of the term 'revolutionary' here applies to Laski's later desire for 'revolution by consent' and should not be confused with violent revolution, which was never his intention. See H. A. Deane, 'Laski, Harold J.', *International Encyclopaedia of the Social Sciences*, Vol. 9, 1968, 32.
54. See K. Martin, *Harold Laski*, p. 71.

2. The administrator and policy-making: The prescriptive strand

It should be re-emphasised that the connection, or fusion, between policy-making and administration is more subtle in this prescriptive strand than in the descriptive one. Graham Wallas acknowledged that statesmen *and* administrators are involved in policy-making and they need equally to improve their methods of thought. Although his prescriptions for policy-making are relevant to men faced with decisions in any sphere of life, he was interested particularly in 'social judgment' – that is, policies made by government representatives on behalf of the nation.[55] The connection between policy-making and administration, then, is based on Wallas' belief that public administrators contribute to the policy-making process and – like statesmen – they must seek to understand and improve the process. Sheldon's writing focused specifically on business administration, but the subtle relationship between policy-making and administration was retained. He stressed the desirability of creating connecting links between policy-making and administration. His emphasis on a *connection* between policy-making and administration contrasts noticeably with the American doctrine which supported the opposing wisdom of *separation*.

In Wallas' case he was a classics master at a boys' school for several years in the 1880s, before being appointed Lecturer and later Professor of Political Science at the London School of Economics. Notwithstanding his immersion in academic teaching, he retained an essentially practical and realistic approach to political science and administration which he nurtured by engaging himself in practical affairs, including his membership of the Royal Commission on the Civil Service (1912–15). Early in his university teaching career, he developed a keen interest in human nature and he was instrumental in channelling the study of policy-making in this direction and away from political institutions. Wallas' approach was not new, for thinkers of the past from Plato to Hobbes and Bentham had set out their views of human nature in politics.[56] Indeed, in Bentham's case, he had embodied an important psychological analysis in his works as well as a detailed code for the administrative institutions of government.[57] But there had been little

55. See G. Wallas, *Social Judgment* (London) 1934, pp. 15–16.
56. See G. Wallas, *Human Nature in Politics*, p. 35. See also T. Hobbes, *Leviathan*, 1651. Republished (London) 1968.
57. Bentham's psychological analysis is contained in *An Introduction to The Principles of Morals and Legislation*, 1789. Republished (Darien, Conn.) 1948.

further development in the psychology of politics since Bentham's works and, instead, political institutions had received the focus of attention in Britain and the United States, as Wallas was aware in 1908 when he wrote: '. . . nearly all students of politics analyse institutions and avoid the analysis of man. The study of human nature by the psychologists has, it is true, advanced enormously since the discovery of human evolution, but it has advanced without affecting or being affected by the study of politics.[58]

Wallas found the modern neglect of the study of human nature in politics a most unsatisfactory state of affairs because fresh psychological and biological knowledge had accumulated since Bentham's time emanating from Darwin's *Origin of Species* onwards. Accordingly, the premises on which Bentham's psychology of man rested were outmoded.[59] Wallas' lifelong endeavour became to reveal the true nature of man – the policy-maker – in the light of the new psychological and biological information and then to propose how the process of policy-making might be improved.

His prescriptions fall into two classes relating to *group* and *individual* decisions. In the case of his advice on group decision-making, Wallas took as his background two policy decisions reached during the First World War. In both case-studies, group decision-making was weak and the incompetence was brought to light in two official documents which investigated the decisions, namely: the First Report of the British Dardanelles Commission (1917) and the Report of the Mesopotamia Commission (1917). The Mesopotamia Report concerned group co-operation between a body of Ministers and public officials who were not congregated in a Whitehall council room but dispersed in Simla, Bombay, Mesopotamia and London, and communicating mainly by telegraph. These policy-makers were responsible conjointly for the first calamitous advance on Baghdad – that is, for reaching a decision which was proved by the event to have been a mistake. The enquiry into this blunder indicated a lack of systematic exploration of the conditions of proposed action and, also, paralysing officialdom accompanied by a breakdown of medical arrangements which caused unnecessary suffering to the wounded. Evidence of conflict between Ministers and military officers was present, as to the extent of final authority which should have been given to the telegraphed military proposals, together with a tendency to conceal factors in the decision in the hope of obtaining desired ends.

58. G. Wallas, *Human Nature in Politics*, p. 37.
59. Ibid., pp. 36–41.

After reading the two reports of the Mesopotamia and Dardanelles decisions, Wallas attributed the faulty group decision-making to a lack of deliberate systematic thought because, in both cases, it was obvious that individual members of the groups were thinking principally at the subconscious level. Wallas termed this subconscious decision-making *the natural method*. By this method, group decisions are reached by a conflict of wills, which he described thus:

> . . . when men form decisions by means of the 'natural' method of a conflict of wills, followed either by an instinctive compromise or by the instinctive dominance of the stronger will, their mental processes are largely subconscious, and they are unable to give (as those often can who are co-operating in 'artificial' logical thought) an account of them which can be followed by others and tested by logical rules. They are unable to explain either the steps by which their forecast of results was reached, or the relation of their final decision to their forecast of results.[60]

In contrast to the natural method of decision-making, Wallas drew attention to *the artificial method* of decision-making involving logical thought which permits individual decision-makers within a group to give an account of their mental processes. These processes can, if required, be followed by other people and tested by logical rules. However, this artificial logical method of decision-making was absent from both these wartime policy decisions. Wallas was critical of the Mesopotamia and Dardanelles group decisions for another reason besides the lack of artificial thought by individual members of the group. His second criticism was directed towards the absence of training in co-operative thought displayed by the decision-makers. He argued, in respect of the Mesopotamia Report, that a necessary rule in co-operative thought is absolute frankness among the co-operating thinkers. But, the Mesopotamia Report had referred to 'want of frankness'. Another necessary rule is for each participant to train himself not to attach more initial weight to his own ideas than to those of others; he must overcome the impulse of first disliking his colleague for making a new suggestion and then disliking the suggestion because his colleague has made it.

Wallas' prescriptions for group policy-making, then, were to

60. G. Wallas, *Our Social Heritage* (New Haven) 1921, p. 67. Wallas' 'natural' method of decision-making by a conflict of wills is remarkably similar to the ideas of the American political scientist Mary Parker Follett, who lectured in Britain and the United States in the 1920s. In particular, Miss Follett's lecture, 'Constructive conflict' (1925) dealt with conflict and its relation to compromise and dominance. See *Dynamic Administration: The Collected Papers of Mary Parker Follett*, ed. by H. C. Metcalf and L. Urwick (London). Reprinted edn 1965, pp. 30–49.

develop logical thought and to train in co-operative decision-making. In stressing the use of logical thought in group policy-making, he was not advocating a complete change to logical thought but he recommended a *combination* of conscious scientific logic with a certain amount of natural thought – the latter he regarded as both inevitable and helpful. The helpfulness of natural, subconscious thought is that it prevents a narrowing approach to group decision-making and contributes an element of human sympathy. For, over-concentration on scientific logic, Wallas considered as dangerous as the lack of it. To illustrate this danger he cited the example of the Prussian military who, in 1914, made a series of errors in decision-making, which rendered war inescapable. These errors, he claimed, were due to an over-emphasis on technical efficiency which narrowed the decision-makers' vision and excluded human emotion.[61]

Regarding *individual* policy-making by statesmen and administrators, Wallas' thought is dispersed throughout his works from 1908 to 1932, but the same prescription for a combination between the natural and artificial methods of policy-making can be seen. However, his tendency to refer to the artificial and natural methods of policy-making in a variety of terms means that it is easy to overlook the constancy of his prescription. For example, he called the artificial method by terms such as intellectualism, reason, logic and rational thought, and the natural method by the terms of emotion, passion and instincts.[62] Before the First World War, when Wallas published two major books, political science was still strongly influenced by the traditional utilitarian view of 'intellectualism'. He was opposed to this strong emphasis on intellectualism as the primary component in man's deliberations because this traditional viewpoint – to which Bentham subscribed – tended to separate reason and emotion and to exaggerate the function of the former. Modern psychologists, on the other hand, in seeking to counter intellectualism had tended to the other fallacy of over-emphasising emotional behaviour – or instincts.

The true basis for political behaviour, Wallas argued, is a *combination* of reason and emotion.[63] Accordingly, as early as 1908, he strove towards Plato's concept whereby the two parts are consciously co-ordinated. Although he was greatly influenced by Plato's thinking, one of Wallas' objectives was to relate the study of politics to recent psychological and biological discoveries and he extracted from this

61. G. Wallas, *Our Social Heritage*, pp. 60–76.
62. See G. Wallas, *Human Nature in Politics*; *Great Society*; and *Social Judgment*.
63. G. Wallas, *Great Society*, pp. 40–59.

modern knowledge the important idea of conscious *control* over mental processes, which gave added support to the Platonic concept of co-ordination between reason and emotion.[64] From 1908 onwards, therefore, Wallas sought to explain the basis of both men's emotions and logical thought and to impress upon statesmen and administrators the significance of conscious control and co-ordination of these two elements in policy decisions. But, whereas his early books were still exploring the components of human nature, by 1932 he had become so alarmed by the confused thinking of statesmen and administrators on policy matters that he set out more positive prescriptions to improve their judgment, based on this theme of co-ordination of emotion with reason – or the natural with the artificial methods of decision-making.

In 1932, Wallas began his treatise by defining judgment more accurately as 'a choice between imagined actions, which the person judging is either to perform himself or to advise or compel others to perform'.[65] As a process, he confirmed, judgment involves the two psychological actions of:

1. A *rational* or scientific calculation of the probable results of the imagined actions (i.e. reason);
2. An *emotional* preference for one result rather than another (i.e. emotion).

Wallas feared that a wide gulf was forming between knowledge associated with the specialised sciences, such as economics, and judgment in the broader sense of wisdom.[66] Consequently, his advice to the individual administrator, particularly the economist, was to become a 'realist' who balances rational calculation with emotional sensitivity. The realist, he pointed out, deals with normative issues because he employs his character to influence the right choice of ends as well as the calculation of means. It is the administrator, he argued, who is more likely to be the realist than, say a teacher, since the administrator is involved daily in making or advising on real decisions in the real world.[67] The teacher, conversely, is more likely to be an 'analyst' tending towards an objective, rather than a normative, approach. Wallas criticised the analyst for over-stressing logical method and he accused

64. G. Wallas, *Human Nature in Politics*, pp. 198–212.
65. G. Wallas, *Social Judgment*, pp. 16–17.
66. Wallas associated wisdom with the teachings of the ancient Greeks, particularly Plato's *Republic* in which wisdom or judgment is based on a combination of reason and emotion. G. Wallas, *Social Judgment*, pp. 51–61.
67. Wallas quoted Josiah Stamp – civil servant and economist – as a typical realist, see G. Wallas, *Social Judgment*, p. 118.

the new 'laboratory' sciences of the same tendency.[68]

To summarise, we confirm that Wallas provided two sets of prescriptions for the administrator engaged in policy-making. The first set was directed towards group policy-making and the second set of prescriptions towards individual policy-making. In both cases, he advised administrators and statesmen to seek a balance between natural and artificial thought. Such a balance entailed forsaking entire reliance on the subconscious decision process (which he called 'muddling through')[69] but, at the same time, avoiding the other extreme of relying too heavily on the logical process. Wallas' variety in terminology makes it difficult to distinguish immediately the connection, or fusion, between policy-making and administration. For example, he wrote about 'decision'-making and 'judgment' more than policy-making. But, a close and thorough reading of his several texts, particularly *Social Judgment* (1932), indicates clearly that the type of decisions, or judgments, for which he offered his prescriptions were major policy decisions about national issues. In this context of policy-making, he stressed that his prescriptions were intended for administrators as well as statesmen.

Progressing to Sheldon's prescriptions, his terminology was equally confusing on occasions. Since he was writing about business administration, key terms he discussed were 'management' and 'labour'. He broke the 'management' category down into smaller parts to include Administration and Management proper and he defined the terms as follows:

> *Administration*, which is concerned in the determination of corporate policy, the co-ordination of finance, production and distribution, the settlement of the compass of the organization, and the ultimate control of the executive;
>
> *Management proper*, which is concerned in the execution of policy, within the limits set up by Administration, and the employment of the organization for the particular objects set before it . . .[70]

It is the word 'administration' which assumes ambiguity in Sheldon's writing because he used it both as a global term to describe the policy-determining group *and* a word which he substituted for *execution* of

68. Ibid., pp. 102–44.
69. Wallas recognised 'muddling through' as a British habit, see G. Wallas, *The Art of Thought* (London) 1926, p. 179. Later, in the United States, Lindblom used the concept of 'muddling through' for the basis of his discussion on incremental decision-making, see C. E. Lindblom, 'The science of "muddling through",' *Public Administration Review*, Vol. 19, Spring 1959, 79–88.
70. O. Sheldon, *The Philosophy of Management* (London) 1923. Republished edn 1930, p. 286.

policy by Management proper. To avoid confusion, we shall retain a capital 'A' when referring to the Administration group. The fusion between policy-making and administration which Sheldon envisaged took the form of an active communication link between the policy-makers (i.e. the Administration) and the policy executors (i.e. Management proper). In the same way that other contributors to the British Philosophy of Administration were unable to accept a separation of policy-making from policy execution in the sphere of government, Sheldon refused to accept the idea of their separation in industry. He began his article on policy-making (1925) by quoting the American A. H. Church, who, in 1914, had stated that in industry:

> . . . there are two elements present, which though sometimes merging into each other, and always exerting reciprocal influence, are nevertheless quite *distinct* in their essence. The first of these is the determinative element, which settles the manufacturing *policy* of the business – what to make – and the distributive *policy* – when to sell and by what means. The second is the *administrative* element, which takes the policy as decided, and gives it practical expression in buying, making and selling.[71]

Sheldon rejected Church's statement, believing that the policy-making, or determinative, element in industry required the same scientific analysis that administration had been receiving during the twentieth century because they are *dependent*, not distinct, elements. In view of this dependency between industrial policy-making and administration, Sheldon considered that it was necessary to develop the technique of policy-making to meet the scientific progress made in administration. He recognised that policy-making is a more variable process than administration, involving judgment, initiative and personal experience and, therefore, he did not expect that a code of *principles* could be established for policy-making in the same way that it had been formulated for administration. But, he did hold the same view as Wallas that certain *conclusions* about policy-making could be reached and the conclusions Sheldon drew relate to three spheres of policy-making: the definition of policy-making; the conditions of policy-making; and the purposes of policy-making. Although his objective was to point to the connection, or interaction, between policy-making and administration, he first presented these three conclusions about policy-making as follows:

71. O. Sheldon, 'Policy and policy-making', *Harvard Business Review*, Vol. IV, No. 1, October 1925, 1 (author' italics).

Definition of policy-making

Sheldon analysed the term 'policy' before defining 'policy-making'. He identified 'policy' as: '. . . a plan defining an objective for the business and governing the methods to be adopted, under given conditions, in pursuit of such objective; being determined, in harmony with existing policies, by those responsible for the direction of the business, and forming an instruction to the executive management'.

From his identification of what 'policy' is, he reached the following conclusion about 'policy-making': 'policy-making, therefore, is a corporate affair. It does not arise in this or that department; it covers the concern as a whole. It does not legislate for detail, but by setting up objectives and ordaining general methods of operation leaves the initiative in detail to those responsible for applying the policy'.[72]

Sheldon added to his definition of policy-making two further characteristics. The first additional characteristic is that policy-making is the essential means of effective co-ordination in an organisation, while the second characteristic relates to the form in which policy decisions are presented. In discussing policy-making as a means of co-ordination, Sheldon argued that co-ordination was the paramount problem in modern business. Policy-making could overcome this problem by supplying a co-ordination of activities. It is the function of the directors in a business (i.e. the Administration) to make policy, he maintained, since policy-making is an inalienable part of direction. Furthermore, good executive work cannot compensate fully for weaknesses in policy-making and, thus, neglect of the policy duty, in terms of either a lack of policy or wrong policies, creates failure in the business. It is evident from Sheldon's thinking that he retained a greater role specificity concerning policy-making and administration than Haldane, Beveridge and Wallas. But, as indicated earlier, his intention was to stress the need to *connect* the two functions and this led him to oppose Church's concept of *separation*. To improve policy as a means of co-ordination, Sheldon considered that a lack or excess of policy could be avoided by establishing a list of policy subjects, so that policy could be formulated according to this universal list of subjects. As a result, there would be policy (i.e. legislation) to guide the executive in all major matters and this list was one obvious field of policy study in Sheldon's view.

The second characteristic of policy-making is the form in which the decision is presented and published. Policy-making, Sheldon insisted, is not the business of sitting around a table passing minutes on subjects

72. Ibid., 3.

raised on an *ad hoc* basis and recording these minutes in a locked book. Policy statements must be presented in a precise and intelligible form because, as with other instructions, obscurity could defeat the object of making them. He suggested that the qualities of law should be applied to policy, namely: exactitude of diction; precision of wording; and severity of style. Finally, policy should be made available, in published format, to all persons affected by it, for their guidance or reference. Failure to circulate policy in this manner is likely to negate the time and energy contributed to its formulation.

Conditions of policy-making

Sheldon believed that it was possible to identify standard conditions of policy-making. Moreover, he considered it was important to analyse these conditions since failure in policy-making results from wrong conditions as much as from the policy itself. He identified the inappropriate policy conditions as doubt as to where the responsibility for determining policy lies; vagueness in policy; policy being settled too early or too late and, most commonly, a maladjustment between policy-making and the execution of policy. He attributed the reasons for these poor conditions to the 'hallowed' atmosphere which surrounds policy. The term suggests the idea of something unapproachable and vague which can hide a multitude of purposes and, sometimes, sins. Policy can relate to trivia, can camouflage conflicting facts and can imply a finality to a matter barely commenced. The scientific conditions of policy-making, therefore, was another field which he associated with policy study.

Purposes of policy-making

Sheldon argued that policy-making is necessary because it serves two purposes. These purposes are the establishment of objectives for the business as a whole, and, the definition of the general principles which shall govern the various branches of the executive management involved in achieving these objectives. From these policies, he noted that other decisions will be taken but they are not 'policies' as such. Rather, they are the interpretation of policies. They are not even 'minor' policies, for to call them by this name would devalue 'policy' of its primary characteristic of original and ultimate decision. He prescribed that a business should be governed primarily by an overruling and co-ordinated policy from which the head of each organisation unit can plan his own particular activities.

Having made a threefold assessment of policy-making embodying its definition; its conditions; and its purposes, Sheldon turned to the connection between policy-making and execution. He maintained that unless a policy is communicated effectively to executives, its application suffers. One method of communication is the publication of policy decisions, but he urged investigation of other methods of communication between policy-making and execution. Indeed, he recommended that these communication methods should form a third field of policy study, stating: '. . . we have not as yet grasped, to anything like the degree necessary . . . the best means for, the proper linking-up of policy and action . . . The channel between the policy-makers and the executive staff does not function effectively; it is choked up or it is broken.'[73]

Policy conditions, he insisted, are as important to the well-being of an organisation, as the policy itself. Good conditions involve an adjustment between policy-making and its execution, which can occur only if a communication channel, or a fusion, is available between these two elements.[74]

Some concluding observations to this prescriptive strand of the British Philosophy of Administration doctrine of a fusion between policy-making and administration are relevant. Wallas emerges as a constructive thinker on judgment – or the making of policy – preceding some of the more famous writers, such as C. I. Barnard (1938), H. A. Simon (1945), G. Vickers (1965) and Y. Dror (1968).[75] For example, his advice on policy-making for statesmen and administrators bears close resemblance to Barnard's concept of decision-making based on the identification of conscious, logical thought and subconscious thought. Barnard first developed his ideas in a lecture (1936), but subsequently embodied them in his book (1938) beginning his analysis of decision-making thus: 'The acts of individuals may be distinguished in principle as those which are the result of deliberation, calculation, thought, and those which are unconscious, automatic, responsive . . .'[76]

And, like Wallas, Barnard drew attention not only to the distinction between logical and non-logical thought but also to the need to combine

73. Ibid., 5.
74. Ibid., 1–6.
75. C. I. Barnard, *The Functions of the Executive* (Cambridge, Mass.) 1938. Thirtieth edn 1968; H. A. Simon, *Administrative Behavior: A Study of Decision-Making Processes in Administrative Organization*, 1945. Republished (New York) 1965; and Sir G. Vickers, *The Art of Judgment: A Study of Policy-Making* (London) 1965. Paperback edn 1968; and Y. Dror, *Public Policymaking Reexamined* (San Francisco) 1968.
76. C. I. Barnard, *Functions of the Executive*, p. 185.

these two psychological actions.[77] Similarly, Wallas' prescriptions provided a key to the process, or stages, of decision-making primarily associated with H. A. Simon's work (1945). Although Simon set out a more sophisticated and detailed account of the processes in decision-making, they both rejected rational, economic man and replaced him by a more realistic *administrative* man. But, Simon proceeded to concentrate on the rational part of the decision-making process by identifying objective rationality and suggesting the limitations to obtaining such rationality. In so doing, he paid less concern than Wallas to emotional behaviour in decision-making.[78] After Simon, D. Easton (1953) embodied several of Wallas' thoughts into his treatise; for example, he complained that American political science over-stressed emotional behaviour and undermined reason. This was Wallas' argument in the context of British politics, although he alternated between criticising the emphasis on reason at the turn of the century to the lack of reason in group policy-making some time later. Despite this alternation to suit the mood of the country, Wallas' prescription remained constant for a *combination* of reason and emotion in policy-making rather than an excess of either one or the other. Easton demonstrated a similar tendency in his work by criticising the over-emphasis on emotional thought and what he termed 'the flight from reason'. Easton also acknowledged Wallas for moving political science from the traditional institutional, or 'situational', approach to the 'psychological' approach.[79]

Finally, G. Vickers (1965) analysed policy-making – or judgment – in which his purpose, if not his methods, are identical to Wallas' earlier aim. Vickers stated the purpose of his book thus: '... to describe, analyze and understand the processes of judgment and decision, as they are encountered in business and public administration and particularly those exercises which we regard as contributing to the making of "policy" '.[80]

However, he does not comment on Wallas' earlier views on judgment but takes his impetus directly from the work of H. A. Simon,[81] which is a pity since Vickers' comments on Wallas' thinking, in the light of his own concept of judgment, would have been a valuable contribution to modern policy studies. It has been established that Wallas originated new ways of thinking about policy-making for statesmen and administrators. But, there are several weaknesses

77. Ibid., pp. 305–6.
78. H. A. Simon, *Administrative Behaviour*.
79. D. Easton, *Political System*, pp. 3–36, 202.
80. Sir G. Vickers, *Art of Judgment*, pp. 15–16.
81. Ibid., pp. 21–2.

inherent in his prescriptions. Firstly, the fact that his theme extended in a loose form throughout several books from 1908 to 1932 means that there is no one concise book giving advice to statesmen and administrators on policy-making or judgment. Wallas' final work *Social Judgment* intended to set out this advice, but not only was it incomplete, being published posthumously by his daughter, but it was of a very general nature as compared with the more systematic works of Simon (1945), Vickers (1965) and Dror (1968). Furthermore, although Wallas' consistent theme was for a balance between reason and emotion in policy-making, he gave only this broad prescription, omitting detailed advice on how control and conscious co-ordination of these two processes might be achieved. It is true that he suggested training in group policy-making but, on the whole, he provided only a skeleton framework for judgment and failed to supply further prescriptions to go within it.

Secondly, Wallas' use of two case-studies about Mesopotamia and the Dardanelles as the background to his prescriptions for group policy-making was an excellent idea and possessed considerable potential for a depth analysis of policy-making. Again, however, he displayed a lack of systematic study. Instead of clearly and fully setting the policy-making scene in both cases, he quoted only brief and random evidence from the official reports to support his argument, leaving the reader to complete the missing information.

In the sphere of industry, Sheldon supplied more detail about policy-making and its interrelation with administration. He rejected policy-making and policy execution as elements which exist separately and noted their interrelationship. Accordingly, he argued that policy studies need to be developed to meet the progress in administrative studies and he began by suggesting his own conclusions for policy studies. His suggestions indicated three fields of policy study which required attention, namely: (1) a universal list of policy subjects; (2) the scientific conditions of policy-making; and (3) methods to enhance communication between policy-makers in industry (i.e. the Administration) and policy executors (i.e. the Management proper). Thus, his article concentrating on a connection between policy-making and administration was an important contribution to the British Philosophy of Administration. However, Sheldon took a more authoritarian attitude to policy-making than Haldane, Beveridge and Wallas. He stressed only the connection between policy-making and administration without acknowledging the extent to which executives contribute to policy-making. Another weakness was Sheldon's assumption that policy should contain the characteristics of law, such as precision and severity of terminology. This prescription incurs the disadvantage that if policy is laid down in legal terms, published and circulated, it is difficult for the Administration to modify its policy without further paperwork and possibly the open contradiction of earlier published documents. Neither can legal policy guides be adapted easily to individual needs, even if they relate only to broad issues, and the risk is created that policy may become harsh and inflexible in its application as a consequence of this legality.

Conclusion

What overall conclusions can be drawn from the British Philosophy of Administration doctrine of a fusion between policy-making and administration compared with the American doctrine of separation and the radical views of the Webbs and Laski? Two conclusions will be discussed, beginning with the question of the realism of the British Philosophy of Administration doctrine. This doctrine centred upon the actual human activity of policy-making by statesmen and administrators, whereas both the American doctrine of separation and the radical British school related to the formal process of policy-making based on theory and institutional analysis. Despite the realism, there is evidence of fragmentation within the British Philosophy of Administration doctrine, as in the case of Wallas' prescriptions for policy-making, which were dispersed throughout several books. There is evidence, also, of a lack of systematic study, with Haldane and Beveridge delivering their views about the fusion between policy-making and administration in addresses or articles without substantiating them in further depth. The fragmentation within the British Philosophy of Administration doctrine was exacerbated by the radical ideas expounded within the same period by Sidney and Beatrice Webb and Harold Laski. Their diverging opinions were apparent to onlookers in Britain as, for example, when Laski took Wallas' place as a temporary lecturer at Cambridge University. Laski's notion of politics was received at Cambridge, where political science was still not a recognised subject, as being: '. . . even more disturbing than the *psychological* approach of Graham Wallas; he thought American *institutions* at least as important as British, and talked more about the Supreme Court than Aristotle . . .'[82]

82. See K. Martin, *Harold Laski*, pp. 48–9, (author's italics).

Laski himself drew a contrast between the Webbs and Wallas, noting that the interest of the former was in institutions, but the latter was not a fighting party man nor had he great interest in the tightness of doctrine or symmetry of institutions. His genius lay, instead, in understanding people and personal relations. [83] It is clear that the Webbs and Laski retained an institutional approach to politics which was closer in many ways to the American approach to policy-making and administration than to the realistic doctrine of the British Philosophy of Administration. Parallels with the American doctrine in the Webbs' writing took the form of their separation of policy-making from administration, their system of checks and balances and their proposal for a committee structure in Parliament similar to the Congressional system. And, although Laski did not favour the separation of policy-making from administration, he had taught for several years in North America[84] and introduced some American ideas into his reforms, such as an election every four years to establish the members of the single legislative assembly.

Although the realistic doctrine of the British Philosophy of Administration was fragmented, and accompanied by the diverging views of the Webbs and Laski, some of its contents gained speedy recognition in the United States. Graham Wallas' thought on human nature, for example, influenced the development of American political science while his prescriptions for policy-making preceded some of the later, more famous, theories about decision-making and judgment. Therefore, the British Philosophy of Administration doctrine of a fusion between policy-making and administration was both forward-looking and influential. Indeed, in terms of being forward-looking, it contained the rudimentary beginnings of a 'systems' approach in which the various parts of government are interdependent systems operating within the constitutional whole. But, because the doctrine was presented unsystematically and in a fragmented fashion, it receded more quickly than the American doctrine based on a separation of politics from administration. The American doctrine still has a well-established place in the history of administrative and political thought, even though it was superseded in the 1940s by the realistic doctrine of fusion.

The second conclusion relates to the constitutional illusions

83. H. J. Laski, 'Graham Wallas', *New Statesman and Nation*, 20 Aug. 1932, p. 199.
84. Laski began his teaching career in North America as a History Lecturer at McGill University, Canada in 1914 before becoming Tutor in History (including the history of political thought) at Harvard from 1916 to 1920. See K. Martin, *Harold Laski*, pp. 26–46.

surrounding British government. The doctrine of the British Philosophy of Administration sought to indicate the constitutional illusions, but not to discard the constitutional conventions underlying them. Although this doctrine belonged to the period 1900–39, it has been revived in recent times. The revival, however, incorporates some of the radical reforms of the Webbs and Laski. For example, the Fulton Report (1968) noted the constitutional illusions, but it argued that the conventions themselves are no longer relevant and should be eliminated gradually. The Fulton Committee stated:

> . . . we think that administration suffers from the convention, which is still alive in many fields, that only the Minister should explain issues in public and what his department is or is not doing about them. This convention has depended in the past on the assumption that the doctrine of ministerial responsibility means that a Minister has full detailed knowledge and control of all the activities of his department. This assumption is no longer tenable. The Minister and his junior Ministers cannot know all that is going on in his department, nor can they nowadays be present at every forum where legitimate questions are raised about its activities . . . In our view, therefore, the convention of anonymity should be modified and civil servants as professional administrators, should be able to go further than now in explaining what their departments are doing, at any rate so far as concerns managing existing policies and implementing legislation . . . On balance we think it is best not to offer any specific precepts for the progressive relaxation of the convention of anonymity. It should be left to develop gradually and pragmatically . . . [85]

Following the Fulton Report, the Minority Report on the Constitution (1973) challenged the illusion that the 'all-knowing' Minister runs his own department and enquired whether it is not departments that run Ministers?[86] But, in neither modern document is any reference made to, or any apparent awareness of, the earlier discussions between 1900 and 1939 on these issues, which confirms the lack of knowledge in Britain about her own administrative history.

The realism of the British Philosophy of Administration doctrine, then, is reiterated today – in part – but some of the detailed examples within it have become outmoded with the further expansion of twentieth-century government. Not only are some of the constitutional conventions less relevant, but Beveridge's analogy of the Victorian marriage is now out of date. The Fulton Report, again with no apparent

85. *The Civil Service, Vol. 1. Report of the Committee (Fulton) 1966–68* (London) 1968, pp. 93–4.
86. *Royal Commission on the Constitution 1969–1973*, Vol. II. Memorandum of Dissent by Lord Crowther-Hunt and Professor A. T. Peacock (London) 1973. p. 4.

knowledge of previous British administrative thought for the era 1900–39 (although the famous nineteenth-century Northcote-Trevelyan Report is cited), dismantled the analogy by suggesting that modern British public administration requires a *variety* of civil servants to advise the Minister rather than reliance on the Permanent Secretary. The Committee recommended that Ministers should have a 'Senior Policy Adviser', plus additional civil servants on a *temporary* basis to assist on policy matters. This proposal introduces adultery into Beveridge's marital analogy and, also, brings into question another constitutional convention – that of political neutrality by British civil servants. Regarding the latter convention, the Fulton proposal encourages an apex of temporary appointees who, although recruited on merit and not party allegiances, can be dismissed by a new political Minister.[87] The convention of political neutrality has been challenged further in the 1970s by the introduction of temporary policy advisers who are not necessarily civil servants but may be party political assistants operating outside the Civil Service structure. In 1974, for example, Harold Wilson's Labour Government appointed thirty-eight political assistants to Ministers and they were interposed between the Minister and his civil servant advisers.[88] Thus, the simple, straightforward relationship depicted by Beveridge of the Minister relying on his Permanent Secretary has become complicated by a number of temporary civil servants and a growing band of 'party' advisers.[89]

It is important to assess the current trend of temporary policy advisers in the light of the historical doctrines of a separation and a fusion between politics and administration. Government is more complex today than in the period 1900–39 and Ministers may require advice in a number of specialised spheres. But, it will be seen that Britain is adopting the concept of politics as 'party loyalties' as well as 'policy-making' and is assuming characteristics associated with American thought rather than her own traditional background of an apolitical Civil Service. Moreover, Britain is moving in this direction at

87. *The Civil Service Vol. 1 Report of the Committee (Fulton) 1966–68* op. cit., pp. 58–60. In practice, the Fulton Committee's recommendation for 'Senior Policy Advisers' was not implemented, although more departmental policy-planning units have been formed and these will be discussed in Ch. 3.
88. See H. Young 'The invasion of Whitehall', *The Sunday Times*, 21 April 1974 and D. Wood 'The Ministers' men invade Whitehall', *The Times*, 10 June 1974.
89. The giant departments established in the 1960s and 1970s are another factor complicating the Minister–civil servant relationship. They have increased the complexity at the top of the British Civil Service and, it is argued, they could create a new 'triple-decked' hierarchy of Ministers. See P. Self 'The organization of government', letter to *The Times* 17 January 1974.

a time when the United States is seeking to limit and control the number of political appointments in the federal executive branch. A post-Watergate Committee found confusion over the roles of different kinds of political appointees in the federal executive and referred to political appointments as a device to intervene in and manipulate the career civil service for 'partisan ideological purposes'.[90] It is possible that if the current trend continues in Britain towards political appointees, the next British administrative doctrine will be the appeal to separate administration from 'politics' rather than promotion of the doctrine of fusion.

90. F. C. Mosher et al. *Watergate: Implications for Responsible Government* (New York) 1974, pp. 63–76.

Chapter 3

The scientific principles underlying the British Philosophy of Administration

The Haldane Report ... Its significance is to be attributed, not so much to the value of its detailed recommendations, as to its recognition of the need for guiding principles in administration.[1]
R. V. Vernon and N. Mansergh

... there are principles which can be arrived at inductively from the study of human experience of organisation, which should govern arrangements for human association of any kind.[2]
L. Urwick

Chapter 1 has established that the British Philosophy of Administration was composed of science and ethics. This chapter relates to the 'science' component, from which it will be seen that scientific principles played an essential role in British administrative thought. The scientific study of administration was being promoted in both Britain and the United States between 1900 and 1939, which indicates some common ground in the respective administrative developments. But, despite points in common, the traditional American doctrine based on the pioneering work of F. W. Taylor and the scientific management school, followed in the 1930s by the POSDCORB principles, is not indicative of the scientific principles underlying the British Philosophy of Administration. Not only was American scientific management received with scepticism in Britain,[3] but three other important differences can be identified between the scientific study of administration in the two countries.

In the first instance, the individual scientific principles inherent in POSDCORB – the acronym expounded by Gulick in his work for the President's Committee on Administrative Management (1937)[4] – had

1. R. V. Vernon and N. Mansergh, *Advisory Bodies: A Study of their Uses in Relation to Central Government 1919-1939* (London) 1940, p. 49.
2. L. Urwick, 'Organization as a technical problem', in *Papers on the Science of Administration*, ed. by L. Gulick and L. Urwick (New York) 1937, p. 49.
3. See Ch. 1, pp. 13-7.
4. *Administrative Management in the Government of the United States: Report of the President's Committee on Administrative Management* (Washington) 1937.

relevance for British administrative thought. Indeed, these principles were contained in the Haldane Report as early as 1918.[5] Notwithstanding the earlier appearance of the POSDCORB principles in British administrative thought, the stress within the British Philosophy of Administration did not focus upon these particular scientific principles. Instead, Britain pursued her own search for scientific principles and this search emphasised alternative principles or utilised different terminology. These British scientific principles of administration are represented more accurately by the acronym SLOCUS than POSDCORB. However, fragmentation was a recurring weakness of the British Philosophy of Administration and we should point out that, unlike American administrative developments, no acronym corresponding to POSDCORB was put forward in Britain to unify the individual scientific principles. Therefore, we have composed the acronym SLOCUS as a useful tool to consolidate the British principles of Staff, Line, Organisation, Communication and Span of control and to act as a device for making comparisons.

The second major difference between the scientific study of administration in Britain and the United States concerns methodology. The conventional American doctrine grew out of the scientific management school, which demanded measurement and precision with regard to establishing scientific principles. Although the objective of precision was lost from view on occasions in American studies within this period, it can be said that, on the whole, the American methodology was more precise than that underlying the British Philosophy of Administration. One reason why the British methodology was less precise was because the science of administration was rendered less like the physical sciences, or machine-like, by the simultaneous development of ethical idealism which served to 'humanise' the British doctrine. On the other hand, a second, more critical, reason should not be overlooked – that a lack of rigorous, systematic analysis was typical of the writing of contributors to the British Philosophy of Administration.

The final difference between the British and American doctrines relates to the implementation of scientific principles. American scientific principles gained practical expression through the widespread application of scientific management and by the wholesale adoption of the POSDCORB principles – despite a short delay – within

---

5. Ministry of Reconstruction, *Report of the Machinery of Government Committee* (London).

the American federal Civil Service.[6] In contrast, the British Haldane Report, which expressed most of the SLOCUS principles, was extended only partially into the Civil Service and in piecemeal fashion. This partial implementation of the scientific principles underlying the British Philosophy of Administration added to the fragmented nature of the doctrines.

This chapter begins by defining the term 'principle' and explaining the different methodologies adopted in the British and American doctrines. This explanation will be followed by the identification of the POSDCORB principles within the Haldane Report – a government document which appeared many years before Gulick's famous study for the President's Committee on Administrative Management in the United States. Finally, the more relevant SLOCUS principles underlying the British Philosophy of Administration will be elaborated individually from the viewpoint of Wallas, Haldane, Sheldon and Urwick. Concerning the meaning of scientific 'principle' in the American doctrine, the work of F. W. Taylor – the pioneer of scientific management – provides a starting point. Although Taylor interpreted 'principle' in the general sense of a broad foundation, or essence of scientific management, the four principles he specified[7] were based on measurement and exactitude. For example, his first principle of 'the development of a true science' meant that every act of work – whether bricklaying, handling pig-iron or shovelling – can be reduced to a science. But, to activate this underlying principle, Taylor relied on the appropriate quantitative mechanisms of time-study and the slide-rule to establish the laws of the various sciences. Similarly, his third principle of 'the scientific education and development of workmen' required other exact mechanisms, such as instruction cards and functional foremen.[8] When the search for underlying principles spread from American industry to public administration, some of the emphasis on measurement was lost, but a keen degree of exactitude still characterised the American doctrine of a science of administration.

6. POSDCORB formed the basis of President Roosevelt's Bill to reorganise the American executive branch of government, following the recommendations of the Brownlow Committee. Congress feared that the administrative proposals would increase the authority of the President to the extent of rendering him a dictator, and on these grounds the 'Reorganisation Bill' was defeated by Congress. See Sir H. N. Bunbury, 'The problem of government in the United States', *Public Administration*, Vol. XVII, 1939, 17–19. But, some two years later, most of the Bill's content had been made law, so that each POSDCORB principle came to be reflected in the organisation of the federal Civil Service.

7. See Ch. 1, p. 15.

8. F. W. Taylor, *The Principles of Scientific Management* (New York) pp. 64–85.

W. F. Willoughby (1927), for example, commenced his work *Principles of Public Administration* by asserting that there are certain fundamental principles analogous to those of any science which must be observed if efficiency in operation is to prevail.[9] However, by the 1930s the term 'principle' had been used indiscriminately in American administrative thought and practice and it was no longer clear what it meant. L. D. White (1936) clarified the term and, in so doing, he reinstated the idea of precision. His clarification involved listing four definitions of the word 'principle', which are:

1. A *source* of action.

2. A fundamental *truth*, proposition or general statement where the dominant stress is on truth, generality or comprehensiveness.

3. A general law or rule accepted as a guide to *action* or a basis of conduct. In this case, the emphasis is on action in terms of a standard to behaviour rather than on truth.

4. A rudiment or *element* as in the natural sciences where the term has been used to signify an original element. For example, water is the principle of matter. However, the natural sciences make less use of the word 'principle' than in the past.

White argued that the term 'principle' in American public administration had been employed frequently in the third sense of a guide to action rather than representing a search for fundamental truth. Moreover, it had been applied loosely to include personal hunches and behaviour traits instead of being a general rule for action. He proposed that the term 'principle' ought to be restricted to a merger of meanings (2) and (3) which would make it more exact. Its usage, then, would be limited because personal hunches or 'intuition' would be recognised for what they were, but they would not be classified as 'principles' of administration. He explained his clarification thus:

> Would it not be desirable to restrict the use of the term to mean a hypothesis or proposition, so adequately tested by observation and/or experiment that it may intelligently be put forward as a guide to action or as a means of understanding? Without expecting experimental or laboratory verification as a sine qua non, would it not be desirable to

9. W. F. Willoughby, *Principles of Public Administration* (Washington) 1927, p. ix. See also W. F. Willoughby, 'The science of public administration', in *Essays in Political Science in honor of Westel Woodbury Willoughby*, ed. by J. M. Mathews and J. Hart (Baltimore) 1937, pp. 39–63.

understand that a principle implies (1) an original *hypothesis*, (2) adequate *verification*, and (3) in consequence the statement of a proposition possessing the quality of generality and conforming to truth at least in the pragmatic sense? . . . If principle may be thought of in terms of hypothesis and verification, then the frequency of its reference will be greatly reduced, but greatly defined. An intuition will be called an intuition and recognized as such – something personal, the outcome of a unique experiential history, but pointing perhaps to insight and truth.[10]

White, therefore, continued in the American tradition of seeking exactitude with respect to scientific principles of administration. Within the British Philosophy of Administration, the term 'principle' conformed to White's first requirement of *hypothesis*, but the British pioneers were less concerned with *verification* and the testing of scientific principles beyond personal observation. And, on the whole, they did not attempt to separate intuition from scientific principles. In his clarification, White noted this difference in methodology, pointing out that Graham Wallas, Richard Haldane and the French industrialist, Henri Fayol, had formulated hypotheses and reached personal convictions about principles of administration, but they were based primarily on intuition and lacked generality. Realising the extent of personal content in their scientific principles, White professed the wish to learn the 'tangled web of circumstances' behind the administrative insight of these pioneers.[11] In elaborating the SLOCUS acronym, this chapter will attempt to provide some of the personal background to the scientific principles promoted by the British pioneers.

The term 'principle', then, within the British Philosophy of Administration, meant a hypothesis which would serve as a guide to administrative action, but its verification was limited often to personal observation rather than detailed measurement or adequate testing by the collection and analysis of data. However, the difference in precision was not absolute and there were exceptions on both sides of the Atlantic. Lyndall Urwick, a contributor to the British Philosophy of

10. L. D. White, 'The meaning of principles in public administration', in *The Frontiers of Public Administration,* ed. by J. M. Gaus et al. (Chicago) 1936, pp. 18–19 (author's italics). Waldo has criticised White's definition because it leaves unanswered certain questions, such as the relationship between 'experiment' and 'observation' to verification. While this is true, White did lay stress, nevertheless, on verification by some form of replicable procedure as distinct from intuitive hunches or hypotheses which remain untested. D. Waldo, *The Administrative State* (New York) 1948, pp. 167–72.

11. L. D. White, 'Meaning of principles', op. cit., pp. 13–25. Josiah Stamp also confirmed that Wallas' work lacked verification, arguing: '. . . Graham Wallas, in the *Art of Thought,* entirely omitting all reference to the biting need of consistency, and its urge in verification . . .' J. Stamp, *Ideals of a Student* (London) 1933, p. 220.

Administration, strove for exactitude and, indeed, he is so renowned for his development of scientific principles that his administrative work embodying ethical idealism has been overlooked, as Chapter 4 will portray. He criticised the degree of personal content in scientific principles of administration, attributing it to the 'practical man fallacy',[12] which was the name he applied to the inability of administrative pioneers to conceive general principles apart from their personal experience. Because he preferred a more analytical discussion of the structure of organisations, Urwick dedicated considerable energy to expounding scientific principles himself and to restating more logically the scientific principles of 'practical' thinkers, such as Fayol.[13] In the case of the American doctrine, the most important exception to exactitude was the POSDCORB principles. Gulick based them directly on Fayol's earlier work and he appears not to have sought to test or verify them further.[14] Like SLOCUS, therefore, the POSDCORB principles can be taken only as practical guides to action instead of representing proven truths or generalities. In view of the fact that the scientific principles underlying the British Philosophy of Administration had more in common with the POSDCORB principles than with American scientific management, this chapter focuses upon a discussion of POSDCORB and SLOCUS.

1. Precursors in Britain to the American POSDCORB principles

It is well known that the American acronym POSDCORB embodied the following scientific principles of administration for the guidance of the Chief Executive:

P	Planning
O	Organizing
S	Staffing
D	Directing
C	Co-ordinating
O	–
R	Reporting
B	Budgeting

12. For reference to the 'practical man fallacy', see L. Urwick, 'Executive decentralisation with functional co-ordination', *Public Administration*, Vol. XIII, 1935, p. 346.
13. See L. Urwick, 'The function of administration: with special reference to the work of Henri Fayol' in *Papers on the Science of Administration*, pp. 117–30.
14. See L. Gulick, 'Notes on the theory of organization: with special reference to government in the United States' in *Papers on the Science of Administration*, pp. 13–15.

The foregoing principles were first presented in Gulick's memorandum of 1936 for the President's Committee on Administrative Management (the Brownlow Committee) and they are based on Fayol's work (1925).[15] But, a closer examination of the individual principles indicates their existence in the British *Report of the Machinery of Government Committee* (1918).

Planning

The first scientific principle that Gulick proposed was 'planning' based on Fayol's definition 'to foretell the future and to prepare for it; it includes the idea of action'.[16] The Haldane Committee, likewise, was acutely aware of the need to think about the future before acting, although it referred to the principle of 'thought' rather than 'planning'. Nevertheless, it was in order to draw up plans for action that thought, research and the accumulation of facts were required. The Haldane Committee recommended more provision in the British Civil Service than in the past for the systematic application of thought, as a preliminary to the settlement of policy and its subsequent administration. The Committee described the principle as '. . . placing the business of enquiry and thinking in the hands of persons definitely charged with it, whose duty is to study the future, *and work out plans* and advise those responsible for policy or engaged in actual administration'.[17]

In Part I of its Report, the Haldane Committee envisaged the principle in operation as requiring *all* departments of the central executive government to set up better provision for enquiry, research and reflection before policy is defined and implemented, as well as the establishment of a *special* department charged with research and enquiry into certain specific matters. In Part II, the Committee made detailed proposals about how particular departments should extend their enquiry and research activities based on this principle of 'thought' or 'planning'.[18] It will be seen in the second section of this chapter that this concern for 'thought' was the basis of the first SLOCUS principle – 'staff'. Haldane, for example, noted in his autobiography, after reading

15. Ibid., p. 13. Gulick referred to the 1925 edn of Fayol's work, but there was an earlier 1916 edn.
16. This definition is taken from L. Urwick's study, 'Function of administration', op. cit., p. 20.
17. *Report of the Machinery of Government Committee*, p. 6, (author's italics).
18. Ibid., pp.6, 22–35.

several continental works about General Staff in the military context, that the books simply pointed to the importance of careful thought before action.[19] Thought, founded on research and facts, channelled into planning for the future, therefore, was the equivalent in the Haldane Report of the scientific principle of 'planning' motivated by Gulick, and Fayol before him. Fayol, however, elaborated at greater length on the plan itself and how to forecast. He listed the components of yearly and ten-yearly forecasts and, in this respect, he carried the principle of 'planning' further than the Haldane Committee.[20]

Organizing

Gulick defined the principle of 'organizing', again taken from Fayol's work, as 'the establishment of the formal structure of authority through which work subdivisions are arranged, defined and co-ordinated for the defined objective'.[21] In other words, the principle of 'organizing' relates to the setting up of a formal authority structure within an organisation to achieve known purposes. It follows that if serious overlapping of functions exists within an organisation there can be no clear-cut system of formal authority. This was the case in the American federal government executive branch in the 1930s and the President's Committee observed: 'Owing to the multiplicity of agencies and the lack of administrative management there is waste, overlapping, and duplication, which may be eliminated through coordination, con-solidation, and proper managerial control'.[22]

Similarly, in 1918 the Haldane Committee had reported: '... there is much overlapping and consequent obscurity and confusion in the functions of the Departments of executive Government'.[23]

Both Committees saw the answer to the problem of overlapping and division of formal authority as the application of the principle of 'organizing' to the major departments of government. In both countries, it was proposed that the overlapping executive functions should be consolidated by the reconstruction of major departments organised according to the services to be performed (i.e. by purpose or function). The alternative methods of organising departments, such as by the persons or classes to be dealt with (i.e. by clientele), were not

19. *Richard Burdon Haldane: An Autobiography* (London) 1929, p. 185. Urwick also confirmed that the 'staff' principle involved 'planning', see this chapter, p. 98, f. n. 69.
20. H. Fayol, *General and Industrial Management*, 1916 (London) 1969, pp. 43–53.
21. L. Gulick, 'Notes on the theory of organization', op. cit., p. 13.
22. *Report of the President's Committee on Administrative Management*, p. 32.
23. *Report of the Machinery of Government Committee*, p. 4.

favoured by either Committee. In 1937 the United States' President's Committee recommended that twelve major executive departments should be established on the basis of 'purpose'. They were the departments of State, Treasury, War, Justice, Post Office, Navy, Conservation, Agriculture, Commerce, Labor, Social Welfare and Public Works.[24] An almost identical argument had been the key to the Haldane Committee's proposals of 1918 when with respect to British central government, it was urged:

> If the principle which we have suggested . . . that the business of the various Departments of Government should be distributed as far as possible according to the class of service with which they are concerned, be accepted, the business of Government would fall into one or other of the following main divisions:
>
> I. – Finance.
> II. & III. – National Defence and External Affairs.
>   IV. – Research and Information.
>   V. – Production (including Agriculture, Forestry, Fisheries), Transport, and Commerce.
>   VI. – Employment.
>   VII. – Supplies.
>   VIII. – Education.
>   IX. – Health.
>   X. – Justice.[25]

Staffing

The principle of 'staffing', as conceived by Gulick, meant personnel management. By 1937, this principle had become an important requirement within the American executive government. Indeed, the three members of the President's Committee of 1937 – namely; Gulick, Merriam and Brownlow, made it clear that: 'Personnel administration lies at the very core of administrative management . . . Improved plans for governmental organization and management are of little value unless simultaneous recognition is given to the need for attracting, retaining, and developing human capacity in the public service.'[26]

In Britain, the human side of administration received as much emphasis as scientific principles and a set of ethical ideals existed concerning human well-being inside and outside the organisation. In addition to these specific ethical ideals, and the actual experiments in 'human relations' which took place in Britain in the period 1900–39,

24. *Report of the President's Committee on Administrative Management*, pp. 33–36.
25. *Report of the Machinery of Government Committee*, p. 16.
26. *Report of the President's Committee on Administrative Management*, p. 7.

the principle of 'staffing' or personnel management held a place of its own among the scientific principles of the Haldane Committee. In British government, however, this principle of 'staffing' was termed 'establishment' work. The Haldane Committee in 1918 was concerned particularly about correct staffing for the *routine* business of government undertaken by lower officials in the Civil Service and, with this in mind, it included among its suggestions the 'staffing' principle: 'In the Treasury there should be a separate branch specialising in . . . 'establishment' work, and studying all questions of staff, recruitment, classification, etc. and routine business generally. Such a branch would be in close touch and constant communication with the officers in other Departments charged with the duty of supervising the "establishment" work.'[27]

The principle of establishment or 'staffing', therefore, was as much a part of the Haldane Report as it was of the later American acronym POSDCORB.

Directing

The definition Gulick gave to the principle of 'directing' was 'the continuous task of making decisions and embodying them in specific and general orders and instructions and serving as the leader of the enterprise'.[28] The leader of the federal executive is, of course, the President himself and the President's Committee saw it necessary to strengthen the formal authority of the President in order that he could act in accordance with the principle of 'directing'. For, although the aforementioned POSDCORB principles were viewed as administrative tools to aid the President in his job of directing, by equipping him with planning facilities, a more coherent organisation and better personnel management, these tools were not in themselves adequate. The President needed further help to make decisions and, accordingly, the Brownlow Committee called for an expansion of the White House staff to assist the President. It was recommended that a sufficiently large group of able assistants should reside in the President's own office to keep him in close touch with affairs of administration and to provide speedily the knowledge needed for executive decision.[29]

27. *Report of the Machinery of Government Committee*, p. 21.
28. L. Gulick, 'Notes on the theory of organization', op. cit., p. 13.
29. *Report of the President's Committee on Administrative Management*, p. iv. The principle of 'staff' in the United States federal executive branch had its origin in the Taft Efficiency and Economy Commission, 1912, see L. D. White, *Introduction to the Study of Public Administration* (New York) 1926, p. 110.

The POSDCORB principle of 'directing' which was applied in the American federal executive by an expansion of the White House staff, had its parallel in Britain by the name of 'staff'. As noted earlier, this principle of 'staff', and its sister principle 'line', form the opening to the British SLOCUS acronym and they will be discussed in detail in the second section of this chapter. Although 'planning' was an important part of the 'staff' principle, the latter contained a second aspect – namely, the idea of 'command'. It is in this second sense of 'command' that the 'staff' principle related to the POSDCORB principle of 'directing'. For, in the military context, it is the General Staff officers who, freed from *administration,* have the time not only to plan for the future, but also *to assist the leader in his duty of command.* It is for this reason that the British principle of 'staff' was linked closely to the concepts of 'command' and 'administration' as we shall explain later. The British principle of 'staff', then, meant aid to leaders in their task of command and it resembled the scientific principle of 'directing', as interpreted by Gulick and the United States' President's Committee.

Haldane was responsible for extending the 'staff' principle – which involved facilities for both command and planning – into British military and naval organisations. After he had promoted it successfully in these specific organisations, he was eager to see the 'staff' principle introduced within the British Civil Service. However, he sometimes referred to this principle as 'thought'[30], as in the case of the Haldane Report. But, there is no doubt that it was to the 'staff' principle – with its emphasis on command – that the Haldane Committee was referring, when it suggested: '. . . the principle ought by no means to be limited in its application to military and naval affairs. We have come to the conclusion that the business of executive Government generally has been seriously embarrassed from the incomplete application to it of similar methods'.[31]

Accordingly, the Haldane Committee embodied within the 'staff' principle aid to leaders in their task of command similar to that envisaged by the American Brownlow Committee. The British 'staff' principle, however, should not be confused with the POSDCORB principle of 'staffing', or personnel management, which it has been noted was termed 'establishment' by the Haldane Committee.

30. See this chapter, pp. 78–9.
31. *Report of the Machinery of Government Committee,* p. 16.

Co-ordinating

Gulick perceived co-ordinating as 'the all-important duty of inter-relating the various parts of the work'.[32] One of the main problems of American government in 1937 was the breakdown of a fully co-ordinated executive branch responsible to the President, for there existed over 100 independent agencies, departments, authorities and boards. Some of these agencies were irresponsible and freely determined their own policy and administrative law. This large number of agencies in the United States reflected past confrontations between Congress and the executive over their relative constitutional powers. Congress was tempted to turn each new regulatory function over to a new independent commission since, in so doing, the executive authority enjoyed by each independent commission corresponded to a relative weakening of the President's executive power vested in him by the constitution. The principal of 'co-ordinating', as applied to the federal executive branch, went hand-in-hand with that of 'organizing' departments according to main purpose. For, in the United States, the co-ordination of public administration under the Chief Executive – the President – was sought principally by bringing this multitude of independent agencies within the structure of the twelve major departments of government. The Brownlow Committee stressed: 'Any program to restore our constitutional ideal of a fully co-ordinated Executive Branch responsible to the President must bring within the reach of that responsible control all work done by these independent commissions which is not judicial in nature. That challenge cannot be ignored'.[33]

In Britain in 1918, the principle of 'co-ordinating' was also keenly related to that of 'organizing'. Public administration would be improved if the overlapping of functions was consolidated into ten major departments but, in turn, to co-ordinate the business of government an interrelationship was required between these major departments. The Haldane Committee explained: 'The distribution of business between administrative Departments should be governed by the nature of the service to be assigned to each Department. But close regard should be paid to the necessity for co-operation between Departments in dealing with business of common interest.'[34]

However, the principle of 'co-ordinating' was expressed in both the

32. L. Gulick, 'Notes on the theory of organization', op. cit., p. 13.
33. *Report of the President's Committee on Administrative Management*, pp. 31–47.
34. *Report of the Machinery of Government Committee*, p. 16.

Haldane Report and the British Philosophy of Administration, in general, in terms of 'communication' rather than 'co-ordination'. Hence, the Haldane Committee recommended that *within* departments formal arrangements should be made for communication by means of intra-departmental meetings, based on the successful arrangement in the Board of Trade where regular meetings were held between the Minister, the Parliamentary Secretaries, the permanent heads of the department and principal officers. Additionally, the Committee proposed that co-ordination *between* departments should be achieved by standing joint bodies of the departments concerned.[35] It is in this recommendation by the Haldane Committee for meetings within and between departments that the equivalent of the Brownlow Committee's proposal to co-ordinate the executive branch of the American government is to be found.

Reporting

The sixth principle contained in POSDCORB is 'reporting', which Gulick defined as 'keeping those to whom the executive is responsible informed as to what is going on, which thus includes keeping himself and his subordinates informed through records, research and inspection'.[36] The President's Committee of 1937 made little direct use of this principle in its recommendations for the reorganisation of the executive branch of the United States government. Instead, 'reporting' was inherent in the other scientific principles; for example, 'planning' involved research and 'organizing' the major departments by purpose meant the establishment of a clear line of formal authority through which matters could be reported to the President. Similarly, the principle of 'budgeting' included measures to vest authority for the supervision of accounting systems, forms and procedures in the Secretary of the Treasury rather than, as had been the case since 1921, in the Comptroller General who was an independent officer, not responsible to the Chief Executive, Congress or the courts.[37]

In Britain the principle of 'reporting' had a more direct place within the Haldane Report of 1918. It took the form, first, of the Committee's recommendation for adequate 'reporting' procedures to be provided for policy decisions made at Cabinet level, which required executive action.

35. Ibid., pp. 9–10.
36. L. Gulick, 'Notes on the theory of organization', op. cit., p. 13.
37. For details of the office of the Comptroller General, see *Report of the President's Committee on Administrative Management*, pp. 21–2.

Secondly, the principle was manifest in the Committee's proposal that these policy decisions should be reported systematically to the major departments of the British government. To reach these conclusions, the Haldane Committee examined the functions and procedures of the Cabinet, as well as those of the executive departments, and one of its stipulations for improving reporting in the Cabinet was: '. . . the appointment of a Secretary to the Cabinet charged with the duty of collecting and putting into shape its agenda, of providing the information and material necessary for its deliberations, and of drawing up records of the results for communication to the Departments concerned'.[38]

The initial 'reporting' of policy decisions to be acted upon by the executive branch and the secondary 'reporting' of these decisions to the major departments themselves was, then, the British interpretation in 1918 of the sixth POSDCORB principle.

Budgeting

For Gulick the principle of 'budgeting' took the form of 'fiscal planning, accounting and control'.[39] This last POSDCORB principle was written prominently into the Report of the President's Committee of 1937 as fiscal management – about which the Committee observed:

> Sound fiscal management is a prime requisite of good administration . . . From the standpoint of overall control the system of fiscal management of the Government now has four major defects, namely, (1) the inadequate staffing of the Bureau of the Budget; (2) the vesting in the Office of the Comptroller General, which is not responsible to the President, of the settlement of claims, the final determination concerning the uses of appropriations, and the prescribing of administrative accounting systems; (3) the absence of a truly independent and prompt audit of the financial transactions of the Government, whereby the Congress may hold the Executive Branch strictly accountable; and (4) the failure to devise and install a modern system of accounts and records.
>
> Our recommendations for improvement of the fiscal administration of the Government are designed to correct these major faults, to return executive functions to the Executive Branch, and to make it accountable to the Congress.[40]

The concept of fiscal management or the principle of 'budgeting' clearly played a significant role in the Brownlow Committee's proposals for the reorganisation of the American federal Civil Service.

38. *Report of the Machinery of Government Committee*, p. 6.
39. L. Gulick, 'Notes on the theory of organization', op. cit., p. 13.
40. *Report of the President's Committee on Administrative Management*, p. 15.

Financial control was an essential element, also, of the British Haldane Report. The Chancellor of the Exchequer had the role in British government not only of raising revenue but also of controlling expenditure. It was believed that to relate these two functions permitted a sound financial system. The Treasury, as the Department of Finance, therefore, exercised financial control over the spending of other departments of government. In exerting this financial control, the Chancellor of the Exchequer was not supposed to encroach on the broader responsibilities of his departmental colleagues. Yet, a traditional antagonism had built up between the Treasury and other executive departments, and the Haldane Committee proposed that a closer personal relationship should replace this ill-feeling. Referring to the antagonism the Committee suggested:

> ... if a new situation in this respect is to be brought about, the obligation upon spending Departments to formulate a full and reasoned statement of their proposals must be recognised as placing upon the Treasury a corresponding obligation not to assume a negative attitude in the first instance towards suggestions for improving the quality of a service or the efficiency of the staff which administers it . . . In addition to this closer personal relationship and fuller knowledge of the circumstances of other Departments, we think that the Treasury would benefit by the establishment of an Advisory Committee which they could consult, either on general questions affecting the public service at large, or on specific proposals from Departments. Such a Committee should be permanently constituted . . .'[41]

The Haldane Committee, like the later American Committee on government administration, insisted that financial control or the principle of 'budgeting' was a prerequisite to good administration.

We have argued that the principles represented by the American acronym POSDCORB had earlier expression in the British *Report of the Machinery of Government Committee*, 1918. In fact, the President's Committee acknowledged that there was nothing revolutionary in its proposals.[42] Yet, it is common in administrative thought in Britain and the United States to associate the POSDCORB principles solely with the 1930 era – with Luther Gulick and the President's Committee on Administrative Management of which he was a member – and to ignore the earlier British work. The reason for this association is that the acronym POSDCORB could be recalled easily. This book adopts the same approach to the scientific principles underlying the

41. *Report of the Machinery of Government Committee*, pp. 18–20.
42. *Report of the President's Committee on Administrative Management*, p. iv.

British Philosophy of Administration by suggesting the acronym SLOCUS. For, although the POSDCORB principles each had a place in the Haldane Report, they did not represent the true British emphasis on scientific principles of administration, or terminology, which developed during the period 1900–39. Before proceeding to the SLOCUS acronym, however, an important point should be noted. Other scientific principles were promoted within the British Philosophy of Administration besides SLOCUS; for example, Josiah Stamp defined the principle of 'consistency'[43] while the Royal Commission on the Civil Service (1912–15),[44] on which Graham Wallas served, restated the eighteenth-century principle of 'division of labour' associated initially with Adam Smith (1776).[45] But, in spite of evidence of additional scientific principles of administration, SLOCUS has been taken as the embodiment of the primary principles inherent in the British Philosophy of Administration.

2. SLOCUS rather than POSDCORB represents the scientific principles underlying the British Philosophy of Administration

The SLOCUS acronym separates into five main principles and the development of each will now be traced:

S   Staff
L   Line
O   Organisation
C   Communication
U   –
S   Span of Control

---

43. J. Stamp, 'The contrast between the administration of business and public affairs', *Journal of Public Administration*, Vol. I, 1923, 162–8. Stamp's emphasis on 'consistency' is discussed in the context of bureaucracy. See Ch. 5, pp. 222–3.
44. See *Royal Commission on the Civil Service, Fourth Report of the Commissioners* (London) 1914, p.28.
45. Long before the twentieth-century stress on scientific principles, Britain had demonstrated a scientific approach to management; for example in the work of Adam Smith, *The Wealth of Nations* (1776) and Charles Babbage, *The Economy of Manufactures* (1832). See L. Urwick, *The Development of Scientific Management in Great Britain*, (London) late 1930s, pp. 13–20, and L. Urwick and E. F. L. Brech, *The Making of Scientific Management*, Vol. II: *Management in British Industry* (London) 1946, p. 217.

Staff and line

The first two principles of 'staff' and 'line' are dependent upon each other and for this reason they are treated together. It was Haldane, Sheldon and Urwick who were responsible for seeking to introduce these principles into public and business administration and each writer's approach is presented individually.

Haldane's approach to the principles of 'staff' and 'line'

Between 1905 and 1912, Haldane was War Minister. When he first accepted the post under Prime Minister Campbell-Bannerman, he admitted to knowing little about military affairs and nothing about army organisation, even though he was responsible for the War Office and the organisation of the British Army. Despite his lack of military knowledge, Haldane was as convinced as F. W. Taylor in the United States that certain *principles* of organisation existed, explaining that he regarded army organisation as a fascinating field to be operated on by applying first principles as soon as he had discovered them.[46] Moreover, the British Army needed reorganising because, at the turn of the century, public respect for the Army was at an exceedingly low ebb, since in both the Crimean War and the South African campaign it had shown itself to be grossly inefficient. After considerable delay and much experimentation in methods of organisation, the Esher Committee had been appointed in 1904 to advise on the reconstitution of the War Office.[47] On coming to office in 1905, Haldane showed his approval of the recommendations of the Esher Committee by selecting as his Military Private Secretary to assist him at the War Office, Colonel Ellison, former Secretary to the Esher Committee. Both men had in common a serious interest in German military organisations. Haldane's interest developed as a result of reading philosophy and theology at the University of Göttingen, where he became fluent in German. Ellison, on the other hand, had been trained in German military surroundings and had studied military history and organisations thoroughly. Accordingly, in his search for scientific principles of administration, Haldane began to read about German military organisations and it was the German concept of General Staff which influenced him most. In his own words:

46. *Richard Burdon Haldane*, p. 183.
47. See Sir C. Harris, 'Lord Haldane at the War Office', *Public Administration*, Vol. VI, 1928, 341.

With Ellison I set to work hard, and we soon hit on fresh ideas. From an early stage I began to study the great principles on which Continental military organisations had been founded, as set forth by Clausewitz, Bronsart von Schellendorff, and Von der Goltz, with the description of Napoleon's mind in Yorck von Wartenburg's book, written from the standpoint of the German General Staff . . . these works merely illustrated the necessity of careful thought before action. This was a lesson which I learned early, and to apply it to the new question of Army reorganisation was a natural step.[48]

To follow up his reading Haldane, with Ellison, visited Berlin in 1906 and from Haldane's account of this visit a clear definition of General Staff emerges. The definition rests on an understanding of the division of the German Army staffs into two parts – *command* and *administration*. The General Staff assisted with *command*, strategy and tactics for war (i.e. operations of war and the training for them). Other staff officers assisted with *administration*, such as transport and supplies to maintain the Army. It was the concept of a General Staff which impressed Haldane and this was the true definition of 'staff'. The General Staff of the German Army was an intelligence, planning and advisory body for war operations, assisting commanders at all levels.[49]

Haldane adopted the principle of a General Staff for the British Army. Hitherto, a General Staff had been established only within the War Office following the Esher Committee recommendations, but Haldane extended the principle throughout the British Army by an Army Order and a Memorandum which he wrote personally and published in September 1906. Not content with this progress, he sought the further expansion of the 'staff' principle into naval organisation and, in 1911, he advised the then Prime Minister, Asquith, to make a sweeping reform of the Admiralty on this basis. Haldane was willing to reorganise the Admiralty himself, but Winston Churchill was keen to move from the Home Office to the Admiralty and he succeeded in this ambition. Accordingly, Haldane remained at the War Office, but he reached an agreement with Churchill that he would

48. *Richard Burdon Haldane*, pp. 184–5.
49. Staffs in some form have existed in military organisations for centuries. However, the General Staff was developed first by Prussia in 1866 following a military disaster. See H. Gordon, *The War Office* (London) 1935, pp. 95–116. By Haldane's time, the General Staff consisted of a permanent department in Berlin which studied strategy, and a body of officers who assisted commanders in the field to plan and direct operations. Although commanders retained full authority and responsibility for the conduct of war operations, their General Staff officers relieved them of the burden of sifting and collating information and of arranging the details arising from the commander's overall plan.

advise on a 'staff' system for the Navy and this he did.[50] Furthermore, as indicated under the POSDCORB principles, he recommended through the medium of the *Report of the Machinery of Government Committee* a modified version of the General Staff principle for the British Civil Service, whereby selected persons in all departments – as well as a separate Ministry of Research and Information – should assume the role of thinking about the future and making plans, apart from administration.[51]

It is important to note that Haldane was chiefly responsible for introducing the principles of 'staff' and 'line' into British administrative thought and practice, although he did not use these terms. He referred simply to the General Staff principle but, in Fig 2, we show the 'line'[52] relationship with the General Staff. Haldane was stimulated by reading about German military organisations, including the work of General Bronsart von Schellendorff, and acted upon this organisational stimulus, but his contribution has been overlooked by the glare of publicity given to later writers. Urwick, for example, did not publish his views until 1933 and, although he acknowledged Bronsart von Schellendorff as 'the founder of the modern general staff theory in military organisation', his tribute to Haldane's application of the principle took the form of small footnote: '. . . also quoted by the late Lord Haldane of Cloan in a Memorandum announcing the formulation of a General Staff for the British Army, *London Times*, September 13, 1906'.[53]

In the United States, J. D. Mooney and A. C. Reiley (1931) gave their interpretation of 'staff' and 'line' in both the military and the business spheres, although it differed somewhat from that of Haldane.[54] Again, in 1937 J. D. Mooney related the principles to military organisation, but he omitted to refer to the founding fathers Bronsart von Schellendorff and Haldane.[55] Similarly, it is little appreciated that 'staff' as conceived by Haldane contained the seed of 'planning'; the principle usually

50. *Richard Burdon Haldane*, pp. 199–232.
51. See this chapter, pp. 78–9.
52. This vertical 'line', or chain of command, in military organisation should not be confused with 'the front line' meaning the fighting troops who historically stood in line and had physical contact with the enemy. The latter line is a horizontal one – for example, the 'infantry of the line' or the 'cavalry of the line'.
53. L. Urwick, 'Organization as a technical problem', op cit., p. 76.
54. J. D. Mooney and A. C. Reiley, *Onward Industry! The Principles of Organization and their Significance to Modern Industry* (New York) 1931, pp. 60–76. Mooney and Reiley referred to three phases of 'staff' – informative, advisory and supervisory. They gave less weight than Haldane to planning as part of the 'staff' function.
55. J. D. Mooney, 'The principles of organisation', *Papers on the Science of Administration*, pp. 91–8.

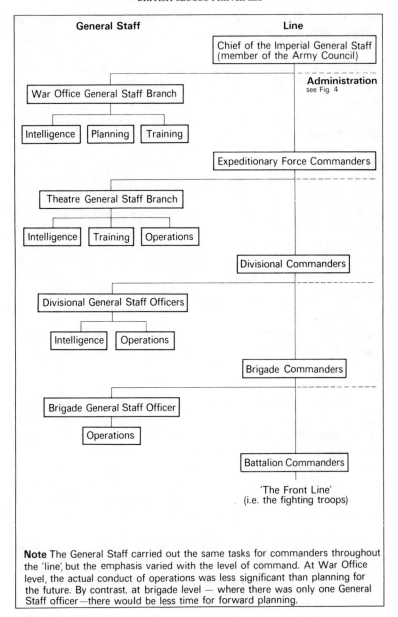

Fig. 2. The General Staff principle applied by Haldane to the British Army, 1906.

attributed to F. W. Taylor (1911),[56] Henri Fayol (1916) and Luther Gulick (1936).

Sheldon's approach to the principles of 'staff' and 'line'

Sheldon set out scientific principles of administration in his two main works (1923) and (1928).[57] The latter book was a combined effort by four of the managerial staff, including Lyndall Urwick, at the Rowntree Cocoa Works, York. It is interesting that in 1928, it was Oliver Sheldon who wrote the section on scientific principles and not Urwick, although the latter became more famous for them. But, at this time Sheldon was better known, for not only had he acquired a reputation for business organisation as a result of his publication of 1923 but he was also Organisation Manager at the York Works, reporting directly to the Chairman, Seebohm Rowntree, and assisted by Urwick. It is in his earlier publication (1923) that Sheldon discussed 'staff' and 'line', but he did so in the course of defining the following four types of organisations based on certain scientific principles:

1. 'Staff' and 'line' organisation: according to the principle of specialisation.
2. Functional organisation: according to the principle of function.
3. Departmental organisation: according to the principle of decentralisation.
4. Committee organisation: according to the principle of conference.[58]

Only the 'staff' and 'line' type of organisation is relevant here, although the other three types will be mentioned again briefly later in this chapter. Sheldon kept closely to Haldane's concept of 'staff', but he described it in the context of business organisations, defining the 'staff' and 'line' type of organisation in the following words: 'It is based on a strict demarcation between thinking and doing; between the actual execution of production, which is the "Line", and the business of analysing, testing, comparing, recording, making researches, co-

---

56. 'Planning' was an essential part of American scientific management. For example, Taylor proposed, in the case of the machine shop engaged in miscellaneous work, that a special planning department should be created to lay out the work in advance. See F. W. Taylor, *Shop Management* (New York) 1911, p. 64.

57. O. Sheldon, *The Philosophy of Management* (London) 1923, reprinted edn 1930, and C. H. Northcott, O. Sheldon, J. W. Wardropper and L. Urwick, *Factory Organization* (London) 1928.

58. O. Sheldon, *Philosophy of Management*, p. 113. The order in which Sheldon presented these four types of organisation has been altered, in order to place the 'staff' and 'line' type first.

ordinating information, and advising, which is the "Staff" . . . The essential point in this principle of organizing is the non-executive and separately organized position of the "Staff".[59]

Sheldon explained more concisely than Haldane how the principles of 'staff' and 'line' could operate outside military organisations. There is 'staff' work in every organisation, he pointed out, but it is normally done by executive officers who are responsible also for the action taken as a result of their investigation. By contrast, in the 'staff' and 'line' organisation proper executive work is performed by Executive officers and staff work by Staff officers. Sheldon did not contemplate the 'staff' and 'line' type of organisation existing in a vacuum, however, since he maintained that no organisation is founded on a single principle. The 'staff' and 'line' organisation could be incorporated, for example, with departmental organisation or functional organisation and in Fig. 3 he illustrated the principles of 'staff' and 'line' combined with the functional type of organisation. The distinguishing feature of 'staff' and 'line' organisation, he argued, is the assumption that the executive manager, whether a *functional* superintendent or a *departmental* manager, has inadequate time for the investigation, analysis and constructive thinking which are necessary for the progress of the organisation. These line officials need advice and it is the staff body who provides it.[60]

Both Sheldon and Haldane envisaged the principle of 'staff' as an organisational method to permit a particular group within an organisation to have the responsibility, time and facilities for constructive thought, research and planning ahead. Indeed, Sheldon set out in an appendix the analogies between factory organisation as he had exposed it and the machinery of government as viewed by the Haldane Committee. On the question of the 'staff' principle, he made the following comment on the Haldane Committee's Report:

The Report concludes with a summary of recommendations, two of which appear to suggest broad principles of organizing which are true of industry as of the State. They read as follows:

'(a) Further provision is needed in the sphere of civil government for the continuous acquisition of knowledge and the prosecution of research, in order to furnish a proper basis for policy.

---

59. Ibid., pp. 114–15.
60. Ibid., pp. 115–22. Figure 3 corresponds to Sheldon's Fig. 4, p. 121.

(b) The distribution of business between administrative departments should be governed by the nature of the service which is assigned to each department. But close regard should be paid to the necessity for co-operation between departments in dealing with matters of common interest.'

Stated in the terms used hitherto, this would appear as a recommendation for a functional form of organization, supplemented by the necessary staff organization, and welded together by the requisite co-ordinating machinery – a proposal which has already been advanced.[61]

Sheldon appeared surprised that the recommendations of the Haldane Committee should correspond with the organisation of the factory, but once having recognised the fact, he suggested that the training of industrial administrators should include the study of the machinery of government.

Urwick's approach to the principles of 'staff' and 'line'

Urwick had the opportunity to consider scientific principles of administration in two capacities before joining the Rowntree Works in April 1922. Firstly, during the First World War, he demonstrated his ability for organising work and, in 1915, he was appointed Staff Captain (Administrative Staff officer) of the 75th Infantry Brigade and from this date until late 1918 he held several staff positions in the British Army in which he concentrated upon organisation. After the war, he returned to England and, on account of his father's illness, he assumed responsibility for the family partnership in the Worcestershire glove factory of Fownes Brothers. By day he worked at the factory applying the principles of administration he had found effective in the Army, and at night he read books on management and, in this respect, he had been stimulated by F. W. Taylor's *Shop Management* which had been recommended to him during his army service. By the time he joined the York Cocoa Works, he possessed considerable knowledge of scientific principles of administration in thought and practice. Working with Sheldon in the small 'Organisation Office' which reported directly to B. S. Rowntree, Urwick gained further experience of administrative principles.[62] To some extent, he was a recapitulator of administrative ideas and in the early 1930s when he had left the Cocoa Works, he devoted time to improving the approach of other administrative writers. In particular, he was unhappy about the principles of 'staff' and 'line' as he found them. He was aware of a considerable lack of clarity

61. Ibid., pp. 144–144 D. Quotation p. 144 C.
62. L. Urwick, Personal letter to the author dated 28 Feb. 1975.

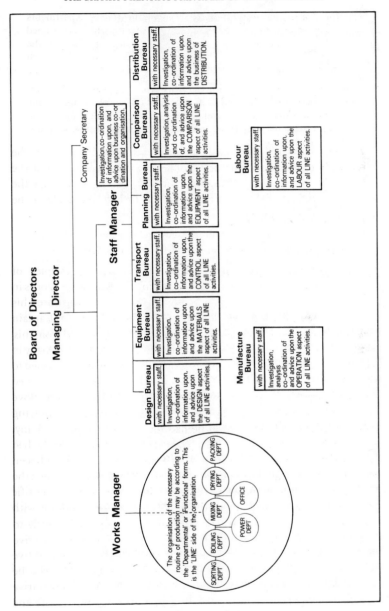

Fig. 3. Sheldon's diagram of the 'staff' and 'line' form of organisation in industry.

concerning the principles and he listed seven different interpretations of 'staff' by individual authors. He bypassed Haldane's definition with respect to military organisation, but he included Sheldon's definition (1923). The seven versions are as follows:

a deal with one particular phase of business.
b give expert advice to the line officers. The primary functional divisions are Sales, Engineering, Manufacturing and Finance.
c are in charge of a single staff function or certain similar or supplementary functions.
d are engaged in the business of analyzing, testing, comparing, recording, making researches, co-ordinating information and advising
e furnish the means of developing standards and plans for which a regular line position leaves no time.
f give special types of services.
g are responsible for investigations, study and designing . . . Routine executive direction of performance usually requires the rapid shifting of attention from one immediate problem to another, leaving little time either for reverie or for continuous concentrated attention to a single idea.[63]

Urwick attempted a complex military treatise to restore the principle of 'staff' to its original meaning based on a General Staff. Confusion had arisen in the writings of businessmen because the 'staff' principle was equated with *specialisation*; hence any function which was specialised was believed to be a 'staff' function. It was this dominating idea of specialisation attached to the 'staff' principle which Urwick sought to clarify. To achieve his clarification, he did not return to Haldane's thought, but quoted numerous passages from the British *Field Service Regulations*.[64] Like Haldane, he had experience of the British Army and found no difficulty in relating military principles to other forms of organisation. But for the average student without military experience, both today and in the first part of the twentieth century, it is not easy to understand the complicated terminology of the British Army with its ranks and names of formations such as brigade, battalion and so on, and harder still to transfer these principles from their military environment into the business situation. If anything, Urwick created greater confusion for the layman, for while Haldane restricted his interest to the General Staff, Urwick was determined to go into lengthy military detail to explain that in many modern armies there are two types of staff – General Staff

63. L. Urwick, 'Organization as a technical problem', op. cit. p. 58.
64. Ibid., pp. 62–88.

and Administrative Staff or their equivalent. The weakness in the writings of American businessmen, like H. S. Dennison and Mooney and Reiley, was that they had failed, apparently, to notice two meanings of the word 'staff' and so Urwick quoted this time from a United States Army manual to indicate two types of staff:

> *General staff officers* assist the commander by performing such *duties pertaining to the function of command* as may be delegated to them by regulations or given them by the commander. *Technical and administrative staff officers* assist the commander *and his general staff* in an advisory capacity in *matters pertaining to* their *special branches*.[65]

In business thought, the *two* staff relations had been merged, mistakenly, into the *one* phrase of 'staff' and 'line'.[66] Urwick provided further military examples from the British Army to illustrate the two separate functions of the General Staff and the Administrative Staff. The General Staff are *not specialists*,[67] he explained. They relieve the chief of the details of command and, on his behalf, maintain personal contact with the 'line'. The Administrative Staff – which embraces *specialist and technical staff officers* – advise on matters of army administration only, including specialised and technical subjects, such as personnel administration and medical treatment respectively (See Fig. 4).[68] In fact, General Staff officers assist the commander to integrate this specialised knowledge into his overall plan.

The General Staff is the proper meaning underlying the 'staff' principle, Urwick confirmed. In business, the parallel 'staff' position would be an assistant to a 'line' executive and not a specialist. But,

65. Ibid., p. 61. The terminology in the British and American Armies differed, although in both Armies there were two types of staff officers. This difference in terminology partly accounts for the misunderstandings about 'staff' and 'line'. For example, see Mooney and Reiley *Onward Industry!* pp. 331–40.
66. Urwick developed this argument in his later essay, 'The nature of line and staff', *Management: A Book of Readings*, ed. by H. Koontz and C. O'Donnell (New York) 1964, pp. 212–14.
67. A General Staff officer has a general rather than a specialised education. In the British Army, some specialists do become General Staff officers for a time, but they have to prove in examination that they can cope with the tactical aspects of military operations and the broad spectrum of General Staff functions. Accordingly, General Staff officers may be regarded as *generalists* rather than specialists.
68. In addition to advising, *specialist and technical staff officers* may *give some direct orders* to the specialised and technical troops. Thus, a situation of dual allegiance is created, whereby the specialised and technical troops owe allegiance both to a 'specialised' authority and to the 'line' commander. For example, a senior medical staff officer may also control the field hospitals and medical stores in the geographical area under the jurisdiction of the commander he serves. By contrast, *General Staff officers do not have authority in their own right* but convey their commander's orders.

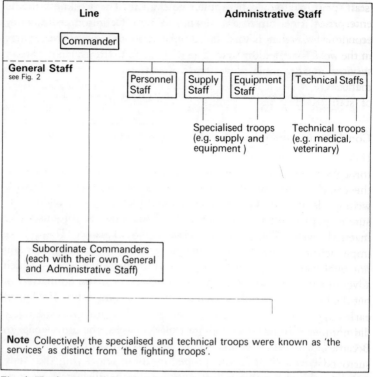

Fig. 4. The functions of the Administrative Staff in the British Army during the First World War. Note Urwick's diagrams contained in 'Organization as a technical problem' in *Papers on the Science of Administration* are highly complex and, therefore, we offer this diagram.

because of the confusion in terminology, the true 'staff' principle had received little implementation in business organisations. It had been blurred by the idea of specialisation.[69] Urwick urged that the proper

69. Moreover, since specialisation was an integral part of Taylor's concept of functional foremen, the 'staff' principle had become confused with Taylor's concept. He had suggested that eight foremen should replace the single foreman and they would each be a specialist in their own function – that is, route clerk, instruction clerk, time and cost clerk, disciplinarian, gang boss, speed boss and inspector. From the viewpoint of the 'staff' proper or the General Staff, Urwick pointed out the difference: '. . . the "staff" officer, as an individual, is the purest example of the segregation of planning from execution which can be found. It is a purer example than Taylor's functional foremen, because they had authority for "line" decisions in respect of their functions, as in the case of the specialist . . .services.' L. Urwick, 'Organization as a technical problem', op. cit. p. 82. See also F. B. Gilbreth, *Primer of Scientific Management* (London) 1912, p. 10.

'staff' principle should be applied in the Civil Service and business enterprises. He stressed that, owing to the increasing complexity of economic life, the individual civil servant or businessman – the general in the field – needed the help of 'staff' officers to integrate specialised services at the point of action. By a long and intricate military manoeuvre, Urwick brought his readers back to Haldane's concept of 'staff' based on the functions of a General Staff.[70]

Conclusion to the principles of 'staff' and 'line'

Haldane was responsible for extending the principle of 'staff' throughout the British Army but, despite his success in *implementing* the principle, he did not *document* it very thoroughly. Most of his writing about the General Staff principle is contained in his autobiography and it is embellished with a great deal of personal material about his life and work. Moreover, although he began to implement the 'staff' principle as early as 1906, his autobiography was not published until 1929 – a year after his death. Furthermore, he advocated that the principle should be extended into the Civil Service, but the Haldane Report was ambiguous on the point. It referred to the earlier application of the principle in military and naval experience, but did not mention the word 'staff' as Haldane did in his autobiography. Because of this looseness in terminology, the principle of 'staff' became surrounded by ambiguity. Neither did the Haldane Report explain by examples *how* the principle had proved successful in military and naval experience and *why* the same type of success was likely in the Civil Service. In other words, the Haldane Report neglected to state clearly the principles of 'staff' and 'line' *before* recommending them for introduction into the Civil Service, and failed to show the differences and similarities which would occur in their transference from the military and naval setting into the Civil Service.

Because no clear parallels were given between the workings of the principles in the military and the business environments, it is not surprising that ambiguity arose when businessmen tried to adopt the principles of 'staff' and 'line'. Sheldon made a good attempt at explaining the principles in the context of business administration, but by the time he had integrated 'staff' and 'line' with the three other types of organisation he identified, they remained – and still remain today – highly complex concepts to understand. This ambiguity and complexity shrouded the contribution of the British Philosophy of Administration

70. L. Urwick, 'Organization as a technical problem', op. cit, pp. 57–88.

to the 'staff' and 'line' principles and, although Urwick restated the principles in the 1930s, his paper reduced the *ambiguity* by clarifying the nature of 'staff' but it did little to relieve the *complexity*.

Finally, it is easy to see that a confusion could occur between the command–administration separation on which the 'staff' principle is based and the politics–administration separation. A closer view of the former indicates that it was intended to be a method of preventing the confusion and conflict which may occur when generalists and specialists work together rather than being a legislative–executive separation. Applied to the Civil Service and industry, Haldane and Urwick envisaged the command–administration separation as being a clear-cut way of assisting 'line' civil servants or managers at various levels in an organisation *to plan and implement* well-considered schemes of action, supported by the necessary technical and other specialised services. In contrast to the American doctrine of a legislative–executive separation discussed in Chapter 2, it was not an attempt to separate policy-making from policy implementation.

Organisation

The third SLOCUS principle is 'organisation' and the emphasis in this case is on the organisation as a whole. What is its purpose and on what basis is it subdivided? What does the term 'organisation' mean? Haldane was conscious of the need for a clearly defined organisational purpose and Sheldon and Urwick, in their turn, were keen to define and analyse the term 'organisation'. Each of these approaches to the principle of 'organisation' will be discussed.

Haldane's approach to the principle of 'organisation'

Haldane had two administrative obsessions. The first was his stress on the need for thought before action on which the principles of 'staff' and 'line' were founded. His second dominating concern was that organisations should have a clear purpose and be organised according to purpose. It may appear naive to us today that Haldane should wish to promote the concept of organisational purpose, for we might argue that surely organisations are brought into being only because of some known and definite purpose. However, Haldane knew what a vital difference an analysis of organisational purpose could make to the continuing success of an organisation. He took his lesson from the Esher Committee of 1904, for in its illuminating report, this

100

Committee pointed out that the purpose of the War Office had become obsolete. The Committee observed: 'For many years the War Office has been administered from the point of view of *peace*, so that it is necessary to make a complete break with the past and constitute it with a single eye to the effective training and preparation of the Forces for *war*.'[71]

The humiliating war experiences suffered by the British Army in the Crimean War (1854–56) and the South African campaign (1899–1902) were a partial result of the War Office's inappropriate purpose. Endless references to obtain authority had been necessary and a mass of routine paper work had diverted the War Office from its larger purpose of war. Haldane, as War Minister, was vividly aware in 1905 of the inefficiency which had been caused by the submergence of the War Office's real purpose and the influence of this realisation was one of the motivating forces behind his administrative thought. Sir Charles Harris, Permanent Head of the Financial Department of the War Office, wrote a tribute to Haldane after the latter's death in which he referred to the visit made by Haldane and Ellison to the German War Office in 1906. Harris drew attention to the profound effect on Haldane of the fact that the German Army was organised for war not peace and that its organisational arrangement permitted an instantaneous passage from peace conditions to war.[72]

Sir Charles Harris appears to have overlooked the Esher Committee's recommendation in 1904, with respect to the British Army, of this same principle of organisation according to purpose. It is possible, however, that this principle came to the Esher Committee through its Secretary, Colonel Ellison, who was already familiar with German military organisations. Whatever the source of inspiration in Haldane's case, it is clear that he was influenced strongly by the principle of organisation by purpose. Indeed, in 1920, he recalled his recognition of this principle when addressing a group of civil servants. Haldane advised the Society of Civil Servants that:

> . . . every department should possess an exact knowledge of the purpose for which it does things, and should proceed to do them . . . I remember being immensely impressed when, as an innocent person of virgin mind, I went to the War Office. They said – we must form an army. Here are the fine old Yeomen and the grand old Militia. These must remain intact. Then there are the Volunteers – a splendid set; you must respect them and their integrity. And then there are the Regulars, with their

71. P. and G. Ford, *A Breviate of Parliamentary Papers 1900–1916* (Oxford) 1957, pp. ix–xiv, 23 (author's italics).
72. Sir C. Harris, 'Lord Haldane at the War Office', op. cit., p. 341.

traditions. When I asked what was the army to consist of, the answer was – 'Oh, it can be made up out of these'. But it seemed to me, even in my innocence, that the first question was – what may we want an army for? And the second question was, when we had found that out, what sort of instrument do we require for carrying out this purpose?[73]

Although he did not envisage war when he first entered the War Office in 1905, Haldane set to work to prepare the British Army as if war was imminent. Later it was acknowledged that if he had not reorganised the British Army according to the purpose of war, or if the Army had been less prepared, the First World War might have had disastrously different results for Britain.[74]

It is possible now to see a pattern emerging in Haldane's administrative thought. As a newcomer to administrative problems, he absorbed his scientific principles of administration from three major sources. The first of these sources was the Esher Committee of 1904, the second source was his Military Private Secretary, Colonel Ellison, and his last source of inspiration came from the German military organisations which he had studied in theory and practice. With zest and energy, he built these principles into the British War Office and the British Army and carried them on as guides to action in British public administration in general. It is hardly surprising, then, to find the principle of organisation by purpose among the suggestions made by the Haldane Committee in 1918 for the reconstruction of the Civil Service. The Committee's Report opens with Haldane's ideas to the fore in the discussion of the problems of the executive departments of government:

> . . . many . . . Departments have been gradually evolved in compliance with current needs, and . . . the purposes for which they were thus called into being have gradually so altered that the later stages of the process have not accorded in principle with those that were reached earlier. In other instances Departments appear to have been rapidly established without preliminary insistence on definition of function . . .[75]

73. R. B. Haldane, 'The machinery of government', *The Civil Servant and his Profession* (London) 1920, p. 33.
74. See the Rt. Hon. Viscount Grey of Fallodon, 'Lord Haldane', *Public Administration*, Vol. VI, 1928, 332–3. Another tribute to Haldane's organisation was made by General Sir Ian Hamilton. After pointing out the poor condition of the British Army when Haldane came to office, Hamilton wrote: 'Came Haldane the Organiser, and cut, pruned, shuffled, grafted, drafted . . . When I look back on this period . . . I do really feel uplifted to think I was privileged to watch his address, his artistry, his perseverance, and even to lend at times a hand. The war was won when Haldane stepped into the War Office . . .' Gen. Sir I. Hamilton, *The Soul and Body of An Army* (London) 1921, pp. 6–7.
75. *Report of the Machinery of Government Committee*, p. 4.

The Machinery of Government Committee, drawing strongly on Haldane's experience of military practices, sought to rectify the obsolete, or indistinct, purpose of executive departments. It proposed to establish ten departments whose purpose, or function, would be to perform a major *service* to the community;[76] for example, the Ministry of Education would be responsible for the service of education. The Committee realised that a certain amount of natural overlap would result between the major and secondary purposes of departments but, nevertheless, its proposal offered a reinstatement of organisational purpose to executive departments and a means of removing the severe overlapping of functions which existed in the British Civil Service following the First World War. The Committee rejected the alternative method of organising departments according to the *persons* or classes to be dealt with, on the grounds that this would lead to 'Lilliputian' administration.[77]

In practice, the Haldane Report recommendations for the ten executive departments of government were not implemented. A Ministry of Health was created, but the general principle of reorganising the work of the departments according to the service to be performed did not materialise. There was not a Ministry of Production, a Ministry of Employment nor a Ministry of Justice[78] established at that time. Indeed, it was pointed out later that the haphazard adoption of the Haldane Report recommendations is a reminder that technical efficiency often takes second place to political expediency.[79] Undaunted, Haldane continued to press his argument for organisation by purpose in the British Civil Service and, again in 1923 in his Presidential address to the new Institute of Public Administration, he stressed that if confusion in public administration was to be avoided government departments must have their scope clearly defined according to

76. See this chapter, p. 80 for a list of the ten departments proposed by the Haldane Report.
77. *Report of the Machinery of Government Committee*, pp. 7–8.
78. Haldane was Lord Chancellor between 1912 and 1915, and in this position he had the opportunity to see how overburdened the Lord Chancellor was, having a number of traditional functions to perform including administration, besides exclusively judicial ones. Haldane argued that the main work of the Lord Chancellor was to head the great tribunals and, as such, he could not act as a proper head of a large administrative department. Therefore, he proposed a separate Department of Justice, headed by a Minister of Justice, to absorb the administrative work of the Lord Chancellor. He made this proposal, for example, in his evidence to the Royal Commission on the Civil Service in 1915, see *Royal Commission on the Civil Service: Appendix to Sixth Report of the Commissioners* (London) 1915, pp. 650–9, and in *Richard Burdon Haldane*, p. 324, as well as in the Haldane Report.
79. See R. V. Vernon and N. Mansergh, *Advisory Bodies*, pp. 51–4.

function. He argued that it was nearly four years since he had been Chairman of the Machinery of Government Reconstruction Committee, but subsequent study had not led him to wish to depart from its conclusions. The broad plan for the reorganisation of the executive government set out in the Committee's Report seemed still, he insisted, the kind of plan to be adopted if progress in public administration was to be achieved.[80] Haldane, then, continued to maintain unswerving dedication to the scientific principle of organisation by purpose, seeing it both as an objective to be pursued by organisations and a method of organising. As an objective, he was aware that to be successful, organisations need to pursue relevant and not outdated purposes. And, as a method of organising, the principle of 'purpose' took priority for the Haldane Committee, and for Haldane personally, over the alternative method of organising by 'persons' or clientele to be served.

Sheldon's approach to the principle of 'organisation'

In 1923, Oliver Sheldon, working in the field of factory organisation, considered that it would be useful to conceptualise the various methods of organising factories. He incorporated the methods he identified into four conceptual types of organisation, namely: (1) 'Staff' and 'line' organisation. (2) Functional organisation. (3) Departmental organisation and (4) Committee organisation. To some extent, these types of factory organisation had their counterpart in British public administration and it has been shown already that the 'staff' and 'line' type corresponded to the Haldane Report proposals for 'staff' facilities within the British Civil Service.[81] Similarly, Sheldon's functional organisation was equivalent to the Haldane Committee's recommendation to reorganise the executive departments of government according to major 'purpose' or function. However, there was some divergence between the Haldane Committee's bases of organisation and those inherent in Sheldon's four types of organisation. The main divergence[82] was that Sheldon referred to departmental organisation, based on the principle of decentralisation, as a separate type from functional organisation, based on the principle of function. By contrast, the Haldane Committee used the title 'Departmental

---

80. R. B. Haldane, 'An organized Civil Service', *Journal of Public Administration*, Vol. I, 1923, 8.
81. See this chapter, p. 92.
82. Another divergence was that Sheldon did not identify a type of factory organisation based on 'persons' or clientele, which was the alternative method considered by the Haldane Committee.

Organisation' simply as a heading to describe subsidiary matters connected with the organisation of departments by major function or 'purpose'.[83] In other words, the Haldane Committee made no major distinction between departmental organisation and functional organisation whereas Sheldon did. In view of this conflict in terms, Sheldon's four types of organisation will not be discussed further, as to do so would undermine the value of the Haldane Report and the method of organisation by purpose which it proposed. However, this brief reference to Sheldon's four types of organisation has been reintroduced to indicate the ambiguity in key terms which existed between 1900 and 1939 in connection with scientific principles of administration – and which continues today.

Fortunately, Sheldon expanded his views about organisation in 1928 and this later work provides a more suitable, and less conflicting, source from which to draw his contribution. He offered an excellent definition of the term 'organisation', followed by an analysis of the effectiveness of an organisation. These aspects are outlined and it will be seen that they resemble subsequent ideas put forward in the 1930s by American administrative theorists, such as C. I. Barnard, H. A. Simon and others.

Definition of organisation

Sheldon opened his treatise with a broad definition of organisation:

> An organisation comes into being as an outcome of several persons joining together to further a given project. The larger the enterprise, the more complex the organization, but, however small it may be, and whatever its object, there an organization exists. An organisation is not something one can hold or reject at will; it comes automatically into existence, when a common object is adopted by a group of co-workers.[84]

The above broad definition of organisation is followed by a more precise one embodying what Sheldon considered to be the six essential elements of organisation. These six elements are summarised before his narrower definition of organisation is given:

(i) *Organisation is a process*   Organisation is a conscious purposeful activity. It is the building of a structure according to plans and specifications. Furthermore, since the structure is designed by men and women, organisation is a continuous process, needing the constant care of those responsible for it. As each new activity begins, it must be properly situated in the organisation. The finest organisation will

83. *Report of the Machinery of Government Committee*, pp. 7–14.
84. O. Sheldon et al., *Factory Organization*, p. 8.

collapse unless the care with which it was originally planned is exercised continually.

(ii) *Organisation is the determination of duties* Skill in organisation consists largely in fitting men and jobs together suitably, but the original starting point in planning an organisation is the analysis and distribution of the work. Any alteration to the proper division of work, to suit the particular capabilities of an individual, may be desirable, but it is a departure from the ideal and can function satisfactorily only for a temporary period.

(iii) *Organisation is only a means to an end* An organisation is a means to an end and organising is the devising of the best methods for accomplishing that end. It follows, therefore, that the end must be definite and known to all concerned, if it is to be the criterion by which to judge the effectiveness of the means. An organisation is not an end in itself. The methods of working are determined in order that they may contribute directly to the achievement of the ends set up. By allocating duties to various individuals or groups, the organiser automatically determines to some extent the methods of working.

(iv) *Organisation must ensure co-ordination* Without full co-ordination of the activities, the ends of the organisation are not being pursued effectively and economically. Organising is itself a co-ordinating activity. It is the linking together of various units to achieve the result planned for the business as a whole.

(v) *Organisation depends on persons as well as jobs* Although the organiser will plan his organisation in the first place irrespective of persons, the success of his plan must depend on the ability of each official who performs a 'job'. Therefore, the job cannot be regarded as wholly distinct from the person or persons performing it and the duties to be undertaken must be related to the persons appointed to undertake them.

(vi) *Organisation presumes that certain means are available* An organiser's task finishes when he stipulates that a certain activity must be carried out by a certain individual or unit and it is presumed that certain means are available to carry out that activity. How an individual or unit performs the work (e.g. whether it is done by hand or by machine) is not directly the responsibility of the organiser, although changes in operating methods may lead him to make changes in the organisation.

On the basis of these six characteristics, Sheldon constructed his final and narrower definition of organisation as: '... the process of assigning duties to individuals or groups, selected for the purpose, so as to achieve specified ends effectively and economically through the co-ordination and combination of all their activities'.[85]

Effectiveness of an organisation

Sheldon identified the *elements* of an organisation in his definition, but if an organisation is to be assessed for *effectiveness*, a further measure is required. According to Sheldon, an organisation is effective when it accomplishes the following four aims:

(i) *To enable work to be done economically and easily* A poor organisation is one in which the execution of work is unnecessarily complicated, circumlocutory or haphazard. An effective, or sound, organisation is one in which every activity is initiated and carried through with the minimum of trouble and the maximum of effect. It is not enough to apply this criterion to one single activity. An organisation is sound only if all the activities of the enterprise are carried out simultaneously under these conditions.

(ii) *To enable central control* No organisation can be considered completely sound unless the Chief Executive has the means to co-ordinate from the top. He must control the decision as to how the organisation shall be built up, so that he can regulate every extension and work out every change in the light of the plan he is pursuing for the *whole* enterprise. A complex organisation cannot be built up and maintained as a serviceable working unit unless each part complies with one design and the ideas of each builder are subordinated to one central purpose.

(iii) *To ensure expansion despite changes* The organisation-builder must create a fabric which can endure through the years. He cannot afford to design his organisation to the needs of the moment and the people of the present. He must build a permanent organisation; yet the structure is not composed of brick and stone. It is a *living* structure and human life contains the seeds of decay. It is short-sighted, therefore, to plan an organisation to fit the personnel at any given time. An ideal organisation, if it is to be stable, must be planned to provide for the exercise of normal capacities; it cannot provide a niche for the abnormal.

85. Ibid., pp. 10–13.

(iv) *To make full use of available human power*   Although the organiser cannot build his edifice on the basis of individual idiosyncracies and peculiarities, he must locate the human power in such a way that each person contributes consistently to the work of the organisation as a whole. This location of human power requires the organiser to distinguish between different types of minds: the analytical mind, the empirical mind, the scientific mind, the mind that commands and leads, the accurate mind, etc. Each cog in the organisational wheel is a human being and conditions must induce human beings to work easily and efficiently. Friction, insecurity, worry, lack of facilities for the full exercise of powers are grit which clog the wheels of the machine. The organiser is the most responsible of the welfare workers for, by efficient organisation, he can remove many of the causes of discontent which are liable to arise in everyday work. Thus, efficiency in work is to carry out the most enlightened labour policy.

It should be noted in Sheldon's scheme that, although the Chief Executive co-ordinates the organisation from the top, the organiser is any organisational member assigned the role of organising. He stated some of the qualities desired in the organiser as a highly analytical mind, a long-distance mind and an appreciation of the human factor.[86]

If Sheldon's analysis of organisation is compared with that of C. I. Barnard (1938) in the United States, a clear similarity is visible. For, like Sheldon, Barnard defined formal organisation, identified its essential elements and discussed the same concept of an effective organisation.[87] Likewise, Simon, Smithburg and Thompson in their American publication (1950) defined formal organisation as: . . . a planned system of cooperative effort in which each participant has a recognized role to play and duties or tasks to perform. These duties are assigned in order to achieve the organization purpose rather than to satisfy individual preferences, although the two often coincide'.[88]

Sheldon's definition of organisation and the measure he put forward to test its effectiveness was intended to draw attention in Britain to the importance of good organisation, for he believed that British industry needed to obtain effective results if it was to compete with its foreign

86. Ibid., pp. 13–18.
87. C. I. Barnard, *The Functions of the Executive* (Cambridge, Mass.) 1938. Thirtieth edn 1968, particularly Chapters VI and VII.
88. H. A. Simon, D. W. Smithburg and V. A. Thompson, *Public Administration* (New York) 1950. Twelfth edn 1968, p. 5.

rivals. Modern industrial conditions, he argued, no longer permitted careless or haphazard organisation.[89]

Urwick's approach to the principle of 'organisation'

The nearest the British Philosophy of Administration came to reaching a 'theory', as distinct from a set of administrative doctrines based largely on personal experience and intuition, was in connection with the scientific principle of 'organisation' (and also the principle of 'communication'). Sheldon's conceptual analysis of four types of organisation together with his clear definition of organisation and the requirements for its effectiveness, achieved a degree of theoretical presentation often absent from the British doctrines. Urwick developed further the scientific principle of 'organisation' which Sheldon had started to elaborate and, like Sheldon, he believed that a clearly defined theory of organisation, if assimilated by industrial managers and public administrators, would help to improve administration in Britain. After his return from the First World War, Urwick began to deliver public lectures on scientific principles of administration, which included audiences of the British Association for the Advancement of Science, the Industrial Lecture Conferences arranged by Mr B. S. Rowntree, and meetings of the Institutes of Industrial and Public Administration. He collected some of his addresses together, and in 1933, published them in a book,[90] which contained his original thoughts on 'The Pure Theory of Organization'.

Definition of organisation

Urwick took a slightly different approach to Sheldon in his definition of organisation. Instead of listing the main elements of organisation, he put forward three separate definitions which incorporated various elements. His three definitions are as follows:

(i) *The substantive definition of organisation* Urwick maintained that, in the first place, organisation is used as 'a substantive connoting *a group of people united for a purpose.* In this sense an organisation comes into being wherever such a grouping takes place. The larger the group, the more complex will be its character. But however small the group may be and however rudimentary its arrangements for collaboration, there an organisation exists. It is not something which is a matter of volition, which can be accepted or rejected at will. It comes

89. Sheldon et al., *Factory Organization*, p. 8.
90. See L. Urwick, *Management of Tomorrow* (London) 1933.

into existence automatically, when a common object is pursued by a group of co-workers'.

(ii) *The specific definition of organisation* 'In addition to its use as a general substantive to describe the group as a whole, "organisation" is also frequently employed specifically to describe the body of arrangements which exist for securing collaboration between the members of the group; in this sense it connotes *the system or methods established'*.

(iii) *The definition of organisation as a process* Organisation in this sense is defined as *'dividing up all the activities* which are necessary to any purpose and arranging them in groups which are assigned to individuals'.[91]

Urwick appears to reflect some of Sheldon's thinking (1928), particularly in the case of the substantive definition of organisation. However, the influence of these two administrative thinkers upon each other was mutual, for although Urwick was Sheldon's assistant in the 'Organisation Office' at the Rowntree Works having joined the firm a few years after Sheldon, he had had a more varied army career than Sheldon. He was, then, Sheldon's junior in service but senior in age and to some extent in experience.[92] In defining 'organisation', Urwick and Sheldon differed in terminology and what Sheldon listed as *the determination of duties*, Urwick called *a process*. But, despite differences in terms, they shared the same aim, which was to set out a theory of organisation to help British industry and government to understand the nature of organisation and to carry out the scientific reforms necessary to withstand foreign competition. Also, the increased size of organisations and the administrative implications of size was a factor motivating Urwick to provide a theory of organisation and he stressed:

> The very large business aggregations which are increasingly character-
> istic of our times are creating problems of administration of a size and
> quality not previously contemplated by industrial leaders . . . There is
> thus a strong case for an attempt to build a pure theory of organisation
> and to direct that attempt particularly towards business organisation . . .
> It must be based on a widespread study of past and existing enterprises
> both in business and in other walks of life.[93]

Urwick incorporated into his pure theory of organisation, certain specific principles of organisation, such as 'staff' and 'line' and 'span of

91. Ibid., pp. 52–3 (author's italics).
92. L. Urwick, Personal letter to the author dated 28 Feb. 1975.
93. L. Urwick, *Management of Tomorrow*, pp. 55–6.

control'. Other contributors to the British Philosophy of Administration, like Haldane and Wallas, had been advocating scientific principles of administration since the turn of the century, but they took a less theoretical and analytical approach than Sheldon or Urwick. By the 1920s and 1930s, with the impact of Henri Fayol in France and Mooney and Reiley, Luther Gulick, H. S. Dennison and other administrative theorists in the United States, the idea of scientific principles to be implemented at *managerial* level (as distinct from *operative* level as in much of Taylor's work) had become highly popular. Indeed, Urwick wanted British organisations to adopt more scientific principles than existed already and his theory of organisation was, in part, a prod to Britain to structure her organisations on firmer scientific grounds. The international popularity of 'management principles' brought about a convergence of terminology from Britain, France and the United States and Urwick's theory of organisation acted, also, as a restatement of common scientific principles. However, in clarifying *international* scientific principles, he went further than the other contributors to the British Philosophy of Administration, who stressed ethical ideals of administration as constantly as scientific principles. Urwick, while being interested in psychology and human problems of administration before and during his career at the Rowntree Works, became more concerned in the 1930s with universal scientific principles (i.e. the technical or structural elements of the organisation) which he believed could be studied separately from the human elements. His work of the 1930s, therefore, began to diverge from the main British Philosophy of Administration towards the establishment of an independent science of administration.

Conclusion to the principle of 'organisation'

Central to the principle of 'organisation' is the idea of purpose. Haldane emphasised the importance of structuring an organisation according to purpose and of maintaining a relevant purpose, while Sheldon and Urwick made organisational purpose a chief factor in their theories of 'organisation'. It can be seen, therefore, that the concept of organisational purpose played three roles within the British Philosophy of Administration. First, it was an organisational *objective* to be pursued; in other words an organisation should analyse its purpose to ensure that it is not pursuing an obsolete goal. Moreover, the purpose of an organisation should be made known to all members. Second, purpose was a *method* of organising as distinct from the method of

111

persons or clientele. The main purpose is broken down into tasks and the tasks are assigned to individuals or groups whose joint efforts help to achieve that main purpose. Finally, purpose was part of the *definition* of organisation, since it was recognised by Sheldon and Urwick that whenever persons join together in common purpose, there an organisation exists. The emphasis on organisational purpose, then, was a foundation stone of the British Philosophy of Administration and it later became the basis of administrative, or organisational, theory in both Britain and the United States.[94]

Several interesting factors should be noted in connection with this principle. Haldane's reorganisation of the British Army according to purpose (i.e. war) had proved effective and in 1918 the Haldane Committee adopted the principle, but for a few years Haldane faced antagonism because he had observed German methods of organisation. His visits to Germany, particularly a visit to Berlin in February 1912 as War Minister, and his hospitality towards a German visitor Herr Ballin in July 1914, provoked attacks upon his integrity. Many British people, including the Press, failed to realise that since he had lived in Germany as a university student and had a deep understanding of the German language, his interest in Germany was based on a cultural and administrative admiration for German knowledge rather than any attempt to be a 'traitor' as some Britons accused him. By August 1914, a large section of the British public had turned against Haldane and he felt he ought to resign his government post as Lord Chancellor, but the Prime Minister refused to accept his resignation. Abuse continued to be directed towards him, however, and the solution came in 1915 when the Prime Minister, Asquith, formed a coalition government in view of the emergencies of war, which demanded the resignation of all existing Ministers. Although Haldane's advice was sought on government committees, he did not take public office again until 1924 when he was reappointed as Lord Chancellor, having made the transition from the Liberal Party to Labour. Throughout the personal abuse at the onset to the First World War, he remained in good spirits; confident that he had reorganised the British Army for its purpose of war and he later explained:

94. Organisation of the executive departments of government according to purpose was also confirmed by W. Beveridge, when he argued that departmental disputes were caused mainly by acute cases of the overlapping of functions. Beveridge referred to the Haldane Committee's recommendation as 'the theoretically perfect scheme', see Ch. 5, pp. 219–20. W Beveridge, *The Public Service in War and in Peace* (London) 1920, p. 52.

I was never depressed by even the most violent abuse. I knew very well that the reorganisation of the Army was likely to turn out to have been thoroughly made, and on lines which would fit it for the task ... I knew, too, that the strategical principles which had been adopted since 1911 by the Admiralty in harmony with those of the Army would enable the two Great Services to work together for victory ... So it proved in the end. But before the War ended in our victory I had, of course, a disagreeable time. I was threatened with assault in the street, and I was on occasions in some danger of being shot at. But on the other hand I had a multitude of loyal and devoted friends whose hopes had through the years rested on my efforts.[95]

Another interesting factor is that there was less divergence by the radical administrative thinkers – Sidney and Beatrice Webb and Harold Laski – from the scientific principle of 'organisation'. Earlier, we suggested that the Webbs differed in important respects from the central doctrines of the British Philosophy of Administration,[96] but in this instance they agreed with the Haldane Report's recommendation to reorganise the executive government according to major purpose. Not only was Beatrice a member of the Haldane Committee but the Webbs proceeded to introduce into their own radical reforms for the political and administrative institutions of British government, the idea of organisation by major purpose. They even favoured Haldane's lifelong pledge for a separate Ministry of Justice[97] and proposed it within their Political Parliament and its Executive which would be concerned with the courts of justice. The Webbs also adopted the other main departments of government recommended by the Haldane Committee as the foundation of the Social Parliament. But, as pointed out in Chapter 2, they envisaged *two* departments for each major service (one to administer and one to control), as well as standing committees of the Social Parliament corresponding to these major departments of Finance, Health, Education, etc. Despite these important constitutional differences, the Webbs adhered to the departments listed in the Haldane Report (1918).[98]

95. *Richard Burdon Haldane*, pp. 238–89. See also, C. Falls, 'Haldane and defence', *Public Administration*, Vol. 35, 1957, 245–53.
96. See Ch. 1 p. 31 and Ch. 2, pp. 45–54, 67–71.
97. Although Haldane urged the establishment of a Ministry of Justice, the earlier recommendation for such a Ministry had been made by J. Bentham. See *Law Reform Now*, ed. by G. Gardiner and A. Martin (London) 1964, p. 7.
98. See S. and B. Webb, *A Constitution for the Socialist Commonwealth of Great Britain* (London) 1920, pp. 120, 138. Laski also confirmed his approval of the recommendations of the Haldane Report, see H. J. Laski, 'The Civil Service and Parliament', *The Development of the Civil Service* (London) 1922, pp. 32–6, and 'The Tomlin Report on the Civil Service', *The Political Quarterly*, Vol. II, No. 4, Oct.–Dec. 1931, 514.

However, there was a weakness in the principle of organisation by 'purpose' as contained in the Haldane Report. The Haldane Committee ignored the disadvantages of organising by purpose and gave only one alternative method of organising by persons or clientele. By contrast, Gulick in his later study of administration for the United States government set out fully both advantages and disadvantages of some four methods of organising – namely: by purpose, process, persons and place.[99] This criticism of the Haldane Report is explained best by a quotation from H. A. Simon (1945):

> The British Machinery of Government Committee . . . considered purpose and clientele as the two possible bases of organization and puts its faith entirely in the former . . . The reasoning which leads to these unequivocal conclusions leaves something to be desired. The Machinery of Government Committee gives this sole argument for its choice:
>
>> 'Now the inevitable outcome of this method of organization (by clientele) is a tendency to Lilliputian administration. It is impossible that the specialized service which each Department has to render to the community can be of as high a standard when its work is at the same time limited to a particular class of persons and extended to every variety of provision for them, as when the Department concentrates itself on the provision of the particular service only, by whomsoever required, and looks beyond the interest of comparatively small classes.'
>
> The faults in this analysis are clearly obvious. First, there is no attempt to determine how a service is to be recognized. Second, there is a bald assumption, absolutely without proof, that a child health unit, for example, in a department of child welfare could not offer services of 'as high a standard' as the same unit if it were located in a department of health . . . It is not necessary here to decide whether the committee was right or wrong in its recommendation; the important point is that the recommendation represented a choice, without any apparent logic or empirical grounds, between contradictory principles of administration.[100]

Simon regarded the methods of organisation by purpose, clientele and so on as contradictory and competing bases of organisation and he blamed this contradiction partly on the ambiguity surrounding the key terms. Evidence of such ambiguity is apparent within the British Philosophy of Administration for there was some divergence, as well as an overlap, between Haldane's bases of organisation and those inherent in Sheldon's four types of organisation.[101]

99. L. Gulick, 'Notes on the theory of organization', op. cit., pp. 21–30.
100. H. A. Simon, *Administrative Behaviour: A Study of Decision-Making Processes in Administrative Organization*, 1945. Republished (New York) 1965, pp. 28–35.
101. See this chapter, pp. 104–5.

Finally, with respect to the approaches by Sheldon and Urwick to the principle of 'organisation', it should be remembered that they both owed a debt in their work to B. S. Rowntree. Rowntree did much to promote the development of human well-being in British administrative practice and he was also an advocate of scientific principles of administration. Not only did he launch conferences at which the latter topic was discussed but he also fostered his managerial staff's interest in the subject.[102] Yet, Rowntree wrote little on administration beyond his simple, practical book *The Human Factor in Business* (1921).[103] Rather, his example of running the Cocoa Works at York on scientific lines and his encouragement to his managers, stimulated Sheldon and Urwick to contemplate and document their theories of organisation.

Communication

The British Philosophy of Administration drew attention to the importance of 'co-ordinating' the various tasks within an organisation and this chapter has shown that the POSDCORB principle of 'co-ordination' had existed earlier in the Haldane Report. British writers, however, did not lay stress on formal 'co-ordination' to the extent of the later American theorists; for example, J. D. Mooney (1937) regarded 'co-ordination' as the beginning and end of all organised effort – for him it was the principle which contained all the other administrative principles.[104] British administrative thinkers, although aware of the need for formal 'co-ordination', believed more strongly in the broader idea of 'communication'. The scientific principle of 'communication', as promoted within the British Philosophy of Administration, often incorporated both formal and informal methods of co-ordination and the principle took two major forms.[105] It represented first a demand for greater *oral* communication in modern organisations, as distinct from formalised communication in *writing*. Both Graham Wallas and Richard Haldane, for example, exposed the dangers of excess paper

102. See A. Briggs, *A Study of the Work of Seebohm Rowntree 1877–1954* (London) 1961, pp. 118–19, 268–73. Urwick has also confirmed the value of B. S. Rowntree's pioneering work at the York factory and the benefit to the development of British management thought and practice of the Rowntree conferences, which commenced in 1919. L. Urwick, Personal letter to the author dated 1 Apr. 1975.
103. B. S. Rowntree, *The Human Factor in Business* (London) 1921, Second edn 1925.
104. J. D. Mooney, 'The principles of organization', *Papers on the Science of Administration*, p. 93.
105. L. Gulick in the United States later made reference to co-ordination by *ideas* as well as *formal* co-ordination, see L. Gulick, 'Notes on the theory of organization', op. cit., pp. 37–8.

work and formal methods of administration and, thus, they did not concur with Weber's insistence that written reports were an unavoidable element of modern bureaucracies. In practice, British administration had suffered from an excess of written communication[106] and Wallas and Haldane considered that a move from written communication to oral discussion, or 'dialectics', was necessary for twentieth-century administration.

Secondly, the scientific principle of 'communication' incorporated the concept of committees. In organisations, committees permit both communication and co-ordination to take place and the role of committees formed an important aspect of SLOCUS. However, the British Philosophy of Administration did not promote the usefulness of committees to the extent of Sidney and Beatrice Webb and Harold Laski, for the Webbs' constitutional reforms were founded on government by committees.[107] The SLOCUS principle of 'communication' in its aspect of 'committees', in fact, pointed strongly to certain weaknesses, as well as advantages, in committees and this principle is now outlined and analysed.

Wallas' approach to the principle of 'communication'

As early as 1914, Graham Wallas stressed the principle of 'communication' from both a scientific and an ethical viewpoint. As a scientific principle, communication was a guide for the structuring of organisations and it consisted of setting up small groups for the purpose of oral communication. Wallas' grievance was that twentieth-century organisations were too impersonal, relying heavily on written communications. Ethically, he envisaged verbal communication as a means of releasing some of the unused powers in human beings and meeting some of their unsatisfied needs. His argument, then, was that modern organisations should return to *personal* methods of communication based on group-dialectics. This traditional method involves a small number of persons, preferably between two and eight, who meet together for organised oral discussion and this form of communication was the basis of Greek philosophy as seen in the dialogues of Plato. Modern organisations, Wallas argued, had neglected this form and had concentrated instead on the *impersonal* method of communication by writing.

106. The excess emphasis on written communication in British administration is discussed in Ch. 5 in connection with bureaucracy.
107. See Ch. 2, pp. 45–54.

Wallas referred to four advantages of group-dialectics for twentieth-century organisations. First, group-dialectics or verbal communication through small groups enables an extension in the range of thought and ideas circulating within organisations. For example, an idea assessed by any one *individual* may not appear relevant, but in a *group* discussion the idea is thrashed out and it may assume a new significance. Second, written words are often too clumsy to explain a delicate idea, whereas personal intercourse is more expressive. The third advantage of group-dialectics which Wallas stated was its capacity to 'humanise' government offices. The official should be known as a man, he argued, and for this to occur, he should do part of his work by verbal methods. However, Wallas realised that it would be no use placing half a dozen clerks round an office table and expecting them to be able to think with the same degree of effort as a newly elected town councillor or a Cabinet Minister faced with the opportunity of his lifetime. These junior civil servants would require not only the *occasion*, but also *motives* for thought. It was Wallas' belief that the psychological nature of man needed oral expression, and small discussion groups set up in the British Civil Service would provide this expression and so humanise the official. But in some cases, particularly in the lower ranks of the Service, stimulus, or motives, for oral discussion would be required and the type of stimulus he suggested included releasing office-bound civil servants to take part in some external activities, such as public enquiries or making oral statements before Parliamentary or Cabinet committees.

The fourth advantage he saw in oral communication was its potential to overcome official habits of thought, such as rigidity, narrowness and the tendency to develop a sense of 'corporate interest' contrary to the public interest.[108] He considered that an atmosphere of free, intellectual thought, such as could be sustained in group-dialectics, would minimise the dysfunctions of habitual thought. Moreover, he was not satisfied that civil servants were intellectually alive and argued:

> . . . a Government office has serious intellectual defects . . . Not only are the training and experience of the official apt to be narrow and 'bookish', but the problems which, consciously or subconsciously, he sets himself to solve may be less comprehensive than those raised in a search for the public good. He may consciously avoid, or half-consciously flinch from, the tormenting effort of new thought . . . The written debate which goes

---

108. G. Wallas, *The Great Society: A Psychological Analysis* (London) 1914, pp. 249–304. Also *Human Nature in Politics*, 1908. Republished (London) 1962, pp. 276–81.

on in a Government office does not put such a strain upon the temper as does the spoken debate of Parliament or a committee . . . this very absence of strain may prevent an . . . official from acquiring that minimum degree of consideration for the feelings of others which oral intercourse produces in all but the most thick-skinned. The total effect, therefore, of a modern official organisation based solely on writing, is the combination of great efficiency in the handling of detail on established lines with the existence of an 'official atmosphere' which may be incompatible with some of the finer intellectual requirements of government, and has, in fact, often produced a general dislike of official methods among the outside public.[109]

Wallas associated the advantages of group-dialectics with business and other organisations, as well as the Civil Service. To business organisations, he suggested that less reliance should be placed on the single, *individual* mind and more on *concerted* discussion. And, in the case of the British Cabinet, he recommended that the Cabinet should be reduced in number from twenty-two members (as it was in 1914) to some ten or twelve to enable efficient oral discussion. To conclude Wallas' approach to the principle of 'communication', it may be said that he was critical of modern methods of communication. They relied excessively on impersonal communication by writing and on individual thought rather than the intercommunication of ideas within groups. In the nineteenth century, conversely, the old trades of tailoring, shoemaking, cabinet-making and others were based in workshops where small groups of between six and twenty persons worked in an atmosphere without machinery noise and without the presence of the employer. This atmosphere encouraged free talk and communication of ideas, but in modern industrial society men cannot talk freely unless groups are organised for this purpose. Metal trades, for example, are too noisy and clerical workers, under the eye of the supervisor, are prevented from conversing. Therefore, modern organisations require, Wallas believed, councils, committees and small organisational groups to facilitate the flow of ideas, to humanise the official, to reduce the tendency to rigidity and corporate self-interest, and to co-ordinate the various actions within the organisation as a whole.[110]

Haldane's approach to the principle of 'communication'

Earlier, it was noted that the British War Office at the turn of the century had become diverted from its main purpose of war by a

109. G. Wallas, *Great Society*, pp. 286–7.
110. Ibid., pp. 249–304.

mass of routine paper work.[111] The Esher Committee of 1904, which had investigated the inefficiency of the War Office, pointed out that 'the complexity of regulations is now so great that their interpretation alone leads to a mass of useless correspondence'.[112]

Haldane, as War Minister, corrected the defects in war administration, as far as possible, by implementing the 'staff' principle and readjusting the purpose of the War Office towards war rather than peace. However, the reliance on written communication in war administration and its stifling consequences led him to assert the same argument as Graham Wallas had proposed partially in (1908) and expanded in (1914). Haldane, in 1912, was called as a witness before the Royal Commission on the Civil Service. His experience in the War Office had given him knowledge of administration which he, and the Commissioners, considered would be helpful in their examination of the British Civil Service. By coincidence, Graham Wallas was the Commissioner questioning Haldane when the latter declared his faith in oral discussion. This cross-questioning is recorded at length, since it illustrates clearly Haldane's approach to the principle of communication:

G. Wallas:	'You have had in the War Office a large experience ... of the custom of dealing with big official business before a council of heads of departments, namely, the Army Council?
R. Haldane:	Yes.
G. Wallas:	There to a larger extent than in other offices the business instead of going up through the ordinary hierarchy and reaching yourself, before it reaches you, or at any rate when it reaches you, is considered round a table by the heads of departments?
R. Haldane:	Well, in theory it is so, but as a matter of fact we found in the War Office such a bad tradition for numerous minutes and red tape that we have set ourselves to get rid of the traditional minute altogether . . . I keep my room open all day in order to discourage written minutes. Whenever I get an opportunity I talk to the people together, military and civilians, and talk the matter out if possible in my presence, and then I send them away to talk it over among themselves . . .The result is that, though I think there are still too many written minutes, we have less than we used to have and

111. See this chapter, p. 101.
112. P. and G. Ford, *Breviate of Parliamentary Papers*, p. 22.

we often substitute an informal talk for the system of a formal discussion round a table.

G. Wallas: And your opinion is that the alteration of oral discussion for written minutes not only saves time, but is a valuable stimulus to thought?

R. Haldane: It is absolutely valuable, I think'.[113]

Wallas and Haldane, over a similar time period, had drawn the same conclusion regarding communication in organisations. They both saw the need for less written communication and more oral discussion within small groups. Furthermore, both men believed that the British Cabinet would be more effective if it was reduced in size. The Haldane Report of 1918, although making no reference to Graham Wallas, repeated his earlier recommendation that the Cabinet should consist of no more than ten to twelve persons,[114] for the effectiveness of the Cabinet was seen to be an important influence on public administration.

Haldane, in addition to seeking to promote oral communication in administration, favoured the concept of committees as a formal method of communication and co-ordination. Two types of committees are discernible from his administrative thought. These are *co-ordinating* committees and *advisory* committees and both types serve a communication purpose. First, the co-ordinating committees were recommended by the Haldane Committee to co-ordinate administrative activities *within* departments (i.e. intra-departmental meetings) and *between* departments (inter-departmental meetings). These formal co-ordinating committees were suggested for communication within the Civil Service, but informal communication also had its role to play. The Haldane Report stated with respect to inter-departmental communication: 'Sometimes this communication will need to be so close that there will have to be standing joint bodies of the Departments concerned . . . Sometimes regular or informal communication on specific questions will suffice. But contact of some kind is vital . . .'[115]

Second, advisory committees were suggested by the Haldane Committee in order to link the Minister and his department with the

113. *Royal Commission on the Civil Service. Appendix to First Report of the Commissioners*, p. 84 (author's italics).
114. *Report of the Machinery of Government Committee*, p. 5. In the 1920s Henri Fayol also pleaded for a small number of Ministers in the French Cabinet. H. Fayol, 'The administrative theory in the State', *Papers on the Science of Administration*, p. 108.
115. *Report of the Machinery of Government Committee*, pp. 10–11.

consumer – that is the section of the public affected by the government service. These committees were to be purely advisory, acting as a formal two-way communication channel between the departments and the public. They were in no way intended to impair the full responsibility of Ministers to Parliament. Indeed, the type of administrative boards and commissions with independent executive powers which risked to destroy ministerial responsibility were criticised by the Committee. Advisory committees were simply a public relations mechanism to increase public confidence in government administration. A few advisory committees existed already in 1918; some were statutory committees, such as the Consultative Committee of the Board of Education and others were discretionary, as in the case of the Consumers' Council of the Ministry of Food. The Haldane Report proposed that advisory committees of this nature should become an integral part of the normal organisation of departments in the British Civil Service.[116]

Sheldon's approach to the principle of 'communication'

Oliver Sheldon, in his typology of factory organisation, included the Committee type. In the same way as the 'Staff and line' organisation, the Committee type is supplementary to other forms of organisation, such as the Functional type based on function or purpose.[117] Within his typology, Sheldon analysed the role of committees and he identified four kinds – namely: *co-ordinating* committees, *advisory* committees, *executive* committees and *educative* committees. Two kinds – the co-ordinating and advisory committees – had been mentioned in the Haldane Report with regard to the Civil Service, but the other two kinds – executive and educative committees – are explained in the following definition by Sheldon of committees:

> Committees can only be of four kinds; firstly, executive, in the sense of making decisions upon matters brought before it. Such a committee can decide but cannot act. It must appoint some officer to carry through and supervise the execution of its decision . . . Secondly, a committee may be

116. Ibid., pp. 11–12. Beveridge also stated his approval of the role advisory committees, including the Consumers' Council, had played during the First World War in keeping British government departments in touch with knowledge about the subjects with which they deal. Like the Haldane Committee, he recommended their extended use in the British Civil Service, although he pointed out that they should not be allowed to affect the direct responsibility of the Minister or his consequent responsibility to Parliament. W. Beveridge, *The Public Service*, pp. 59–62.

117. See this chapter, p. 92.

advisory, in that it brings together certain selected individuals to whom an official who requires special guidance in a difficult situation may refer . . . Thirdly, a committee may be educative in that it forms a means whereby an official may keep his staff regularly notified of events and policies, and thereby introduce them to the larger problems of management . . . Fourthly, a committee may be coordinative, in that it brings together certain individuals, representing certain definite functions or parts of functions, for the purpose of ensuring that the work of each function is conducted upon lines corresponding to and harmonizing with the work of other functions.[118]

The advisory committees recommended by the Haldane Report, as a normal part of Civil Service organisation, embodied the roles allocated by Sheldon to advisory and educative committees. In other words, the Civil Service advisory committees were intended to provide *both* information and guidance to government departments regarding the service they perform to the community. Apart from this difference, and the wider analysis of committees offered by Sheldon, the Haldane Committee and Sheldon believed in formal committees as a means of communication and co-ordination within organisations. Sheldon's analysis was extended to point out the necessity of structuring committees on a scientific, rather than a casual, basis. By scientific, Sheldon meant that a committee should be established only for a definite and defined purpose and that each organisational member should know his exact relation to any committee. Despite the usefulness of committees, Sheldon, like Haldane and Wallas, recognised the value of informal communication, stating that friendly conversation with the officials on whom the administrator can put most reliance when any difficulty arises will be as effective as the statutory establishment of a committee. However, he added that no organisation is complete without some committees, although their establishment should be related to the existing fabric of the organisation.

Urwick's approach to the principle of 'communication'

In the 1930s, Urwick wrote one of his finest and most original studies of administration, *Committees in Organisation*, yet it is virtually unknown. His book provides a comprehensive and systematic approach to the principle of 'communication' through the medium of committees and he wrote it in the belief that a scientific study of committees was essential to the development of administrative thought. Committees

118. O. Sheldon, *Philosophy of Management*, pp. 122–5.

had proliferated in Britain by the 1930s and general ciriticisms concerning them were frequent. Such generalisations, he pointed out, were too vague and if administration was to be based on scientific principles, a scientific enquiry into committees was required. Urwick first defined the term 'committee', and then divided his enquiry into two main parts. The first part deals with the characteristics of committees and the second part examines committees in action. His definition of a committee is contained in his opening paragraph, in which he stated:

> In any form of organisation duties and responsibilities may be assigned to a group of persons acting conjointly in a corporate capacity. Such a group is usually described as a committee. Committees are used widely both in business and in government. This country is governed by a committee – the Cabinet. Every limited liability company operating in business has, for its governing authority ... a committee in the shape of its board of directors ... Apart from these various types of governing authority, committees are found at many lower levels of organisation in every variety of enterprise.[119]

Urwick broke down his analysis of the characteristics of committees into four sections, which are – the structural characteristics of committees; the psychological characteristics of committees; the disadvantages of committees; and the reasons for the use of committees. In view of the proliferation of committees in British administration by the 1930s, it is useful to single out from Urwick's study the disadvantageous characteristics of committees. He specified three disadvantages of committees. In the first case, he argued that they are often irresponsible because it is impossible to hold a conjoint body responsible in the same way as an individual can be held responsible for action or the lack of it. This comparative freedom from responsibility enjoyed by a committee offers opportunities for pursuing secondary objectives. The second disadvantage of committees which Urwick identified is that they are bad employers. The collective character of a committee's responsibility makes it difficult for a subordinate to escape criticism, and when a scapegoat is required it is often a subordinate. Finally, committees are costly. They prove an expensive form of organisation because the salaries of the collective members are involved, the cost of accommodation, the cost of the members' preparation time, the expenses of the secretary in preparing and issuing agenda minutes, reports and so on.

In the second part of his work, Urwick made a study of committees in

119. L. Urwick, *Committees in Organisation* (London) 1930s, p. 2.

action and his approach was to list the main activities of organisations and to decide, on the basis of the characteristics of committees, to what extent they are suitable to discharge these activities. For example, the activity of co-ordination should be implicit in the organisation structure and the remedy may lie in correcting poor leadership rather than in creating a co-ordinating committee.[120]

Conclusion to the principle of 'communication'

The principle of 'communication' is a clear indication of the merger of human and structural elements in British scientific principles. Verbal communication, especially in small group situations, was seen to satisfy human needs by enhancing the psychological well-being of organ- isation members, as well as being a device within the structure of organisations for informing, advising and reducing excess paperwork and other dysfunctional consequences of red-tape. Wallas and Haldane both recognised the limitations that accrue from an over-emphasis on the impersonal method of communication in writing, particularly its ability to create inefficient administration, such as the constant issuance of written minutes. They favoured discussion in *small* groups, as an alternative to written communication and, even, as preferable to oral discussion in *large* groups. Haldane, as War Minister, broke the tradition of Army Council meetings, with their written minutes, and concentrated on smaller face-to-face discussions. And, although Wallas included councils and committees in the concept of 'group-dialectics', he stressed that large governmental committees with a chairman and written minutes were not a true dialectic group. The subject of small groups in organisations and red-tape will be discussed further in Chapters 4 and 5 when we examine the ethical ideals underlying the British Philosophy of Administration and bureaucracy.

In practice, committees increased in both public and private administration in the period up to 1939. In the British Civil Service, frequent use was made of advisory committees, which was in the spirit, if not a consequence of the recommendation of the Haldane Report. The Ministry of Health, for example, utilised some 125 advisory committees between 1919 and 1939 and, during the same period, the Board of Trade relied on 76 advisory bodies. However, advisory committees were not made a normal part of departmental organisation, as the Haldane Report had urged, in the sense that an individual

120. Ibid., pp. 3–48.

Minister was responsible for a committee's work.[121] By the 1930s, Urwick had certain reservations about committees and listed their disadvantages as well as their advantages. Wallas and Haldane, in their enthusiasm for oral communication, had given no systematic account of the disadvantages of committees. Wallas had made passing reference to a few limitations of large governmental committees and councils, but no full analysis of the disadvantages, the advantages and the relevance of committees was available until Urwick's publication in the 1930s. Nevertheless, the British Philosophy of Administration was sensitive to the need for both formal communication, such as committees, and friendly informal communication within organisations. By contrast, the Webbs and Laski by their more *institutional* approach put their faith in *formal* committees and paid little attention to *informal* methods of communication, except in the form of social surveys conducted outside the organisation.[122] In the Webbs' case, their excessive reliance on committees served as a major weakness in their constitutional reforms.

Span of control

The final principle to be included in the British acronym SLOCUS is 'span of control'. This principle was well known in Britain and the United States in the 1930s, but it made an earlier debut in Graham Wallas' *The Great Society* (1914). As in the case of 'communication', Wallas proposed the scientific principle of 'span of control' on *psychological* grounds and for this reason he did not approach the principle with the same degree of exactness which Urwick and later administrative theorists adopted.

Wallas' approach to the principle of 'span of control'

Wallas did not label his principle 'span of control', but proposed the elements of the idea without giving it a definite title. He believed in what he called 'human' rather than 'mechanical' direction in organisations, although he observed that 'human' direction was largely accidental instead of being an intentional feature of organisations. Hence, his intention became to set out guidelines for the purposeful structure of organisations on human lines, and the key principles he

121. See R. V. Vernon and N. Mansergh, *Advisory Bodies*, p. 53.
122. See B. Webb, *Our Partnership* ed. by B. Drake and M. I. Cole (London) p. 13 for reference to social surveys. See also S. and B. Webb *Methods of Social Study* (London) 1932.

proposed for the building of these organisations were 'communication' and 'span of control'. In the case of control in organisations, Wallas maintained that a superior must direct and control his subordinates so as to develop in them loyalty and affection towards him. More than this, human direction must take account of each subordinate as an *individual* and preserve the self-respect of each individual organisational worker. To maintain this self-respect, the control system in an organisation should enable a superior to *know* his subordinates without the effort of having to *remember* them. The whole character of a subordinate should be known; his best work; faults which are out of character and the like, so that it becomes pointless for a subordinate to try to create an artificial 'good impression' during inspections by a superior. Such a control system, however, would depend on the capacity of each superior to know his men well, some superiors having better ability than others in this respect. Therefore, the 'span of control' of a superior will vary according to his capacity to get to know his subordinates well and Wallas expressed his views on the variation in the 'span of control' thus:

> The number of subordinates with whom an official can maintain that complete and subconscious ease of acquaintance which is necessary for 'human' (or 'humane') direction, varies, like the range of acquaintance of a workman with his fellows, greatly with the conditions of the service and the idiosyncracies of the superior official. Mr. Phipps of the English Board of Education, in giving evidence before the Royal Commission on the Civil Service ... refers to 'heads of clerical sections' in his office who are 'kept in close touch from day to day with the Chief Clerk', and says, 'there are eleven of these heads of sections – not more than the Chief Clerk can keep in touch with'. Another very successful and humane directing official whom I know, is by exception, able to keep in touch, in Mr. Phipps' sense, with a much larger number, perhaps thirty, direct subordinates ... The limit of men's powers in this respect depends, to a quite important degree, upon their natural 'memory for faces', and, if Professor Muensterberg's plan of psychological tests for office is ever generally adopted, a test of that type of memory might well be applied to candidates for certain kinds of directing work. I, myself, if I were submitted to such a test, would be certainly rejected.[123]

Wallas did not propose an *exact* formula for the 'span of control' like later British and American theorists. In particular, the principle was subjected to rigorous mathematical analysis by Graicunas in his contribution to *Papers on the Science of Administration* (1937), when

123. G. Wallas, *Great Society*, pp. 356–61.

he attempted to determine a standard 'span of control'.[124] Rather, Wallas' proposal was that the designers of organisations should keep before them the fact that organisational members need to preserve their self-respect, and to achieve this goal the control system in the organisation should permit a superior to know his subordinates intimately and to judge their work on this basis.

Urwick's approach to the principle of 'span of control'

Urwick referred to the scientific principle of 'span of control' in several of his works[125] but, unlike Wallas, his promotion of the principle was not on psychological grounds to grant self-respect to the individual workers, but on administrative grounds to facilitate co-ordination in organisations. Urwick lifted the principle out of its psychological context where it had become known as 'the span of attention' and renamed it the 'span of control'. In his paper 'Organisation as a technical problem' he included in his discussion of the principle of 'span of control', a chart by the Lithuanian administrative theorist, Graicunas, to support the mathematical conclusion that no human brain should attempt to supervise directly more than five or six other individuals. Graicunas' theory illustrated that an individual who is co-ordinating must take into account in his decisions not only the reactions of each subordinate as an *individual* but also the subordinate's reactions as a member of any possible *grouping* of persons which may arise during work. Such groupings add to the complexity and difficulty since, as Graicunas' chart indicated, the number of relations which the superior must consider increases by geometrical, not arithmetical, progression. Convinced by Graicunas' reasoning, Urwick was absolute that the scientific principle of 'span of control' should not be broken, in the sense that a superior should not try to control more than five or six workers, unless in very special cases.[126] Abuse of this principle, he maintained, would lead to problems of co-ordination and would weaken

---

124. V. A. Graicunas, 'Relationship in organization', *Papers on the Science of Administration*, pp. 181–7. Graicunas was described as a French management consultant. However, Urwick has pointed out that Graicunas was a refugee from Lithuania, who had emigrated to the United States. Urwick helped Graicunas, whose English was poor, to write his contribution to *Papers on the Science of Administration*. L. Urwick, Notes to the author, dated Sept. 1976.
125. L. Urwick, *Management of Tomorrow*.; 'Executive decentralisation', op. cit., and 'Organization as a technical problem', op. cit.
126. Urwick pointed out in another paper, that at lower levels of organisation where specific tasks lend themselves to easier control, the number of subordinates of any one superior may be increased to eight or twelve. L. Urwick, 'Executive decentralisation', op. cit., 348.

the control system in an organisation.

Urwick viewed the principle of 'span of control' as a formal co-ordinating device, in addition to committees, and he gave examples of the principle in practice. His first example related to the administration of the British Army during the First World War. Kitchener, who had superseded Haldane as War Minister, did not enforce scientific principles of administration in the way that Haldane had, and Urwick used Kitchener's lack of scientific administration as his first example of the working of the principle of 'span of control':

> It is now common knowledge that Kitchener, despite his immense services to the Empire in the early days of the Great War, was not wholly a success as an organiser at the War Office. He was impatient of formal principles of organisation, relying largely on his own immense energy and force of character. The control of the Army in Great Britain in peace is divided into seven commands. In the first year of the war five more campaigns were started in different parts of the world. Thus, as Sir William Robertson very properly pointed out on his appointment as Chief of the Imperial General Staff, he was being asked to deal with eleven or twelve Commanders-in-Chief. On his advice a Commander-in-Chief, Home Forces, was appointed and things ran more smoothly from that moment, since the number of separate commanders with whom the War Office had to deal was reduced by six at a stroke of the pen. It is interesting to speculate how far the overload of work which reduced the effectiveness of Kitchener's administration was due to failure to recognise the importance of this simple principle.[127]

The second example of the principle of 'span of control' is seen from Fig. 5, which Urwick included in his paper (1933).[128] The figure outlines the administrative organisation of the British government as it was in the 1930s. In the Cabinet alone, the Prime Minister had to co-ordinate the work of seventeen Ministers and there were as many, if not more, departments not represented in the Cabinet, which Urwick considered too many. Thus, like Wallas and Haldane before him, he called for a reduction in the size of the British Cabinet to permit a realistic 'span of control' and hence to improve co-ordination in British government administration. Moreover, Urwick drew attention to the provision of a number of separate departments dealing with functional questions in relation to Scotland which, he argued, denoted the persistence of local sentiments and traditional arrangements, despite altered circumstances and the growing complexity of government.

127. L. Urwick, 'Organization as a technical problem', op. cit., 52–7 and notes to the article, 'Executive decentralisation' op. cit., 385–6.
128. This figure was labelled Figure IV in L. Urwick, 'Organization as a technical problem', op. cit., p. 56.

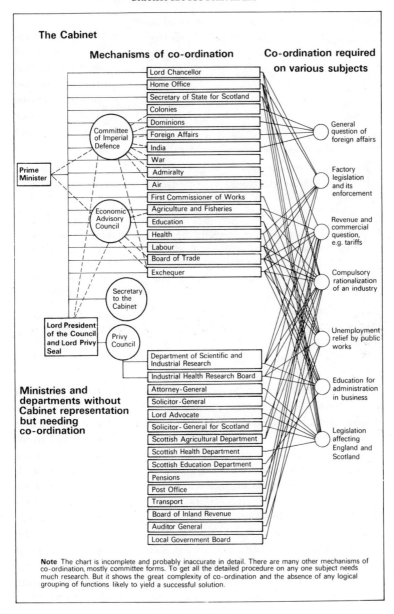

The Cabinet

Mechanisms of co-ordination

Co-ordination required
on various subjects

Lord Chancellor
Home Office
Secretary of State for Scotland
Colonies
Dominions
Foreign Affairs
India
War
Admiralty
Air
First Commissioner of Works
Agriculture and Fisheries
Education
Health
Labour
Board of Trade
Exchequer

Committee
of Imperial
Defence

Economic
Advisory
Council

Prime
Minister

Secretary
to the
Cabinet

Lord President
of the Council
and Lord Privy
Seal

Privy
Council

**Ministries and
departments without
Cabinet representation
but needing
co-ordination**

Department of Scientific and
Industrial Research
Industrial Health Research Board
Attorney-General
Solicitor-General
Lord Advocate
Solicitor- General for Scotland
Scottish Agricultural Department
Scottish Health Department
Scottish Education Department
Pensions
Post Office
Transport
Board of Inland Revenue
Auditor General
Local Government Board

General
question of
foreign affairs

Factory
legislation
and its
enforcement

Revenue and
commercial
question,
e.g. tariffs

Compulsory
rationalization
of an industry

Unemployment
relief by public
works

Education for
administration
in business

Legislation
affecting
England and
Scotland

Note The chart is incomplete and probably inaccurate in detail. There are many other mechanisms of
co-ordination, mostly committee forms. To get all the detailed procedure on any one subject needs
much research. But it shows the great complexity of co-ordination and the absence of any logical
grouping of functions likely to yield a successful solution.

Fig. 5. Urwick's diagram of co-ordination in British government administration.

Conclusion to the principle of 'span of control'

Wallas and Urwick, between 1900 and 1939, were suggesting the same principle of 'span of control' but for different reasons. Wallas emphasised 'humane' control while Urwick's main objective was to improve formal co-ordination in organisations. Taking Wallas' approach to the principle first, it was typical of his desire to amalgamate the structure of organisations with a concern for the well-being of employees. However, his approach embodies two weaknesses. First, he associated the effectiveness of the principle of 'span of control' with a *superior's ability* and neglected to consider the point which Urwick made later that the 'span of control' also depends on the type of *tasks* being carried out by subordinates. For example, if tasks are uniform or the subordinates are not involved in complex work relationships, a superior can supervise more subordinates than if the work is diverse or highly interrelated. Second, Wallas' reference to tests to determine a senior official's natural 'memory for faces' is apt to be self-defeating. For, as Wallas pointed out, he had poor memory himself and yet he was an excellent university teacher, reaching the highest levels at the London School of Economics. Surely, tests of memory, if implemented, might prohibit good administrators from being offered senior posts?

Turning to Urwick's approach to the principle, it is seen that he brought a greater scientific exactness to the principle of 'span of control' in the 1930s. This exactness led H. A. Simon (1945) to deal a crushing blow to the principle and it was a double-headed blow. Under the first head, Simon argued that the principle of 'span of control' could be contradicted by an equally valid scientific principle of administration. The contradictory principle, or proverb of administration, was that administrative efficiency is enhanced by keeping to a minimum the number of organisational levels through which a matter passes for decision. This second principle raised a dilemma which Simon phrased in these terms:

> The dilemma is this: in a large organization with interrelations between members, a restricted span of control inevitably produces excessive red tape, for each contact between organization members must be carried upward until a common superior is found. If the organization is at all large, this will involve carrying all such matters upwards through several levels of officials for decision, and then downward again in the form of orders and instructions – a cumbersome and time-consuming process.
>
> The alternative is to increase the number of persons who are under the command of each officer, so that the pyramid will come more rapidly to a peak, with fewer intervening levels. But this, too, leads to difficulty,

for if an officer is required to supervise too many employees, his control over them is weakened.[129]

The second head to Simon's criticism of the principle of 'span of control' related to the divergence in the optimum number of subordinates which a superior can control. Some proponents of the principle has stated three or five subordinates; others eleven as a suitable number, and yet they had provided no explanation of the reasoning leading them to that number. Simon argued that the principle, as stated, shed no light on the crucial question of 'span of control'.[130] But here Simon was not altogether correct, for Graicunas had given mathematical reasoning to support his theory. Furthermore, if Simon had been familiar with Wallas' version of the principle, he would have noted a deeper psychological reasoning underlying it and recognised that no *exact* formula was intended in Wallas' formulation. Urwick's later paper was useful in drawing attention to this principle and in advocating its use in British administration, but his emphasis on exactness made him inflexible over this matter of individual capacity to control. For, while five or six subordinates may be a suitable number for one superior to control when tasks are interrelated, other individuals may be capable of handling a larger number.

Conclusion

This chapter has identified five important scientific principles of administration which had points in common with the American POSDCORB principles, but portray more accurately the nature of the British Philosophy of Administration. The search for scientific principles within British administrative thought yields four general conclusions. Firstly, the British concern for scientific principles of administration was an advancement in administrative thinking. Although certain scientific principles had been put forward in Britain from the eighteenth century in isolated works, such as Adam Smith (1776), it was not until this century that a number of individual scientific principles was introduced into British administrative thought. For example, from 1905 onwards Haldane studied and then applied scientific principles of administration to the British Army and Navy, before recommending their extension into the Civil Service. It is true that Frederick Taylor had begun an earlier, more intensive, search

129. H. A. Simon, *Administrative Behavior*, p. 28.
130. Ibid., pp. 26–8.

for scientific principles in American industrial organisations, but the British Philosophy of Administration nevertheless provided some independent views about scientific principles of administration which have been overshadowed by the American doctrine of a science of administration. Moreover, these British views were supported by the radical thinkers, Sidney and Beatrice Webb and Harold Laski, particularly with respect to the Haldane Report. In this instance, therefore, there were no significant diverging opinions to undermine the influence of the British Philosophy of Administration.

Secondly, although homogeneity prevailed within British administrative thought regarding scientific principles of administration, fragmentation still served to diminish the importance of the British contribution. Not only were the five individual scientific principles not co-ordinated into an acronym like POSDCORB, but they were drawn together only in the Haldane Report of 1918.[131] If this government Report had been implemented more speedily and comprehensively, akin to the Brownlow Committee's proposals in the United States, fragmentation of the scientific principles in British administrative thought would have been lessened. The failure to implement the Haldane Report was as much a disappointment to Haldane[132] as it was to Sidney and Beatrice Webb and Harold Laski. But, the Haldane Report did receive partial expression in administrative practice. In the case of the principles of 'staff' and 'line', an increase in facilities for thought and investigation in the British Civil Service ensued, although it was not a conscious development and no national Ministry of Research was formed. In the United States, L. D. White (1936) later observed that it was a pity no such Department had been established, since it could have been responsible for *testing* some of the hypotheses underlying the British administrative system and he lamented that the recommendation had 'died stillborn' – a victim of retrenchment.[133] The principle of 'organisation' gained marginal acceptance in the creation of the new Ministry of Health, and the principle of 'communication' was applied by certain alterations to the Treasury and its methods of communicating with other departments, as well as by the appointment of a Secretary to the Cabinet. The size of the British Cabinet was not

131. In contrast, in the United States by the 1930s, the POSDCORB principles were co-ordinated in the famous book by joint editors L. Gulick and L. Urwick entitled *Papers on the Science of Administration*.
132. See the Rt. Hon. Lord Bridges, 'Haldane and the Machinery of Government Committee', *Public Administration*, Vol. 35, 1957, 262.
133. See R. V. Vernon and N. Mansergh, *Advisory Bodies*, pp. 52–3 and L. D. White, 'Meaning of principles', op. cit., p. 22.

reduced, however, until after 1939, with the exception of the first National Cabinet of 1931 which contained ten Ministers.[134] The use of advisory committees increased, also, in British public and business administration.

It is interesting to consider what accounted for the piecemeal implementation of the Haldane Report. When it appeared on 7 January 1919, ten days after the General Election, it received a glowing acknowledgement in the Press and was in such demand by students of government in Europe and the United States that it went quickly out of print. Yet, Lloyd George's Government appears never to have given detailed attention to the Report as a whole, for what have been described sketchily as economic and political reasons.[135] After the lukewarm official reception to the Report, Haldane, who had been a prime mover in calling for the setting up of the Machinery of Government Committee and had drafted the major part of the Report, looked for alternative outlets for the expression of scientific principles of administration. One such outlet was the Institute of Public Administration and, although the first impetus for its foundation came from the Society of Civil Servants in 1918, Haldane was associated closely with the early discussions and lectures leading to its establishment and was the Institutes first President. The fact that a large number of senior civil servants were members of the Institute meant that, unofficially, scientific principles of administration filtered into the Civil Service.[136] Another vehicle for implementing the scientific principles underlying the British Philosophy of Administration was Urwick's work as Director of the International Management Institute in Geneva from 1928 to 1933.[137] In this capacity, he spread knowledge about scientific principles, notably in the sphere of business administration, which included but extended beyond the particular principles which we have summarised as SLOCUS.

The third conclusion relates to two additional factors, besides fragmentation, which caused a reduction in the significance of the scientific principles promoted within the British Philosophy of Administration. The first factor is that British administrative pioneers,

134. R. V. Vernon and N. Mansergh, *Advisory Bodies*, pp. 51–4.
135. L. D. White suggested certain recommendations were not implemented because of the need for retrenchment, see this chapter, p. 132, while R. V. Vernon and N. Mansergh have suggested political reasons but do not elaborate on them, see *Advisory Bodies*, p. 50.
136. See the Rt. Hon. Lord Bridges, 'Haldane and the Machinery of Government Committee', op. cit., 262–3.
137. See 'Urwick, Lt. Col. Lyndall', *International Who's Who* (London). Thirty-sixth edn 1972–73, p. 1714.

such as Graham Wallas and Richard Haldane, failed to present systematically their ideas about scientific principles. Wallas stated his views in texts which embodied psychology, sociology and politics with administration. Haldane, with a similar disregard for systemisation, interspersed scientific principles with personal details of his life in his autobiography. Added to this lack of systematisation was the absence of verification of the scientific principles which, coupled with their fragmentation, marred the authoritativeness of the British contribution and its development as a coherent body of thought. The second factor to affect the development of the scientific principles underlying the British Philosophy of Administration was ambiguity in terminology. Haldane carried forward the same basic ideas from his military experience into the Civil Service, but he was not consistent in his terminology. Hence, the 'staff' principle was termed loosely 'thought' and 'research' in the Haldane Report, which no doubt was a reason why Beatrice Webb referred to the Report as reflecting 'Haldane's incurable delight in mental mistiness'.[138] Wallas was no more explicit, having identified clearly the principle of 'span of control', but giving it no specific name. Likewise, there was some ambiguity in key terms between the Haldane Report in the context of public administration and Sheldon's thinking about business administration. This ambiguity within the British Philosophy of Administration was exacerbated by a general confusion which grew up in Britain surrounding administrative developments in other countries. Although Britain basically rejected American scientific management, both countries were applying science to administration with varying degrees of exactitude. Again, at the European level, the science of administration was applied to the combination of industries, but this time it was called 'rationalisation'. All three movements applied science to administration, but the distinct differences in method were often overlooked. Sheldon distinguished between the British science of administration and American scientific management (i.e. a science predominantly for *administrators* to follow rather than *operatives*) and between rationalisation and American scientific management (i.e. science applied to the *combination* of industries as distinct from *individual* industries), denoting both the common factor of the application of science to administration and the distinctions in methodology and application which characterised

---

138. See the Rt. Hon. Lord Bridges, 'Haldane and the Machinery of Government Committee', op. cit., 254.

them.[139] None the less, confusion arose between the terms, and 'rationalisation' was used by some British writers to imply the application of science to administration generally instead of in the specific sense of relating to the combination, or merger, of industries.[140] The ambiguity in terminology associated with the British scientific principles between 1900 and 1939 has remained to the present time. The principles of 'staff' and 'line', for example, have been acknowledged recently as being 'one of the most confusing branches of management theory'.[141]

Despite the fragmented character of the British scientific principles, the ambiguity in terminology and a universal decline in the 'principles of management' approach to the study of organisations, there is evidence today of the endurance – albeit incognito – of the earlier scientific principles. The final conclusion draws attention to this evidence. For example, the principles of 'staff' and 'line' were reiterated by the British Fulton Committee (1968) in its proposal that planning and research units should be established in executive departments for long-term policy planning:

> . . . to identify and study the problems and needs of the future and the possible means to meet them; it should also be its function to see that day-to-day policy decisions are taken with as full a recognition as possible of their likely implications for the future. The Planning Unit should not carry any responsibility for the day-to-day operations of the department.[142]

In other words, the Fulton Committee, without historical reference to the Haldane Report, argued for 'staff' separate from 'line' officials in the British Civil Service to undertake research and long-term planning. The main proposals of the Fulton Committee were accepted but, once again, those relating to 'planning units' were not among them. But, as in the case of the Haldane Report, further planning facilities did emerge, so that by 1972 planning units existed in ten departments of

139. Sheldon made this distinction in two separate articles, see O. Sheldon, 'The art of management: from a British point of view', *Bulletin of the Taylor Society*, Vol. VIII, No. 6, Dec. 1923, 211, and 'The significance of rationalization', *Harvard Business Review*, Vol. VI, No. 3, Apr. 1928, 264–9.
140. Rationalisation was utilised in the more general sense of the application of science to administration by, for example, Sir H. N. Bunbury, 'Rationalisation and the processes of administration', *Public Administration* Vol. VIII, 1930, 275–82.
141. P. Self, *Administrative Theories and Politics* (London) 1972, p. 121.
142. *The Civil Service Vol. 1. Report of the (Fulton) Committee 1966–68* (London) 1968, p. 57.

government for the purpose of research and planning.[143] A second example of the survival of traditional scientific principles of administration is 'organisation' by purpose, which is still popular today in Britain and the United States. In 1970, this principle formed the basis of a British government White Paper on the reorganisation of the Civil Service, but again no reference was made to the earlier suggestion in the Haldane Report. The White Paper (1970) announced:

> . . . the object has been to ensure that the broad framework of the central machinery in terms of Ministerial and departmental functions complies with the Government's strategic policy objectives. In practical terms, this means the application of the functional principle as the basis for the allocation of responsibilities: government departments should be organised by reference to the task to be done or the objective to be attained, and this should be the basis of the division of work between departments rather than, for example, dividing responsibility between departments so that each one deals with a client group.[144]

Likewise in the United States in 1972, President Nixon adhered to the principle of 'organisation' by purpose in his proposal to reorganise the American Civil Service. He suggested that the streamlining of the executive branch should take the form of the establishment of four new giant departments relating to the major purposes, or goal objectives,[145] of government: a Department of Natural Resources, a Department of Human Resources, a Department of Community Development and a Department of Economic Affairs.[146] Similarly, the introduction during the 1960s into the American federal government of the Planning–Programming–Budgeting System (PPBS) was based on the clearer definition of organisational purpose. The use of PPBS as a modern tool

143. The ten departments with 'planning units' in 1972 were: (1) the Ministry of Agriculture, Fisheries and Food; (2) The Board of Customs and Excise; (3) the Ministry of Defence; (4) the Department of Education and Science; (5) the Department of Employment; (6) the Foreign and Commonwealth Office; (7) the Department of the Environment; (8) the Department of Health and Social Security; (9) the Board of Inland Revenue; (10) the Department of Trade and Industry. See G. K. Fry, 'Policy-planning units in British central government', *Public Administration*, Vol. 50, Summer 1972,139–55. See also P. Self, *Administrative Theories*, pp. 121–146 for a recent analysis of 'staff' and 'line' in government.
144. White Paper, *The Reorganisation of Central Government* (London) Oct. 1970, p. 4.
145. At the American Society for Public Administration (ASPA) North-East Regional Conference 1972, a series of talks was given by A. Dean, D. M. Fox, J. Fesler and H. Mansfield on the President's reorganisation proposals. It was pointed out that the proposed new giant departments were based on the old principle of 'organisation' by purpose, although the terms 'goal objectives' or 'program goals' are often used today.
146. *Papers relating to the President's Departmental Reorganization Program* (Washington) Feb. 1972, p. 1.

of management has spread since from the American federal government to a wide application in American government and industry, as well as in British administration.[147]

The foregoing examples illustrate that scientific principles developed in British and American administrative thought and practice during the period 1900–39 still have relevance today. In this respect, there can be said to be *advocates* of the 'principles of management' – that is, people who cling to the old guidelines for structuring organisations, but there are also *rejectors* of the scientific principles of administration. H. A. Simon (1945), March and Simon (1958), H. Seidman (1970) and P. Self (1972) all have criticised scientific principles of administration.[148] However, they do not reject them completely, and even Simon after his scathing attack, looked to see what he could salvage from the principles. It can be concluded, then, that in both countries there is evidence of some survival of the earlier scientific principles of administration. The essential difference between the British and American doctrines in the era 1900–39 was that the British Philosophy of Administration *combined* the simultaneous study of ethical ideals with scientific principles and thus avoided the mechanistic, or machine-like, approach to organisations characteristic of American administrative developments.

147. See D. Novick, 'Brief history of program budgeting', in *Current Practice in Program Budgeting (PPBS)* ed. by D. Novick (London) 1973, pp. 19–28.
148. See H. A. Simon, *Administrative Behavior*, pp. 20–36; J. G. March and H. A. Simon, *Organizations* (New York) 1958, pp. 12–33; H. Seidman, *Politics, Position, and Power: The Dynamics of Federal Organization* (New York) pp. 3–36; and P. Self, *Administrative Theories*, Chs. 1 and 4.

Chapter 4

The ethical ideals underlying the British Philosophy of Administration

'The spiritual phase tends to dominate that which is apt to be mechanical . . . It is this that I hope for in the new Civil Service. The higher the ideals the more penetrating will be its influence'.[1]
R. B. Haldane

'The whole body of ethics needs to be reworked in the light of modern corporate relations, from Church and company to cadet corps . . .'[2]
J. Stamp

Ethical ideals were accorded as significant a place within the British Philosophy of Administration as scientific principles. They took the form not only of a *general* concern for ethics, but also of *particular* ideals to be pursued and upheld by the Civil Service and industry. This chapter defines what is meant by an 'ethical ideal' and shows the development of the particular ethical ideals underlying the British Philosophy of Administration. Although these ideals were expounded by the individual pioneers Wallas, Haldane, Sheldon, Urwick and Stamp, they did not remain vague aspirations in the minds of administrative thinkers, but gained partial substance from practical experiments into human well-being in organisations conducted by corporate bodies in Britain from the First World War onwards. These corporate experiments are included in this chapter and they will be compared with the more famous Hawthorne experiments in the United States.

The simultaneous emergence of scientific principles and ethical ideals within the British Philosophy of Administration contrasts sharply with the American experience whereby the doctrine of the science of administration preceded by some two or three decades the doctrine of human relations. Despite this contrast in the development of administrative doctrines, their content with respect to human relations was remarkably similar. For example, the British Philosophy

1. R. B. Haldane, 'Preface', *The Development of the Civil Service* (London) 1922, p. xii.
2. J. Stamp, *The Science of Social Adjustment* (London) 1937, p. 69.

of Administration, supported by the corporate experiments, was deeply concerned with monotony in modern organisations, which was a starting point in the later Hawthorne experiments in Chicago. Again, observations were made in Britain about the importance of groups in organisations and group behaviour. The British concern with these and other questions of human well-being was stimulated by Graham Wallas (1914)[3] and the subject was studied, during and after the First World War, by the Ministry of Munitions, the Industrial Fatigue Research Board and the National Institute of Industrial Psychology. Elton Mayo, Professor of Industrial Research at the Harvard Business School and Director of the famous Hawthorne experiments commented about the similar discoveries:

> I have quoted this extraordinarily interesting development in the English work at considerable length for a specific reason. In two instances which I propose to describe, industrial inquiries undertaken in the United States have been driven, step by step, to similar methods and assumptions. This is of some interest, because there was at no time during the early developments of the inquiries any relation between the investigators here and in England. The first instance is a Philadelphia inquiry undertaken in the year 1923 . . . The other instance is the five-year inquiry of the Western Electric Company at its Hawthorne Works in Chicago . . .[4]

But, fragmentation was, yet again, a major limiting factor regarding the British contribution. After an early and valuable start to the study of human relations by individual pioneers of the British Philosophy of Administration, and the corporate bodies,[5] the work was not advanced with the same systematic depth and subsequent analysis which the Hawthorne experiments received in the United States. The Hawthorne enquiries kindled further research and study into human relations in the United States and other countries because they were marshalled into a coherent form, notably by Roethlisberger and Dickson (1939),[6] and were followed up by more research by the Harvard Graduate School

3. G. Wallas, *The Great Society: A Psychological Analysis* (London) 1914.
4. E. Mayo, *The Human Problems of An Industrial Civilization* (New York) 1933, pp. 42–3.
5. The British human relations discoveries have been acknowledged by, for example, R. J. S. Baker, *Administrative Theory and Public Administration* (London) 1972, p. 45; A. Tillett et al., eds., *Management Thinkers* (London) 1970, particularly pp. 201–24 and 275–93; and J. Child, *British Management Thought: A Critical Analysis* (London) 1969, particularly pp. 54–9.
6. F. J. Roethlisberger and W. J. Dickson, *Management and the Worker* (Cambridge, Mass.) 1939. Reprinted edn 1964. The Hawthorne experiments were documented also by E. Mayo, *Human Problems*, pp. 55–121, and E. Mayo, *The Social Problems of An Industrial Civilisation* (London) 1949, pp. 60–76.

of Business Administration. In Britain, excellent work was undertaken by the Ministry of Munitions and the Industrial Fatigue Research Board, but even though lengthy memoranda were published, no volume was produced equivalent to Roethlisberger and Dickson's work to catch the imagination of academics and practitioners. This fragmentation was due partly to the fact that human relations at work was only one of several ethical ideals put forward within the British Philosophy of Administration for organisations to pursue. Other ideals included appraising the direction of society as a whole – and the role of organisations within it – while another ideal was that organisations should assist the community at large by encouraging interest in adult education and other communal activities. This broad approach to ethical ideals led the British doctrine to extend into philosophy and religion, which had the advantage of making administrators aware of their responsibility within and to society. But, it incurred the disadvantage of reducing the impact of British *administrative* thought, since pioneers of the British Philosophy of Administration allowed their views to slip into a wide range of academic disciplines without attempting to amass and analyse them. Another reason for the fragmentation was that there was not the same need in Britain to emphasise human relations because, unlike the United States, there was no necessity to counteract a mechanistic science of administration.[7] The acceptance of human relations as an integral part of British administrative thought explains why less attempt was made to analyse the ethical ideals. This chapter brings together the numerous British contributions and identifies the common ethical ideals. Before these particular ideals are discussed, however, the concept of an 'ethical ideal' must be defined and the American Hawthorne experiments mentioned briefly to ease comparisons with the British experience.

First, the definition of an ethical ideal. Vagueness prevailed during the period 1900–39, and still prevails today, with regard to such concepts as morals, ethics, motives and incentives. Contributors to the British Philosophy of Administration wrote with enthusiasm about particular ethical ideals they wished to see promoted, but they tended to

---

7. The need to counteract the heavy dependence on a mechanistic, or formalistic, science of administration in the United States was stressed by M. E. Dimock, 'The criteria and objectives of public administration', in *The Frontiers of Public Administration* ed. by J. M. Gaus et al. (Chicago) 1936, pp. 116–33; R. A. Dahl, 'The science of public administration: three problems', *Public Administration Review*, Vol. VII, No. 2, Spring 1947, 1–11 and H. A. Simon, 'A comment on "The science of public administration"', *Public Administration Review*, Vol. VII, No. 3, Summer 1947, 200–3.

be careless in their use of terminology – interchanging freely the words 'ethics' with 'ideals' or 'motives' with 'incentives' and rarely defining any of the terms or using them consistently. It is helpful to draw some distinctions between these terms in order to provide a clear framework for the study of ethical ideals. Ethics differs from morality in that conduct may be described as 'moral' when it is maintained or observed as a fact, but, conduct becomes 'ethical' as it rises from fact to ideal.[8] In the case of the British Philosophy of Administration, although notions like right, good or welfare were given partial substance by corporate experiments, on the whole, they began as *ideals* in the thoughts of administrative pioneers rather than as observed *facts*. Ethics, therefore is more appropriate to delineate these aspirations than morals or morality. The combined phrase 'ethical ideals' reinforces the strong trend to idealism[9] inherent in the British Philosophy of Administration and contains the administrative pioneers' tendency to use the words 'ethics' and 'ideals' interchangeably.

The terms 'motive' and 'incentive' must now be clarified. The ethical ideals underlying the British Philosophy of Administration included aspirations for non-economic incentives in the Civil Service and industry, which were believed to encourage altruism, happiness in work and the development of the inner spirit of the worker and of the group, or organisation, to which he belonged. The word 'incentive' was used synonymously with 'motive' to imply stimulus to effort.[10] Incentives, then, were conceived as being of two types – the *non-economic* type, which was intended to create a higher form of life and the *economic*

8. See T. V. Smith, 'Ethics', *Encyclopaedia of the Social Sciences*, Vol. V, 1931, 602.
9. Idealism can be used in a more specific sense to relate to the modern school of idealism associated with great names from many countries including Kant, Hegel, Fichte, Green and Bosquanet. Although Haldane was a self-professed follower of the modern school of idealism, this was not the case with other contributors to the British Philosophy of Administration. Therefore, the specific sense of the term idealism is not intended. See G. de Ruggiero, 'Idealism', *Encyclopaedia of the Social Sciences* Vol. VII, 1932, 568–72. See also *Richard Burdon Haldane: An Autobiography* (London) 1929, pp. 19–20.
10. J. Stamp gave an alternative definition which attempted some distinction between 'motive' and 'incentive' although he did not use it widely:

'I have passed rather easily from 'motive' to 'incentive', whereas if this were a book on ethics as such, I should have drawn a careful distinction, but I think no practical difficulty will arise. My earliest mentor in ethics, the Rev. A. E. Balch, defines a motive as "a desire transformed into a practical incentive to action" (*Introduction to the Study of Christian Ethics*, p. 43). My own practical distinction is that in "motive" the emphasis is on being *pushed* towards the objective, and in incentive on being *pulled* by it.'

Motive and Method in a Christian Order (London) 1936, p. 121.

type which was aimed directly at accomplishing the work in hand. The British doctrine of ethical idealism, therefore, hoped for more than improvements in human well-being within organisations; it hoped to benefit society as a whole. While a broad concern for society can be found in the American doctrine in Elton Mayo's writing on human relations,[11] it became overshadowed by the specific Hawthorne findings about participative supervision and group behaviour. Because of the tendency to stress the Hawthorne experiments out of their general context, we begin our brief reference to American human relations with a broad introduction. But, even after this reinstatement of the Hawthorne experiments in their broader setting, the British Philosophy of Administration will be seen to have embodied an expansiveness which extended widely into problems of modern society and transcended the nature of the American human relations doctrine.

1. The general context of American human relations

The experiments in human relations in the United States began in September 1923, with the enquiry by Elton Mayo and others, into working conditions in the mule-spinning department of a textile mill near Philadelphia. One of the important discoveries to emerge from the Philadelphia enquiry was that rest pauses helped to reduce montony in repetitive work and Elton Mayo carried forward this knowledge to the Hawthorne study.[12] After the Philadelphia enquiry came the work of the Graduate School of Business Administration at Harvard University. The Harvard venture started when a special research committee was formed in 1926 to study effort and fatigue in industry.[13] It was clear to the committee that two distinct, but closely allied, fields of industrial enquiry were needed: enquiries under laboratory conditions into physiological conditions of workers; and enquiries among workers in the industrial situation itself where the total work situation – both physical and social – could be studied. Accordingly, the Fatigue Laboratory was organised to deal with the former studies and the Department of

11. E. Mayo, *Human Problems*, pp. 122–67.
12. Ibid., pp. 42–54.
13. The research received financial aid from the Laura Spelman Rockefeller Memorial (later the Rockefeller Foundation); the same body which provided aid to the British National Institute of Industrial Psychology whose work is described later in this chapter.

Industrial Research was to study the latter. The work of the Department of Industrial Research during the 1920s and 1930s fell into three separate periods. The first time-span of 1926 to 1932 included the Hawthorne enquiry, which was the most important investigation in a programme of intensive exploratory research. The second period lasted from 1932 to 1936 and involved the formulation and testing of hypotheses based on evidence collected during the first time-span. The final period extended from 1936 to 1945 when the discoveries about human relations were disseminated. This dissemination involved Departmental members in weekend discussion groups for business executives and in course-work centring upon problems of human and labour relations, for which case-studies proved particularly effective.[14]

Regarding the actual Hawthorne experiments, these have been described by numerous writers from the 1930s onwards and we do not propose to outline them in detail again. Rather, we shall summarise the main results only of the Relay Assembly Test Room, the Interviewing Programme and the Bank Wiring Observation Room.[15] The Relay Assembly Test Room experiments, involving six female operatives working on the assembly of telephone relays, lasted for five years from Spring 1927. A general increase in the rate of output and the improved worker attitudes which resulted among the six girls were believed, at first, to be due to the rest pauses introduced. Indeed, some of the early hypotheses advanced were that relief from cumulative fatigue or monotony caused these improvements. But, after further tests, an increase in morale was observed among the girls in the test room independent of any particular change in rest pauses or the shorter working hours which had been initiated. As the Relay Assembly Test Room experiments continued, a general conclusion was drawn that the increased output could not be related to physical working conditions alone, but tended to vary in accordance with the workers' personal situations outside work and the interpersonal relations at work. Furthermore, supervision which was sensitive to the health and well-being of the worker was thought to affect output favourably and the Interviewing Programme, begun in September 1928, was intended to study further the quality of supervision at the Hawthorne plant.[16]

14. The Department gave increasing attention to developing case-study material on human relations, such as the book of case-studies by P. Pigors, L. C. McKenney and T. O. Armstrong, *Social Problems in Labor Relations*. See E. Mayo, *Social Problems*, pp. 132–40.
15. Unless stated otherwise, we base our summary of the Hawthorne experiments on the book by F. J. Roethlisberger and W. J. Dickson, *Management and the Worker, passim*.
16. See also E. Mayo, *Human Problems*, pp. 58, 78.

The Interviewing Programme led to new developments in supervisory training as well as conferences on leadership and co-operation. After the main interviewing research, a change in technique was introduced whereby specialised interviewers were assigned to small groups. They noticed evidence of informal leadership among groups in shop departments and the restriction of work due to group pressure for controlled output. As a result of this evidence, the Bank Wiring Observation Room Study was planned with two purposes in mind; to develop a new method of supplementing the interview with direct observation, and to obtain more exact information about social groups within the company. The Bank Wiring Observation Room Study lasted from November 1931 to May 1932 and completed the research programme by the Department of Industrial Research at the Hawthorne plant, Chicago. This study consisted of a detailed sociological analysis of a shop situation in which fourteen men were assembling switch equipment. The investigators noted a restriction of output due to the influence of 'cliques' which had developed within the group of men. These cliques generated sentiments about output which classified members of the group as 'rate-busters'; 'chiselers' and 'squealers', according to whether they produced too much work; too little work or sneaked information to a supervisor about an associate. Thus, the Bank Wiremen showed the experimenters that behaviour at work cannot be understood without considering informal organisation within a group and they demonstrated, also, that workers are not motivated strictly by economic advantages but respond to sentiments and social factors, such as symbols of prestige and status.

The Hawthorne experiments were significant because they were based principally on psychological and sociological assumptions. Up to the 1920s, developments in psychology had progressed separately from the science of administration. In fact, Hugo Münsterberg, well known at Harvard University for his early research in industrial psychology, referred in 1913 to scientific management as 'that other American movement'.[17] For, during most of the period 1900-39, it was the doctrine of the science of administration which predominated in the United States, with developments in psychology and sociology taking a secondary, or at least an independent, role. From the late 1930s, when the conclusions emanating from the Hawthorne experiments were disseminated, this situation changed. The psychological and sociological findings stemming from the Hawthorne experiments were received in the form of the human relations doctrine, which was

17. H. Münsterberg, *Psychology and Industrial Efficiency* (New York) 1913, p. 49.

welcomed as a relief from the mechanistic science of administration.

Some psychological assumptions had been present in the American science of administration, but they were simplistic. For example, Frank and Lillian Gilbreth discussed psychology in connection with scientific management, but it was a rather crude psychology used as a means of promoting scientific management *vis-à-vis* traditional forms of management. They interpreted psychology largely in terms of *individuality*, which was supposed to be realised through the scientific selection of workers as distinct from the 'guess-work' associated with traditional management. Again, individuality was to the fore in scientific management because the individual was the unit measured in relation to output and records kept related to individual output. Incentives were aimed at encouraging personal responsibility, with wages being determined scientifically and paid promptly, instead of the monetary incentives existing under traditional management which lacked standardisation in assessment.[18] Psychology, then, was not ignored by the scientific management school, but it related to simple assumptions including the presumption that monetary incentives, properly determined and paid out, are of overriding importance in inducing workers to produce greater output. Münsterberg regarded the psychology within the American scientific management movement as vague, particularly in relation to the selection of fit men, and argued that, although the followers of scientific management recognised the need for psychological enquiries, they did little to apply the results of psychology to scientific management.[19] Despite the writing and experiments by Münsterberg, who succeeded the famous psychologist William James at Harvard,[20] there was comparatively little psychology applied to industry in the United States before the Hawthorne experiments and what progress was made advanced as a separate movement from the science of administration.[21] The British Philo-

18. W. R. Spriegel and C. E. Myers, eds., *The Writings of the Gilbreths* (Homewood, Illinois) 1953, pp. 341–500. This aspect of the Gilbreths' work was first published as *The Psychology of Management* (New York) 1914.
19. H. Münsterberg, *Psychology and Industrial Efficiency*, pp. 49–56.
20. See L. S. Hearnshaw, *A Short History of British Psychology 1840–1940* (London) 1964, pp. 158, 175.
21. Münsterberg believed that because the followers of scientific management had left psychology in a state of vagueness, it was the duty of the experimental psychologist to examine industry from the psychological viewpoint. Hence, prior to the Hawthorne experiments, some examples of applied psychology included work by Harvard personnel into the Electric Railway Service, the Ship Service and the Telephone Service in the United States. But, on the whole, Münsterberg confirmed that there had been little psychology applied to industry in the United States. H. Münsterberg, *Psychology and Industrial Efficiency*, pp. 63–118.

sophy of Administration, on the other hand, incorporated complex psychological and sociological assumptions with ethical ideals, and they were elaborated alongside scientific principles. These specific ethical ideals are now discussed.

2. Specific ethical ideals underlying the British Philosophy of Administration

The body of ethics emerging from the diverse works of pioneers of the British Philosophy of Administration consists of the following three ethical ideals:

> A higher form of society.
>
> Service to the community.
>
> The happiness and well-being of the worker.

A higher form of society

Wallas' approach to the ethical ideal of a higher form of society

Probably Graham Wallas was the first British administrative writer this century to challenge the direction in which society was moving. *The Great Society* (1914) includes some of his best-developed administrative ideas and yet, as its name implies, the book's over-all intention was to review the progress and objectives of twentieth-century mechanised society. Wallas' concern for society shows him as a sociologist and psychologist, in addition to being an administrative thinker, for he sought to understand the effects of mechanisation in social and psychological, as well as administrative, terms. About sociology, he stated:

> During the last hundred years the external conditions of civilised life have been transformed by a series of inventions . . . One effect of this transformation is a general change of social scale . . . Economists have invented the term The Great Industry for the special aspect of this change which is dealt with by their science, and sociologists may conveniently call the whole result The Great Society.[22]

Wallas began his book with a sociological explanation of the Great Society. He argued that the practical men who had brought the Great Society into existence in the mid-nineteenth century considered, if they

22. G. Wallas, *Great Society*, p. 3.

had stopped to think at all, that they were offering a better existence to the human race. They believed that even if the Great Society should deprive men of some of the romance and intimacy of life, it must increase their security, render famine impossible, since a labourer would be able to buy foodstuffs locally from the world market, and cause wars to be fewer because of their disruptive effect on the international system of credit. But, now that the change had come, the old enthusiasm for the Great Society was waning because the constant possibility of general depressions still prevailed as did the fear of war. More important, there was a deep anxiety as to whether development was proceeding on the right lines, since radiant faces among the people were becoming rare and the majority showed few signs of 'that harmony of the whole being which constitutes happiness'.[23]

'Happiness' is a term which appears frequently in Wallas' writing on the Great Society and organisational life within it. It is based on the ancient Greek concept of harmony of the soul, which was also the basis of his prescription for policy-making, or judgment, contained in Chapter 2 of this book. Inherent in his concept of happiness is the realisation that man lives not only consciously, but subconsciously in the past of memory and the future of expectation, as well as in the experience of the present. To be happy, therefore, a man requires that his consciousness and his subconsciousness are at one and happiness in this sense was the subject of Aristotle's *Ethics*. Wallas returned on several occasions to the works of Aristotle and Plato to support his views, arguing that in some respects their ideas are closer to twentieth-century psychology than those of nineteenth-century thinkers. It was his concern for happiness which led Wallas to take seriously the doubts being expressed about the future happiness of individuals in the Great Society and about the permanence of the Society itself. Regarding permanence, he stressed that the empires of Assyria, Persia and Rome must have appeared permanent to the statesmen who directed them, since they possessed military power, rapid communication systems and accumulated wealth. Yet, the very cohesive forces which created these ancient empires proved at the same time to be damaging forces, for as they became larger these social organisations became too distant to stimulate the affection or pride of their subjects and the methods they adopted became more mechanical and inhuman.[24]

23. G. Wallas, *Great Society*, p. 7.
24. Ibid., pp. 5–10 and G. Wallas, *Social Judgment* (London) 1934, p. 51. Sociologists in other countries had also drawn attention to disadvantages of modern industrial society; for example, Emile Durkheim, *Le Suicide*, 1897. See E. Mayo, *Social Problems*, pp. 3–10.

One might ask what Wallas' broad review of the Great Society has to do with administration, but it is linked closely. By beginning with a macro-view of society – an approach favoured by other British administrative thinkers such as Urwick and Stamp – he was able to envisage not only how organisations fit into society but what is required by individuals within organisations to prevent an inner strain emerging in society due to scale and impersonality. His answer to the problem of maintaining the Great Society was to draw attention to the need for specialised research, particularly in psychology, to reach those who guide social action, notably politicians and administrators,[25] so that they can understand and control the social forces of our time. Therefore, from 1908 onwards, Wallas' aim was to relate modern psychological knowledge to actual problems of current civilised life – policy-making was one such problem and social organisation was another. It was in analysing organisations from a socio-psychological viewpoint that he suggested ethical ideals, as well as scientific principles, for their reconstruction and maintenance.

A higher form of society was an ethical ideal, then, promoted by Wallas in his study of the Great Society. Broadly speaking, this ideal required the adoption of 'happiness' as one of the main bases of social organisation, while in the narrower sense of the Civil Service and industry, it meant attempting to ensure that employees are 'happy'. Happiness in this narrower sense will be discussed again in further detail under the third ethical ideal. Wallas was not directly furthering Bentham's utilitarian concept of happiness since he believed that Bentham's thinking contained serious psychological inadequacies, including the latter's failure to distinguish between the consciousness of the moment and the consciousness which, even during the moment, embodies the past and the future. What Wallas sought was to restructure happiness in modern psychological terms and to re-commend it as the foundation for the Great Society. In this ideal, he was inspired by Aristotle, remarking:

> Aristotle, in one of those conversational flashes which lie in wait for his readers on almost every page of the *Ethics*, says:
>
>> 'Virtue is rightly defined as a Mean, and yet so far as it aims at the highest excellence, it is an Extreme'.
>
> No social Organisation is, we feel, good which does not contain that element which Aristotle here calls the Extreme . . . the Extreme as a

25. Elton Mayo later confirmed the need for developments in psychology and other social sciences to reach administrators involved in human situations and referred to a failure in this respect. E. Mayo, *Social Problems*, p. 18.

personal ideal for those who are called by it, is a necessary complement of the Mean in public policy.

But here we reach the point where our examination of the conditions of Happiness, and indeed, the whole method of psychological analysis, ceases to be a sufficient guide to life. It is rather through Philosophy than Psychology . . . that the call of the Extreme makes itself most clearly heard.[26]

Although Wallas framed his administrative thought in the context of sociology and psychology, he weaved the ethical thinking of the ancient Greeks, particularly Aristotle, into his ideals, so that his final stress rested upon philosophy, which provided him with his guide for society and for administration. He realised that to aim at man's happiness in organisational life was not a guarantee for attaining the good of society. Nevertheless, the production of *happiness* would be more likely to achieve the 'social good' than aiming simply for the production of *wealth* or other organisational goals.[27]

Urwick's approach to the ethical ideal of a higher form of society

Undoubtedly, Urwick is the best known of the British administrative pioneers for his writing on scientific principles of administration in the 1930s. Few people, however, know his early approach to administration which, like that of Wallas, contained a socio-psychological attitude and a quest for a higher form of society. When Urwick was an undergraduate at Oxford, psychology was still a 'suspect' subject and it was not until his army service during the First World War that he gained a real introduction to psychology. He was sent a copy of William Trotter's influential work *Instincts of the Herd in Peace and War* (1916) while he was based with the British Army in France, and from this reading he was determined to know more about psychology. He developed this interest conjointly with the science of administration and his first offer of an appointment with the Rowntree Company in York was as a full-time psychologist. Seebohm Rowntree personally suggested to Urwick that he might like to take the position of Works Psychologist, for which he could prepare by reading psychology for two years in Cambridge under the famous British psychologist, Dr C. S. Myers.[28] Urwick declined the post, proposing that a trained psychologist would be more suitable for the Company and, a short time later, he accepted the position of Organisation Secretary with the Rowntree

26. G. Wallas, *Great Society*, pp. 392–4.
27. Ibid., *passim*.
28. Dr Myers' work is described in this chapter, pp. 180–3 in connection with the British corporate experiments.

Company.[29] He remained interested in psychology, none the less, and a decade before his famous work on scientific principles of administration, he published an article on psychology which included his ethical ideal of a higher form of society.

Urwick began his article by pointing out that some writers, particularly opponents of American scientific management, feared that modern industry would kill the creative impulse in man. They believed this type of management would aggravate the tendency to specialisation which was already a feature of Western civilisation and would prove individually harmful and culturally unsound, because it limits self-expression and creativity. Much unscientific opinion, he continued, was of the view that progress as conceived by economists was based on specialisation and carried within it the roots of its own breakdown and decay. Even psychologists had not been successful in dealing with the question of creativity in industry, for most of their attention had been canalised into the controversies aroused by scientific management. Instead of arguing negatively against scientific management, Urwick took a positive approach to society as a whole:

> 'What we want to know is not whether Scientific Management is on the wrong line, but whether the whole of modern machine technology is on wrong lines . . . The confusion of thought which arises from this canalisation is repeated by non-psychological writers, and who can blame them? The objections raised by Trades Unions to many forms of Scientific Management are often set down hastily to mere ignorance and perversity. But if we take account of the fact that the very existence of the craft unions is threatened by the erasure of the craft distinctions; and that the skilled workers thus risk losing the outlet for the creative impulse, the dignity of skilled work, we cannot help seeing, unless wilfully blind, that the workers are contending for a type of civilisation higher than that which it is intended to force upon them.[30]

Urwick was challenging whether *specialisation* in industry was the true path of progress for man and he formulated this challenge from his experience, not only in the British Army, but also in his family glove business. In the glove factories, the management had offered the workers the opportunity to participate in experiments in scientific management, but they had objected for, although they would possibly have benefited economically, their dignity would have been destroyed. In any case, they considered the whole tendency to be socially undesirable. The task of the psychologist then, Urwick claimed, was not

29. L. Urwick, Personal letter to the author dated 28 Feb. 1975.
30. L. Urwick, 'Experimental psychology and the creative impulse', *Psyche*, Vol. III, No. 1, July 1922, 32-3.

to deal with the immediate aspects of scientific management but to explore whether workers, fearing the risk of a diminished outlet for the creative impulse, were expressing demands for a higher type of society. This exploration would require an exact enquiry into the creative impulse to find out how it arises, how it develops and more particularly how it affects the individual's 'weal or woe'. Such an enquiry, he suggested, would involve psychologists in answering at least the following seven points:

1. What instinctive processes combine in the creative impulse?
2. What individual differences are discernible in the various aspects of that impulse, e.g. susceptibility to monotony, manual dexterity, etc., etc.?
3. Is a return to handicraft possible psychologically, i.e. will the instinct of workmanship function normally with a less efficient method once it knows of a more efficient method?
4. What various tasks are particularly adverse to the impulse, contain no outlet for its expression?
5. What is the effect on various individuals of these different types of tasks, the physiological and psychological costs?
6. What sublimations are possible for the individual in the case of the various instincts analysed under 1? E.g. can knowledge of a machine compensate for handling of a tool?
7. How far for various individuals is there really an aesthetic element in the impulse? Can it be transferred from the object made to the method of making?

It is of course possible to extend the list almost indefinitely. Nor is it to be expected that the necessary experimental work for the solution of a tithe of the questions already posed will be accomplished within a generation. But it is suggested that an analysis of the creative impulse and the effects of machine processes should be an ideal constantly before the minds of psychologists, and that such an individual analysis must be the necessary basis of any real knowledge upon the possibilities and probabilities of various forms of industrial organisation . . .[31]

Urwick ended his detailed article deep in idealism, stressing that the end of industry must remain 'the good life' whatever the economic consequences, and if the methods of industry could be shown to be psychologically harmful to the individual the truth must be stated. Like Wallas, he had before him the ethical ideal of a higher form of society which he thought was what the workers themselves were indicating in their dislike and rejection of aspects of American scientific management and other forms of specialisation inherent in modern machine production. He did not propose a step backwards for Western

31. L. Urwick, 'Experimental psychology', op. cit., 39–40.

civilisation to handicraft. Rather, he suggested the alternative of making a serious study of the creative impulse in man, so that its effect on the individual worker could be ascertained and other channels provided for the direction of creativity. Urwick, therefore, referred more directly to 'creativity' than to 'happiness' as the ideal basis of the higher type of society, but he believed that creativity had an immense effect upon the 'weal or woe' of the individual worker.[32]

Sheldon's approach to the ethical ideal of a higher form of society

Sheldon's main work (1923)[33] contained both ethical ideals and scientific principles for management. Ethically, Sheldon's aspiration was for the reconstruction of society, but such reconstruction had to come from every sector of the community. It is impossible to carry through great social changes, he argued, unless the general feeling of the community provides the impulse. It was this belief in the 'community will' which led him, as will be seen in connection with the second ethical ideal, to recommend that management should help the community to become better educated and more fully developed. Despite the need for every part of the community to be involved in reconstruction, management had the task – until democracy and education were achieved more widely – of directing society. The choice between progress and chaos lies before us, he asserted, but we shall obtain the one or fall into the other according to the intellectual and moral qualities of the people who bear the responsibility of building a worthy industrial and social future. We may found our Jerusalem or create our Babel, discover our Utopia or yield to Nemesis, but it is the role of industrial management to set the tone of national ideals. If industrial leaders are self-seeking and devoted only to material ends, national ideals will tend to follow a similar path.

Industry is not external to society, Sheldon pointed out, and it is, therefore, concerned in the local interpretation of societal ideals. But management must go further than seeking to apply existing ideals, it must inspire fresh ones, for no State or part of a State should rest content with things as they are. He urged: 'No leadership which does not continually hold aloft not only the light of an ideal but the torch whereby other ideals may be found, can expect to lead into a future of great achievement.'[34]

32. Ibid., 27–48.
33. O. Sheldon, *The Philosophy of Management* (London) 1923. Reprinted edn 1930.
34. Ibid., p. 89.

From the overview that management must uphold ideals prevailing in society and at the same time discover fresh ones for progress, Sheldon developed the ethical ideals underlying his *Philosophy of Management*. The philosophy he recommended he saw as a means of building 'the Kingdom of Heaven' on earth, which was his ultimate ideal and another approach to a higher form of society.[35]

Stamp's approach to the ethical ideal of a higher form of society

Josiah Stamp approached this ideal in an innovative manner arising from his devotion to Christianity and from his skill as an economist in the Civil Service and industry. His ideal of a higher form of society centred around his views on equilibrium, since a 'balanced' society was his far-reaching goal. In order that this ideal might be achieved, he believed that a science of social adjustment was necessary to regulate imbalances in society. The science of social adjustment meant the study and control of the impact of science on society, and the type of imbalances he had in mind were those stemming from the application of scientific discovery to areas of society, such as industry. As with earlier British administrative thinkers, like Wallas – his mentor at the London School of Economics where he had been an external student[36] – Stamp was querying to what sort of world science was leading. He was afraid that rapid scientific advance would lead to a stationary ethical development which might endanger civilisation. Scientific discovery itself, he pointed out, has no moral or ethical quality and it is easy to assume that every new revelation contributes to progress.

Stamp's aim (1937) was to warn that scientific discovery and progress are *not* synonymous and the former has to be applied at a suitable time and place, if it is to be absorbed without causing friction to other elements of social life. Without careful application, scientific innovation creates heavy costs in its adoption – costs affecting man's affections, his social life and the tools he uses. Science, he maintained, can have harmful effects if inappropriately applied – leading not only to social dislocation but to economic waste of capital and equipment and increased unemployment. Yet, who is to achieve the much-needed

---

35. Ibid., *passim*.
36. For reference to Stamp's encouragement in his studies by Professor Graham Wallas, see J. H. Jones, *Josiah Stamp Public Servant: The Life of the First Baron Stamp of Shortlands* (London) 1964, pp. 87, 274.

balance between science and society? He noted:

> It is rightly stated that the training of the scientist includes no awareness of the social consequences of his work, and the training of the statesman and administrator no preparation for the potentiality of rapid scientific advance and drastic adjustment due to it, 'no prevision of the technical forces which are shaping the society in which he lives'. The crucial impact is nobody's business.[37]

Stamp wanted to make the science of social adjustment a collective responsibility in the hands of industry and government rather than 'nobody's business', and the technique of social adjustment would involve modifying both the impact of science upon men *and* modifying the nature of man to meet the impact. In the former case, attention would be directed towards finding the right time and place to apply scientific innovation to prevent unnecessary pain in society. But, in the latter case, it meant developing knowledge about man through psychology, sociology, ethics and other sources. By developing knowledge of man alongside pure science, Stamp hoped that it would be possible to prepare man for change, making disequilibrium in society less likely.[38] He continued the theme of the science of social adjustment in other works. For example, in his Presidential address to the Institute of Public Administration in October 1937, Stamp suggested that the public administrator, as an agent of government, should acquire the technique of social adjustment, since the official would be an important instrument in the new society.[39] His ethical ideal, therefore, was for a new and higher form of society in which science and man are in harmony and where the public administrator has a task in helping to achieve balance in society.

Conclusion to the ethical ideal of a higher form of society

Four conclusions can be drawn from the attention paid by contributors to the British Philosophy of Administration to the ideal of a higher form of society. Firstly, the ideal indicates a real fear in this period for the possible disintegration of modern industrial society.[40] The fear was generated by the rapid, and sometimes thoughtless, application of

---

37. J. Stamp, *Science of Social Adjustment*, p. 15. Stamp's own quotation is taken from Professor Hogben, *The Retreat from Reason*, p. 3.
38. J. Stamp, *Science of Social Adjustment*, pp. 1–7.
39. J. Stamp, 'The administrator and a planned society', *Public Administration*, Vol. XVI, 1938, 3–22. Stamp also touched upon the theme of social adjustment in *Motive and Method*, particularly pp. 21–48.
40. Scientists, philosophers, statesmen and preachers, in addition to administrative thinkers, had misgivings about scientific progress and its reactions on society, see J. Stamp, *Science of Social Adjustment*, p. 1.

scientific discovery without concern for its social and ethical consequences. There was fear that developments in ethical thinking and the 'human' sciences were falling behind developments in pure science while, at the same time, there was anxiety that a society conceived by economists and aimed principally at economic progress would destroy itself. Thus, the need to balance or maintain the impersonal and mechanised twentieth-century industrial society was identified. Such maintenance or balance consisted of undertaking research into the 'human' sciences, particularly psychology and sociology, and making sure that this knowledge reaches those who guide society, including the public administrator and the industrial manager.

The second conclusion refers to the collective responsibility expected of industry and government in the guidance of nations. British administrative pioneers took a macro-view of administration, seeing industry and government within the context of national society and not as worlds in themselves. They hoped that industry and government would be concerned with the broad implications of progress in modern society, such as the effects of mechanisation, specialisation and division of labour. Contributors to the British Philosophy of Administration had reservations, therefore, not only about American scientific management but about the whole trend of scientific progress. Indeed, their ethical ideal confirms the move in Britain this century away from an individual *laissez-faire* approach to societal problems to an acceptance of the need for industry and government to assume joint responsibility for the type of society being created.

Thirdly, the key to the higher form of society hoped for by these British administrative pioneers differed slightly. Wallas emphasised happiness; Urwick creativity; Sheldon education and development of all sectors of the community; and Stamp put his faith in the science of social adjustment. Despite this mild difference in emphasis, there was general recognition of the need to consider not only the purpose and direction of society, but also the progress of the individual within modern life. The ideal suggests strong elements of altruism and urges industry and government to aim for more than economic advantages. However, there are limitations as well as advantages in this ethical ideal. By adopting this macro-approach to administration, pioneers such as Wallas and Stamp tended to lose their administrative thought within complex writing on society at large, and Chester Barnard confirmed this weakness. Although he praised Stamp's work and adopted the idea of equilibrium in his own work, he criticised the absence of specific attention to administration, noting:

> If one examines Sir Josiah Stamp's recent book, *The Science of Social Adjustment*, a stimulating and penetrating inquiry into the causes of the disturbance of social equilibrium, one will find scarcely a line to indicate the existence of formal organizations, despite the author's active connection with them; nor a single suggestion regarding the study of them as one of the important fields of scientific exploration looking toward the more apt adjustment of society to changing conditions.[41]

As well as Barnard, Elton Mayo in the United States stressed equilibrium, pointing out that human equilibrium could be affected by conditions outside the factory, such as the impersonality of urban life.[42] However, in the American 'human relations' doctrine, the broad concern for society took a secondary role to the vital discoveries at the Hawthorne plant. By contrast, the British Philosophy of Administration devoted considerable attention to the relationship between society and administration, but the result was a fragmented and less concise approach to administration. Stamp, for example, presented no co-ordinated study of formal and informal organisations akin to that of Barnard, although he did document valuable information about administration within organisations in a series of books and articles.

Service to the community

The ethical ideal that public and private organisations should serve the community as well as perform their administrative functions was put forward between 1900 and 1939, notably by Haldane and Sheldon. The ideal envisaged the British Civil Service and industry as exemplars to the community in the field of ethics, as well as being practical organisations of communal service. And, while Haldane was recommending the ideal to the Institute of Public Administration, Sheldon was encouraging industry to serve the community.

Haldane's approach to the ethical ideal of service to the community

As President of the new Institute of Public Administration, Haldane addressed the Institute in the early 1920s on the ideal of service to the community. He pointed out that he had worked hard for almost ten years as head of two large government departments and he had direct experience of others.[43] Yet, he had not accomplished all he had set out

41. C. I. Barnard, *The Functions of the Executive* (Cambridge, Mass.) 1938. Thirtieth edn 1968, p. 3.
42. E. Mayo, *Human Problems*, p. 172.
43. Haldane was a Minister and not a permanent civil servant, as noted in Ch. 2, pp. 37–9.

to do, for much was a matter of gradual evolution involving both continuity in policy and commonly agreed ideals. Continuity cannot be reckoned upon, he stated, with ever-altering Ministries and so we rely on the Civil Service. With regard to the internal organisation of the Civil Service, Haldane referred his audience to the *Report of the Machinery of Government Committee* (1918) which was the type of plan he envisaged for the progress of the Service in its twentieth-century tasks. But, his view of progress extended beyond the internal reorganisation of the Service to embrace the possibility of an ideal Civil Service. The function of the Civil Service, he emphasised, is to provide the factors necessary for continuity in administration, and it is important to the well-being of the State that the Service is of the highest excellence. Excellence, then, should be one of the primary purposes of the Civil Service.

Haldane considered that excellence in the Civil Service was linked to the British educational system, and in his evidence before the Royal Commission on the Civil Service in 1912, he indicated that a review of the Service would be unsatisfactory unless the whole question of education was studied. His idea of a perfect system was for equal opportunity in education, whereby university education would be open to the talented, irrespective of social background, and the Civil Service would be able to draw upon this wider background. The Commissioners obviously heeded Haldane's suggestion for their Report on the Civil Service (1914) laid stress on improving the general system of education in order to benefit the quality of those recruited into the Service. [44] Yet, the internal reorganisation of the Civil Service as proposed in the Machinery of Government Report combined with the recruitment of suitable staff did not meet Haldane's idealistic image of the Service. He continued:

> What I wish to do is to submit for your consideration the ideals which the Civil Service may seek to realize. What would be an ideal Civil Service and what should it always set before its eyes? Its first and dominant common object ought to be the service of the public in the most efficient form practicable. Virtue is its own reward here as elsewhere. [45]

44. *Royal Commission on the Civil Service: Appendix to First Report of the Commissioners*, 1 Vol. (London) 1912, pp. 78–93. Haldane was qualified to give evidence because he was then Chairman of the Royal Commission on University Education in London, see *Royal Commission on the Civil Service: Fourth Report of the Commissioners* (London) 1914, p. 3.
45. R. B. Haldane, 'An organized Civil Service', *Journal of Public Administration*, Vol. I, 1923, 12.

Haldane was calling forth the development of an organisational 'spirit' or what is known as *esprit de corps* within the Civil Service based on the ethical ideal of service to the community. He considered that the ideal of service depended upon the non-economic motive of self-sacrifice, which was more likely to produce the type of organisational 'spirit' he envisaged than the profit motive. As examples of organisations manifesting this spirit of self-sacrifice for public duty, Haldane named the British Navy and the Army. The motive of self-sacrifice is inculcated, he maintained, through tradition and education – tradition which sacrifices the life of the individual for duty to the State. His stress on an *esprit de corps* created a deep impression on Marshall Dimock in the United States, who had read a similar appeal by Haldane in his evidence to the Coal Commission (1919). Later, Dimock himself published an article on non-economic incentives in relation to American public administration in which he confirmed the importance of an *esprit de corps* and acknowledged Haldane's earlier thinking on the subject.[46]

In the context of the British Civil Service, Haldane hoped that the ideal of service to the public based on self-sacrifice could be stimulated by sacrifices, such as are witnessed when civil servants refuse to exchange modest salaries for more lucrative ones in industry or commerce.[47] He believed that the ideal of public service and other high ideals prevailed among those who had acquired a larger outlook on the 'meaning of life' which comes from knowledge, and he proposed that the State and the Civil Service should seek to encourage such knowledge as an aid to progress. He realised that education could not itself guarantee the motive of self-sacrifice, but he thought it could make it increasingly probable, particularly university education. Therefore, Haldane urged the Civil Service to initiate the ideal of service by requesting more education and training for its members. Also, he recommended that the Institute of Public Administration should keep in close touch with establishments of higher education, especially the universities which he viewed as 'great schools of life and thought'.[48]

With its knowledge increased, Haldane proposed that the Civil

---

46. M. E. Dimock, 'Public administration: the potential incentives of public employment', *The American Political Science Review*, Vol. XXVII, 1933, 628–36.
47. Beveridge had made a similar point about salaries in the context of the vow of poverty which civil servants should take. See Ch. 2, p. 42.
48. Josiah Stamp also laid responsibility at the feet of universities to awaken in students a sense of obligation to the community. J. Stamp, *Ideals of a Student* (London) 1933, pp. 52–9.

Service would be able to take an educative role in relation to the community. He declared his views thus:

> It is not only by rendering highly skilled service to the public in dealing with administrative problems and questions, even of policy, that the civil servant of the future may serve the public. The Civil Service, if itself highly educated, may become one of the greatest educative influences in the general community. It may set a high example and may teach lessons which will have far-reaching influence. I believe in its own interests, not less than in those of the State, it is well that it should set this ideal before itself as one which is of immense practical importance in its tendency to raise the standards in business and in life generally of those with whom it will have to be dealing constantly.[49]

Service to the community by setting a high standard of conduct and by acting as an educative influence within the community was a novel idea, Haldane suggested, but a useful one. For, the future of Britain depends upon the maintenance of high standards, and if the Civil Service can set this example on a large scale it will help Britain to retain a high position among other nations as well as strengthening the position of the Civil Service.[50]

Sheldon's approach to the ethical ideal of service to the community

Whereas Haldane urged the Institute of Public Administration and its members in the Civil Service to develop the ethical ideal of service to the community, Sheldon (1923)[51] spurred industrial management to define the same ideal. The ideal of service to the community had been translated into practical moral expression at the Rowntree Cocoa Works, York, and Sheldon was obviously profoundly affected by the concrete example set by his Chairman, Mr Seebohm Rowntree.[52] Sheldon adopted Rowntree's views on community service and his hopes for industry bear a striking resemblance to the realisation of the ideal in the York 'model' factory.[53]

Sheldon broke the ideal into two parts: one concerned with management's relation to the community at large; the other with management's relation to its own individual workers who, in turn, are

49. R. B. Haldane, 'An organized Civil Service', op. cit., 16.
50. Ibid., 6–16. William Beveridge confirmed the ethical ideal of service to the community in his lecture 'The civil servant of the future', *The Development of the Civil Service* (London) 1922, p. 244.
51. O. Sheldon, *Philosophy of Management*.
52. See B. S. Rowntree, *The Human Factor in Business* (London) 1921. Second edn 1925.
53. Rowntree was a Quaker and, in 1918, Quaker employers in Britain proposed that business should adopt an ethic of service. The Rowntree factory was a 'model' in the sense of epitomising this and other ethical ideals. See J. Child, *British Management Thought*, pp. 46–7.

community members. In the case of the community, he believed that industrial management should aim to serve the community by putting communal well-being before industrial wealth. He clarified this aspect of the ideal by drawing upon Rowntree's work (1921) which associated three objectives with service to the community:

1. Industry should create goods or provide services of such a type and in such measure, as may benefit the community.

2. In the process of wealth production, industry should pay the greatest regard to the general welfare of the community and pursue no policy detrimental to it.

3. Industry should distribute the wealth produced in such a manner as to serve the highest ends of the community.

In other words, Sheldon maintained that an ethical as well as an economic value should be attached to the goods produced for the community. Goods should be assessed in terms of whether they are physically or morally harmful to the community, even if this ethical evaluation is in an inverse ratio to the economic value of the products. He was aware of his idealism and pointed to the inevitable gulf between the actual and the ideal. Nevertheless, he considered that it was management's responsibility to pursue the ideal of service to the community, for however scientific management might become, its primary responsibility is social and communal. Its efficiency is to be judged not only by scientific standards, but also by the supreme standard of communal well-being.

Regarding the second element – management's relation to its individual workers – Sheldon argued that management should not accept responsibility for the individual as a worker and deny its responsibility to him as a social unit. Factory life and life outside the factory are inextricably intertwined. Thus, management's influence upon the worker reflects on the same individual in other capacities and this factor is important, since the worker in industry is also an agent in social progress. The individual is bound by many ties – domestic ties, trade ties, national ties, religious ties – and Sheldon emphasised that there is no reason to suppose that the economic tie has a prior right or that the economic relationship between worker and manager can cancel the worker's relationship elsewhere. The second part of the ideal, therefore, required an endeavour by management to understand the several roles the individual has to play inside and outside his work environment and to develop the 'spirit' of the worker which will affect his spirit as parent, voter and citizen. One way management can arouse this spirit, Sheldon pointed out, is to ensure that the worker has sufficient leisure[54] time and to encourage him to spend this time in benefit to the community by, for example, developing himself through study and social intercourse. Sheldon had observed the increased leisure and study granted to workers at the Rowntree Works by means of the introduction of the forty-four-hour week, the long weekend and the provision by the Company of adult education classes.[55] And it was this kind of ideal, or example, which he envisaged when he referred to management's relation to individual workers who, outside their work, are communal members.[56] It is interesting that aspects of this ideal were confirmed later by the Hawthorne experiments in the United States when it was concluded that workers needed to be considered, bearing in mind the *social* setting in which they lead their lives rather than viewed essentially as 'economic men'.[57]

Conclusion to the ethical ideal of service to the community

Haldane and Sheldon were trying independently to encourage the Civil Service and industrial management, respectively, to take the initiative in setting the ethical ideal of service to the community. The ideal raises several important conclusions for discussion. Firstly, although the ideal relates to service to the community, it cannot be discussed without reference to trade unionism. During the First World War, trade-union representatives were included in many of the control schemes set up in industry due to the pressure of war needs and, hence, after the war they exercised some real control of industry. To an extent, this ideal portrayed the need for employers to take account of the expanding role of trade unions, since the unions were stirring the public conscience and insisting that workers should be treated more humanely. Despite the fact that a number of British industries, including the Rowntree Company, sought to co-operate with trade unions by taking active measures to offer some genuine control to employees through consultative councils and participation in profit-sharing schemes, this ideal reflects a wariness that trade unionism might lead to *sectional* rather than *communal* well-being. Haldane warned the Civil Service

54. Sheldon defined 'leisure' as 'scholē' meaning 'schooling' and he argued that if it is to benefit the community, leisure should approximate closely to its original meaning. O. Sheldon, *Philosophy of Management*, p. 94.
55. See B. S. Rowntree, *Human Factor in Business, passim.*
56. O. Sheldon, *Philosophy of Management*, particularly pp. 70–99.
57. F. J. Roethlisberger and W. J. Dickson, *Management and the Worker*, p. 569.

against slipping into the kind of narrow outlook characteristic of trade unions[58] and, likewise, Sheldon referred to the growing power of trade unions in Britain as a force for good or evil.[59] Both Haldane and Sheldon, then, were appealing in the ideal of service for communal well-being to be placed before all other considerations – whether the narrow interests of management or of trade unions. Little reaction appears to have been registered by the trade unions towards this ethical ideal, except a dislike of profit-sharing schemes because of their tendency to weaken trade-union solidarity.[60]

Another factor of modern society which prompted Sheldon to urge industry to adopt the ideal of service to the community was the split between the ownership and management of industry. He believed that the comparatively recent growth of the 'management' element in industry gave it the chance to move away from the economic motive and to carve its own ethical standards – the ideal of service being the most important.[61] Thus, the ideal of service promoted by Haldane and Sheldon revealed a humane quality in their thought, but the ideal was not without limitations. Both writers failed to give adequate guidelines as to how the ideal of service to the community might be defined and attained. Haldane put his faith in knowledge, particularly at university level, and was instrumental with Sidney Webb in developing the London University and certain provincial universities.[62] But his conception of universities was over-idealistic. Regrettably, they do not necessarily equip their attenders with knowledge of 'the meaning of life' or inculcate the quality of self-sacrifice to the State. Haldane was noble in wishing to see a spirit of organisation, or *esprit de corps*, developed in the Civil Service based on self-sacrifice, but he was simply reawakening the age-old philosophical question of what causes a man to put the interests of his country or community before his own. Haldane, therefore, indicated the need for self-sacrifice, but he did not give an accurate indication of how this motive is developed or maintained in organisations. Similarly, Sheldon's ideal of service

58. R. B. Haldane, 'An organized Civil Service', op. cit., 9–10.
59. O. Sheldon, *Philosophy of Management*, p. 187.
60. See B. S. Rowntree, *Human Factor in Business*, pp. 128–72 and G. D. H. Cole, *British Trade Unionism Today: A Survey* (London) 1939, pp. 65–72.
61. O. Sheldon *Philosophy of Management*, p. 76. For a guide to the growth of the 'management' element in British industry, see O. Sheldon, 'The art of management: from a British point of view', *Bulletin of the Taylor Society*, Vol. VIII, No. 6, Dec. 1923, 209–14. See also J. Child, *British Management Thought*, particularly pp. 51–3.
62. See Sir H. F. Heath, 'Lord Haldane: his influence on higher education and on administration', *Public Administration*, Vol. VI, 1928, 350–60, and B. Webb, *Our Partnership*, ed. by B. Drake and M. I. Cole (London) 1948, pp. 95–102.

tended to be vague and he repeated idealistic aspirations without providing sufficient concrete substance about how the 'community will' might be identified or whose standards shall determine what is communally highest. Rather, he assumed a consensus of opinion among management and the community on highly charged ethical issues and reiterated glowing statements such as: 'Management is finding the light of a new spirit glinting from the pinnacles of its corporate task. That spirit is the spirit of service . . .'[63]

To conclude, it may be said that the ideal of service to the community is a worthy one, but such ethical standards are hard to define – harder than scientific principles of administration. In this case, the aspiration of service tended to over-idealisation, leaving the Civil Service and management the difficult task of defining and pursuing the ideal.

The happiness and well-being of the worker

In the late nineteenth and early twentieth centuries, individuals and the government enquired into the working and living conditions of the British people. At the individual level, enquiries had been conducted privately in the 1890s by Charles Booth and Seebohm Rowntree, who examined the plight of the poor. Several private factories[64] introduced reforms in welfare and industrial conditions and the government became concerned with factory conditions. By 1901, social legislation was extended by the Factory and Workshop Act, which empowered the Secretary of State to make regulations for the improvement of factory conditions. As a result of this Act, a number of investigations were launched into the health and safety of British factory workers and the reports and subsequent regulations dealt with needs such as adequate ventilation and protection from fumes and dust.[65]

---

63. O. Sheldon, *Philosophy of Management*, p. 75. In Sheldon's case, it is helpful to obtain more practical proposals for the ethical ideal of service to the community from B. S. Rowntree's work, *Human Factor in Business*. Mary Parker Follett in the United States was impressed by the Rowntree Cocoa Works. In particular, she praised the Rowntree Co. for explaining to individual workers how their performance could contribute towards creating employment in the community of York. See M. P. Follett, *Freedom and Coordination* (London) 1949, p. 27.
64. The private factories included the Cadbury Bournville Works at Birmingham, as well as the Rowntree Co. See E. Cadbury, *Experiments in Industrial Organization* (London) 1912.
65. See P. and G. Ford, *A Breviate of Parliamentary Papers 1900–1916* (Oxford) 1957, pp. ix–xiv, for details of the governmental enquiries and social legislation. See also A. Briggs, *A Study of the Work of Seebohm Rowntree, 1877–1954* (London) 1961, pp. 16–85. for details of the private enquiries by B. S. Rowntree and C. Booth.

Alongside the private and public enquiries and reforms aimed at improving the well-being of industrial workers, contributors to the British Philosophy of Administration, by their ethical idealism, strove to bring the individual's happiness to the forefront of attention. While the second ethical ideal briefly mentioned the role expected of management towards the individual worker, it was discussed in the context of the worker as a *community* member. This third ethical ideal concentrates more specifically upon the worker's happiness and well-being in his *job*. By studying this ideal from the viewpoint of several British administrative pioneers – namely, Wallas, Urwick and Stamp – the relationship between ethical idealism and 'human relations' becomes more evident. Following these individual viewpoints, the more practical corporate experiments into human relations by the Ministry of Munitions, the Industrial Fatigue Research Board and the National Institute of Industrial Psychology will be described.

Wallas' approach to the ethical ideal of the happiness and well-being of the worker

Wallas' concept of happiness was defined earlier in this chapter. It was his belief that there was less happiness in work the nearer it approached the fully organised mechanical and subdivided 'Great Industry'. Indeed, happiness was the measuring rod he adopted to judge the Great Industry and by comparing the life of the worker under less industrialised conditions with the new twentieth-century worker in industrial Britain, he reached the conclusion that the cause of unhappiness lay partly in the monotony and repetition of movements involved in mechanical, subdivided work. On the basis of this assumption, he elaborated the ideal of the worker's happiness and offered suggestions on how happiness might be introduced into modern organisations. Four major aspirations, or suggestions, can be identified from his *Great Society* which are: happiness via the reduction of monotony; happiness via social groups; happiness via self-respect; and happiness via other non-economic incentives.

Happiness via the reduction of monotony

Wallas' comparison of pre-industrial society with modern society is based on a study of the history of the arts and, in particular, the Sinhalese potter. This potter accompanied his work by an ancient, traditional song which contained directions for apprentices – in the absence of written directives – on how to remember pottery operations in their correct order. The Sinhalese potter owed much of his happiness

164

to the fact that he had skilfully learned the 'right' methods of turning the wheel and throwing the clay. Similarly, Wallas argued, the violinist in the course of playing adopts the 'right' use of his bow which is a more suitable technique than allowing him to please himself, because these arts have been developed in accordance with certain human nervous and muscular conditions. Monotony occurs, he claimed, not as a direct result of repetition in work, since the traditional arts involve repeating the same series of actions, but from the *exact* repetition of movements. Despite the fact that the same actions are repeated, the arts of pottery and violin-playing embody a *variety* of movements, for no touch of the thrower's hand on the revolving clay or sweep of the violinist's arm is alike. Wallas believed that avoidance of exact repetition, as characterised by the traditional arts, could be made a condition of highly organised machine industry to prevent the operator becoming merely a part of his machine. For example, variation could be introduced by altering from time to time the type of machine used by a particular workman or varying the grade of material he handles and if work is still monotonous, it could be alternated with other work. He advocated these forms of variation to reduce monotony irrespective of whether they involved a temporary loss of efficiency, since he was interested in promoting the 'happiness' as well as the 'efficiency' of the worker.

Wallas' concept of happiness based on harmony of the soul, and achieved through variety and skill in work, differed from the type of happiness envisaged within American scientific management. Gilbreth, writing in the United States at about the same time, referred briefly to the worker's happiness, but he conceived it simply in terms of eliminating fatigue and did not relate it to monotony. [66] Hence, Wallas' idea of happiness was an advanced concept, going beyond economic and physiological understanding to encompass a psychological–spiritual interpretation of the worker's happiness.

Happiness via social groups

A man's work does not occupy all his consciousness and his happiness depends also on his relation to his fellow men, Wallas insisted. Quantitatively, a man can 'like' only those to whom he can attach a

66. See W. R. Spriegel and C. E. Myers, eds., *Writings of the Gilbreths*, pp. 336-7. Taylor also conceived happiness in physiological terms. He ascertained the pace of work for a first-class man, rather than an average man, and argued that if such a man can keep up this pace for a period of years without injury to his health, he will become happier. F. W. Taylor, *Shop Management* (New York) 1911, p. 25.

name, face and character without undue effort. Thus, if he is employed in a large business of some 2,000 persons, he cannot form close associations very easily. In armies, it has been found that the comfort and contentment of officers and men depends upon the deliberate formation of groups – companies or platoons – of some twenty-five members. Other examples outside the army of deliberate aims to create groups for regular social intercourse, Wallas pointed out, are the university college or dormitory systems. Furthermore, he stressed: '. . . if no arrangement of the kind has been made by the authorities, clubs or cliques, in forms sometimes inconsistent with other conditions of desirable social life, spontaneously make their appearance'.[67]

Wallas' reference to the need for small groups to be created deliberately or springing up spontaneously in organisations is brief, but nevertheless it is an observation of a 'human relations' nature which arose from his ethical concern for the happiness of the worker. Again, therefore, Wallas was putting forward an idea as early as 1914 which corresponded closely to the later American doctrine of human relations, since the Bank Wiring Assembly Room experiment at the Hawthorne plant identified the role which small groups or 'cliques' play within formal organisations. Moreover, Wallas' administrative thought contrasted markedly with American scientific management, for Taylor's emphasis was directed towards the worker as an individual. Taylor disliked group loyalties and his dislike can be traced to his early working experience as an apprentice in the machine-shop at the Midvale Steel Company, where he was obviously a 'rate-buster', who antagonised his fellow workers. Having been a victim of group bitterness by his colleagues who sought to control output, Taylor's interest focused upon increasing *individual* output and incentives but, in so doing, he neglected to consider the positive value of informal *group* activity.[68]

Happiness via self-respect

In the same way that quantitatively a worker cannot form satisfactory relations on a large scale with his fellow workers, neither can he be supervised on a large, impersonal scale. Wallas derived his scientific principle of 'span of control' from his belief in the importance of self-respect, which cannot be achieved unless supervision is on a scale small enough to permit a close relationship between supervisor and

67. G. Wallas, *Great Society*, pp. 355–6.
68. See F. W. Taylor, *The Principles of Scientific Management* (New York) 1911. Reprinted edn 1913, pp. 48–55.

supervised. This scientific principle of a limited 'span of control' was one method of adjusting the vastness of the Great Society to the smallness of the individual man.[69]   Besides this principle, Wallas indicated another method of preserving self-respect in the case of public officials, which was to bring the official into more direct contact with the community, so that he might receive conscious recognition of his own social worth.[70] Similarly, in the United States, the findings of the Relay Assembly Test Room experiment at the Hawthorne plant indicated the importance of supervision. In fact, the experiment revealed that the relationship of confidence and friendliness established by the girls in the test room meant that little supervision was required. A report on the test room suggested: '. . . the girls . . . have ceased to regard the man in charge as a "boss" . . . they have a feeling that their increased production is in some way related to the distinctly freer, happier, and more pleasant working environment'.[71]

From this recognition, the Interviewing Programme was commenced to study the quality of supervision generally at the Hawthorne plant. Wallas' thinking not only predates the Hawthorne findings about the importance of a close relationship between supervisor and supervised, and the happiness it could bring to the worker, but it also received confirmation from the American experiments.

Happiness via other non-economic incentives

It is evident already from Wallas' writing that he regarded non-economic factors, such as regular social intercourse within small groups and the maintenance of self-respect, as essential to the worker's happiness. However, he became further interested in the question of non-economic incentives, particularly in relation to women in modern industry because their wages were usually lower than those of men for work of the same grade. Surely, therefore, non-economic incentives must play an important part in women's motivation? He decided to test this hypothesis by substituting 'happiness' for the 'wealth-production' criterion and, when he was visiting Harvard University in 1910, he carried out a small industrial study among factory women in Boston. His limited investigation took place under non-controlled conditions and it is one of the earliest enquiries carried out by a British administrative thinker this century. This early study resembles the

69. See Ch. 3, pp. 125–7. Sheldon also emphasised the need for the industrial worker to be treated with respect, see O. Sheldon, *Philosophy of Management*, p. 85.
70. G. Wallas, *Great Society*, pp. 341–61.
71. E. Mayo, *Human Problems*, pp. 77–8.

method used by Elton Mayo and his colleagues in their initial enquiry into labour turnover at the Philadelphia company, when a nurse acted as a 'listening post' and gained confidences from workers.

In his study at Boston laundries and other poorer kinds of factories, Wallas enlisted the help of a lady who collected savings stamps from the female factory workers. She agreed to ask the girls and women at the factories, 'Are you happy?' In nearly every case the answer was 'Yes'; the girls having interpreted the question as meaning, 'Are you happier than you would have been if you had stayed at home instead of going to work?' The girls admitted that they enjoyed their work because they felt they were 'of some use', they were less lonely or they found the time went more quickly at work than at home. Of the small number of girls and women who said they were not happy, some had 'trouble at home' which was so serious that they were unable to forget it at work. Wallas' study, therefore, provided some empirical evidence to support his belief that non-economic incentives affect attitudes towards work.[72]

Urwick's approach to the ethical idea of the happiness and well-being of the worker

Earlier, it was shown that Urwick (1922) identified the need for a psychological enquiry into the creative impulse to find out how creativity, previously expressed in craftsmanship, can find outlets in modern twentieth-century industry.[73] In the same article, he pointed to the pleasure the skills of craftsmanship grant to their owner and he believed that an analysis of the creative impulse would yield further information about the pleasures and pains involved in individual production. But, in the absence of this detailed psychological knowledge, Urwick turned to his army experience from which he drew important conclusions relating to the psychological concept of the 'span of community'. Consciously or unconsciously, he claimed, the Army had been successful in inducing men to co-operate, even in wartime when demands upon their lives and comfort were excessive. It had been able to hold its regiments and divisions together because it provides an acceptable 'span of community' based on groups through which men can realise their ideals. For, ideals which inspire men's actions develop only through social expression within a group of a certain size. Accordingly, an organisation must allow for social groupings within which individuals may achieve the mental and moral evolution which

72. G. Wallas, *Great Society*, pp. 363–6.
73. L. Urwick, 'Experimental psychology', op. cit., 27–48.

will induce them to co-operate. In civilised life, he continued, where the size and nature of the organisation cause its purpose to be lost from view, the necessary *social* expression disappears and *individual* instincts come to the fore, which makes co-operation hard to achieve. As a result of the repression of social instincts, he argued: 'You get a pathological condition of society attributable to overstraining of the span of community, exactly as the individual who is faced with a task beyond his span of apprehension or memory may ultimately develop nervous breakdown.'[74]

In the Army, by contrast, groups such as the section, the platoon, the company and the battalion demand certain allegiances and loyalties from individuals which permit them to channel their individual instincts into social expression. The span of community has been grossly neglected in industry, Urwick insisted, with little attention being paid to the size of the group and its pathological reactions. Like Wallas, Urwick made reference to other non-economic incentives, besides the size of the group, but he phrased these incentives as 'social rewards'. He pointed out that social rewards, such as badges, buttons and colours, have a high motive value and assist in sublimating desires for self-assertion. All these psychological matters require research, he argued, and group psychologists should bear them in mind when conducting their detailed experiments. Urwick, therefore, supported Wallas' views about small groups, particularly of the army type, and about the existence of other non-economic incentives.

Stamp's approach to the ethical ideal of the happiness and well-being of the worker

Writing in the 1930s, some years after Wallas and Urwick, Stamp took up the theme of non-economic incentives in work. However, he did not deal with them directly in relation to the ideal of the happiness of the worker, but discussed them indirectly in the sense that they were essential for the establishment of a Christian order. An order, presumably, which would benefit the happiness of the worker in the long run! Much of Stamp's writing was concerned with Christianity in economic life, which raised issues concerning rewards for work. The Christian order he wished to see evolve would be planned on a national basis, instead of being left to competitive forces, and in this planned order the profit motive would largely disappear. In its place, other motives would be required and Stamp was keen to study what

74. Ibid., p. 42.

alternative motives existed. His awareness of the need to study motives led him to classify economic and non-economic motives according to their economic efficiency and ethical import. In the case of non-economic incentives, Stamp identified the following body of semi-altruistic motives which he believed were already in evidence in Britain in the 1930s:

(i) *Pride of craftsmanship* He noted a marked increase in the extent to which pride of success and of craftsmanship operate beyond the monetary incentive to produce good and plentiful work.

(ii) *Pride of institution* The pride of institution flourishes, particularly if it can be contested against another institution, so that the honour of the company or the concern can function.

(iii) *Pride of uniform* A uniform, for example denoting government service, is worth a definite differential in money.

(iv) *Dignity and security of Civil Service positions* Officials in the Civil Service have the dignity and security of their position in the Service. Also, they are motivated by the stimulus of reputation for efficiency and signs of recognition, which are equal in incentive quality to large additions to salary.

(v) *Love of the work* Work is carried out by public bodies for nothing but the love of it or the esteem of the people. Such work is proof of a large fund of non-economic incentive prevailing in Britain. It is true, however, that such workers have sufficient means which, if lacking, might cause them to be less willing to work for non-economic rewards.

(vi) *Honours in public life* Stamp cited the example of the Japanese delegation who were asked to report on incentives in English public service. They were surprised that able men would work for long periods for the reward of a piece of ribbon and the right to put several letters of the alphabet after their names and that, strangely, the men in question appeared to be quite satisfied with this culmination to their endeavours.

Stamp pointed out that more knowledge was required about the strength of human desire, such as the extent to which it prevails and man's ability to sacrifice for a principle or for an institution.[75] He was alive to the fact that non-economic incentives could be as self-regarding as profit and that 'inverted egoism' is present in much public service.

---

75. Similarly, Haldane showed a concern to understand what induces a man to make sacrifices for an institution or for his country, see this chapter, pp. 156–9.

Nevertheless, he believed that the task ahead was to explore how far non-economic incentives could be substituted for financial incentives, in order that semi-altruistic motives could be developed as a reliable form of motivation in a Christian order.[76]

A corporate approach to the ideal of the happiness and well-being of the worker

Three organisations of a government nature, or with governmental interests, pioneered practical developments towards the happiness and well-being of the worker. These developments by the Ministry of Munitions, the Industrial Fatigue Research Board and the National Institute of Industrial Psychology demonstrate that there was a pronounced interest in 'human relations' in Britain from the First World War onwards, apart from the work of private organisations such as Rowntree and Cadbury. Moreover, these practical reforms and experiments support, and extend, the arguments of the individual contributors to the British Philosophy of Administration.

The Ministry of Munitions

The British interest in human relations, based on the well-being of the worker, began with studies of fatigue in relation to the industrial worker. In 1903, at an Industrial Congress in Brussels, a resolution was passed that the various governments represented should undertake investigations into industrial fatigue. In Britain, evidence was accumulated as a result of enquiries into the working of the Factory and Workshop Act, 1901 which revealed that bad ventilation and long hours attributed to fatigue, but it was not until the First World War that serious attention was paid to the causes of fatigue. [77] Owing to the need for both men, women and young people to be employed in the manufacture of sometimes heavy munitions equipment, the question of workers' fatigue assumed greater significance during the war. In 1915, Mr Lloyd George, then Minister of Munitions, appointed the Health of Munition Workers Committee to advise the Ministry on questions affecting the 'health and well-being of workers in munition factories'. Urgency and the many problems to be investigated caused the Committee to issue a series of memoranda at an early stage in its enquiries covering various aspects of industrial fatigue. By 1917, an interim report, *Industrial Efficiency and Fatigue*, had been published

---

76. J. Stamp, *Motive and Method*, pp. 49–97.
77. See P. and G. Ford, *Breviate of Parliamentary Papers*, p. 198.

together with twenty memoranda[78] dealing individually with a wide variety of industrial questions. Studies of fatigue were not limited to Britain, and the American scientific management movement had made useful studies and recommendations in relation to the reduction of fatigue through rest pauses, suitable ventilation, lighting and other means. However, the scientific management studies remained essentially at the *physiological* level, treating fatigue as a symptom of the physical body.[79] In this respect the Ministry of Munitions, and the later American human relations school, differed from the American scientific management movement since the investigators moved from physiological questions to consider *psycho-sociological* factors. The memoranda composed by the Health of Munition Workers Committee were circulated widely and, although they were concerned with workers in munition factories, the conclusions were deemed useful for solving similar problems in other industries. A study of the Committee's conclusions contained in its various publications gives an indication of the contribution made by the Ministry of Munitions to the understanding of human relations. The most important of these conclusions relate to monotony and non-economic incentives.

Monotony

The Committee's study of fatigue led to the conclusion that the bodily sensations normally associated with fatigue were a fallacious guide for, in reality, fatigue is connected with the nervous system. The signs and symptoms of fatigue thus depend upon the nature of the work undertaken, whether it involves fixed routine or degrees of mental activity. Fatigue, in fact, was seen to spring from three sources – the maintained use of intelligence; the maintenance of steady attention upon one skilled task; and the continued use of special senses, whether by touch or sight. In the case of the latter, fatigue was found to depend upon whether the worker obeys his 'natural rhythms' or if unnatural

---

78. For a list of these memoranda, see Bibliography to this book. See also Ministry of Munitions, Health of Munition Workers Committee Interim Report, *Industrial Efficiency and Fatigue* (London) 1917 and Ministry of Munitions, Health of Munition Workers Committee Handbook, *The Health of the Munition Worker* (London) 1917, pp. 7–12.
79. See W. R. Spriegel and C. E. Myers, eds., *Writings of the Gilbreths*, pp. 303–40. Elton Mayo confirmed that 'Taylor confined his attention, upon the whole, to the problem of irrelevent synthesis or mistaken coordination in our muscular apparatus; there is urgent need to extend this inquiry to discover what irrelevant syntheses of emotions and ideas are imposed upon workers by indifferent education and unsuitable conditions of work'. E. Mayo, 'The basis of industrial psychology', *Bulletin of the Taylor Society*, Vol. IX, No. 6, December 1924, pp. 249–59.

rhythm is imposed upon him by the pace of his machine or his fellow workers. These conclusions caused the Committee to draw a correlation between monotony and fatigue; thus confirming Wallas' belief that monotony affects the industrial worker. The Committee noted that:

> . . . a sense of 'monotony' may diminish the capacity for work. This is analogous to, if it does not represent, a fatigue process in unrecognised nervous centres. Conversely, 'interest' may improve the working capacity even for a uniform monotonous activity, and the interest may spring from emotional states, or, as some think, from states of anticipatory pleasure before meal-time and rest ('end-spurt'), or, again, from a sense of patriotism eager to forward the munitions output.[80]

The Committee, therefore, was keen that latent fatigue in munition workers should be detected, since it affected not only the worker's well-being but also his ability to manufacture the munitions urgently required for war. Closely linked to fatigue was the question of incentives, and patriotism was soon recognised as a forceful non-economic incentive to production. Patriotism alone was inadequate, however, to bring about increased output of munitions and the Committee decided to make incentives a subject for study in its own right.[81] In the early work of the Ministry of Munitions, then, similarities can be seen to the later Hawthorne studies in the United States. The Relay Assembly Test Room experiments were engaged for some time in considering hypotheses relating to fatigue and monotony before broadening out into the Interviewing Programme and the Bank Wiring Observation Room tests. Similarly, the initial interest in fatigue shown by the Ministry of Munitions will be seen to broaden out in the work of the other two British corporate bodies to include other factors affecting the worker's happiness and well-being.

Non-economic incentives

The Health of Munition Workers Committee did not underestimate the importance of economic incentives in its investigations, but there was not the same overriding stress placed upon them as in American scientific management. Indeed, evidence was submitted to the Committee which showed their irrelevance in some cases. For example, a factory which paid distinctly low wages, but provided welfare facilities, showed a rapid and satisfactory output. The Committee concluded, therefore, that welfare facilities not only increased well-being, but also acted as an incentive to work. These welfare facilities

80. *Health of The Munition Worker*, p. 18.
81. Ibid., pp. 16–20.

consisted of such provisions as reduced hours of work, rest pauses, good lighting, hygienic cloakrooms and workshops, canteen facilities, welfare supervision and recreation.[82]

Welfare supervisors were considered a necessity in munition factories, and, indeed, in most modern industries where the employer had neither the time nor the experience to handle problems of the workers' health and well-being. The task of the welfare supervisor was seen to involve the engagement of workers, record-keeping, investigating lost time, sickness and poor output among workers, as well as keeping informed about working conditions and making home visits. In its Memorandum No. 2, the Committee called urgently for the appointment of welfare supervisors, especially in factories where women were employed and within eighteen months, several hundreds of such appointments were made. Also, courses in social welfare were provided by the London School of Economics and other British universities and full particulars about welfare were made available by the Ministry of Munitions. In addition to the welfare supervisor within the factory, the workers' well-being outside the factory was studied. The Committee came to the conclusion that leisure was imperative for munition workers and advised that:

> Steps should be taken, if possible in co-operation with the local authority, to organise (preferably with the assistance of a committee of the munition workers themselves) recreation on a scale sufficient to meet the needs of large numbers. 'Winter gardens' and cafes for refreshment, music, dancing, etc. are attractive, and full use should be made of all public halls in winter and parks and open spaces in summer for entertainments, bands and sports. Social clubs, cinemas, baths, bowling greens, skating rinks, playing fields, etc. are all valuable in this way.[83]

The war was recognised as a unique opportunity to investigate and provide for the well-being of the munition worker, not simply because welfare was an incentive to output but, more important, because the physical and mental vitality of the nation was at stake. Such vitality depended upon favourable conditions for the body, such as rest, cleanliness, exercise and recreation, and relief from mental boredom, monotony and discontent.[84] Many of the conclusions of the Health of Munition Workers Committee and its proposals for the well-being of the worker show an obvious similarity to the private welfare innovations at

82. *Industrial Efficiency and Fatigue*, p. 74, and *Health of the Munition Worker*, pp. 24–7.
83. *Health of the Munition Worker*, pp. 109–23.
84. *Health of the Munition Worker*, p. 13.

the Rowntree Cocoa Works in York. The similarities are more than coincidence, since Rowntree had a considerable influence on the Ministry of Munitions. He is believed to have been responsible for impressing upon Lloyd George the urgency of improving welfare conditions – hence his appointment as Director of the Welfare Department in January 1916. Thus, despite the conclusions reached by the Committee's own expert investigators, there is little doubt that the Ministry of Munitions gained impetus from, and even copied, aspects of Rowntree's 'human relations' approach at the Cocoa Works. By his idealism, therefore, Rowntree affected not only those at the York Works like Sheldon and Urwick but was also instrumental in setting the ideal of the worker's well-being before government – as Asa Briggs has pointed out:

> When he moved from York to Whitehall at the beginning of 1916, Rowntree was anxious from his new vantage point to reconcile the claims of efficiency and welfare, to assist Lloyd George in increasing the flow of munitions while at the same time 'raising the well-being of the worker to as high a point as possible' in all munition factories.[85]

Criticisms were lodged in some quarters against these welfare provisions. The trade unions, for example, viewed the expansion in welfare activity with certain suspicion and expressed resentment by some of their members about the interference of welfare supervisors in their private lives.[86] A more general criticism was that these welfare developments promoted by the government represented a sudden and artificial expansion in welfare – a development which was emerging of its own accord in British industry in the pre-war period[87] It appears, then, that the sudden stress on welfare during the war had drawbacks, particularly if welfare supervisors enquired too deeply into the private lives of munition workers. But, despite a few criticisms, the Ministry of Munitions, through the detailed and statistical investigations of its Health of Munition Workers Committee and through the personal idealism of Seebohm Rowntree, was responsible for setting British industry positively on the path of human relations during the First World War.

85. A. Briggs, *Study of the Work of Seebohm Rowntree*, pp. 117–19.
86. See A. Tillett et al., eds., *Management Thinkers*, p. 178.
87. In the pre-First World War period, at least twenty British firms had established welfare departments, including Cadbury, Fry, Hudson Scott, Reckitt and Rowntree. See E. T. Kelly, ed., *Welfare Work in Industry* (London) 1925, p. 4.

The Industrial Fatigue Research Board

At the end of 1917, the Health of Munition Workers Committee was disbanded, but it had made strides towards improving the health and well-being of British factory employees, particularly the munition workers. In 1918, the Industrial Fatigue Research Board was set up with strong medical and psychological backing to continue some of the work commenced by the wartime Committee and to expand the studies of the worker's health and well-being into all types of factories from iron and steel to cotton and silk.[88] The Industrial Fatigue Research Board was appointed jointly by the Medical Research Committee[89] and the Department of Scientific and Industrial Research and many of its staff were former investigators from the Health of Munition Workers Committee. From 1920 onwards, the Research Board published annual reports summarising its work, as well as many individual reports relating to specific areas of study concerning the worker's well-being and his output.[90]

The methods of study of the Industrial Fatigue Research Board were modified to suit peacetime conditions and more direct observation of factory workers and controlled laboratory experiments were introduced. But, the same concern for the health and well-being of workers was carried forward from the war period to the new era of 'reconstruction' – a point clearly demonstrated by the appointment to the Research Board of Dr C. S. Myers, Director of the Psychological Laboratory, Cambridge. The Board's work was supervised by four specialist Committees of Statistics, Physiology of Muscular Work, Physiology of Vision and Industrial Psychology. Each of the Board's reports was submitted to one or more of these committees and published only on their recommendation.[91] By 1928, the Research Board had become so interested in the health of the worker that its name was changed to the Industrial Health Research Board on these grounds:

> At the time of their formation the Board were confronted mainly with special problems of health and efficiency arising from the long hours

88. Although the findings of the Health of Munition Workers Committee were intended to apply more widely than simply to munition factories, the Industrial Fatigue Research Board purposely selected factories for examination which represented *all* the main British industries. *First Annual Report of the Industrial Fatigue Research Board* (London) 1920, pp. 5–7.
89. This Committee later became known as the Medical Research Council.
90. *First Annual Report of the Industrial Fatigue Research Board*, pp. 5–10.
91. *Eighth Annual Report of the Industrial Fatigue Research Board* (London) 1928, pp. 26–30.

that were worked during the war. Under existing conditions those are of relatively small importance, and the Board's investigations are now, for the most part, directed towards problems far removed from that of fatigue as such. The Board have also felt that the possession of a title expressing what they aim at eliminating instead of what they wish to enhance is something of a disadvantage. A recommendation has accordingly been submitted . . . that the word 'fatigue' should be replaced by the word 'health' and that the Board should in future be known as the Industrial Health Research Board.[92]

Many of the observations and experiments of the Industrial Fatigue (Health) Research Board after the First World War and into the late 1920s were concerned with hours of work, lighting, monotony and a hygienic factory environment in general. From the abundance of reports published by the Board,[93] we have selected extracts from two to indicate the growth of the British human relations approach. The first Report, published in 1923, focused attention on the importance of rhythmic movements to the worker's well-being, and this focus is evident from the experiments at sweet factories. [94] The second Report of 1924, which included details of experiments in a firm of manufacturing chemists, concentrated on monotonous work and how it can be relieved by a variety of tasks and by social relations between workers.[95]

Experiments in sweet factories

Motion study, approached from the viewpoint of the psychologist instead of the engineer, was seen to be useful in the Industrial Fatigue Research Board's investigations. Thus, experiments were conducted by the Board using motion study to relieve fatigue and to make the worker more comfortable. The assumption was not that monetary incentives should accompany increased output – as in the case of Taylor and Gilbreth's use of motion study in the United States – but rather that if the worker's well-being could be enhanced, increased production would probably result as a by-product. An experiment in sweet dipping was one of a series carried out by the Board in sweet factories aimed at

92. *Ninth Annual Report of the Industrial Health Research Board* (London) 1929, p. 3.
93. By the 1930s, the Board had published nearly seventy reports in addition to its annual reports. See individual reports of the Industrial Fatigue (Health) Research Board (London) 1919 onwards.
94. Industrial Fatigue Research Board Report No. 14, *Time and Motion Study* (General Series No. 5) by E. Farmer (London) 1923.
95. Industrial Fatigue Research Board Report No. 26, *On the Extent and Effects of Variety in Repetitive Work* (London) 1924.

achieving the worker's well-being and comfort and we outline it briefly. The process of 'dipping' consisted of putting a centre (an almond, walnut, Brazil nut or caramel) in a basin of melted sugar with the left hand and covering it with the sugar by working it with a fork held in the right hand, and then putting the finished sweet on a tray. The process was monotonous and fatiguing, since the girls who performed the task had to stand over a basin of sugar, kept hot by a gas jet, and repeat the operation 22,400 times a week!

The girls were observed in their work by the Board's investigator who noted that the work materials were not arranged very well. The worker had to leave the bench to empty trays of sweets and fetch fresh supplies of centres. Moreover, girls became irritated by having to wait for fresh supplies of sugar, and so new arrangements were introduced to improve these conditions and help productivity. Another factor which irritated the workers was the constant feeling they they might touch the worker alongside with their arm or upset her tray, apart from the fact that they felt tired at having to stand all day. Accordingly, a bench was designed to give the girl more space and enable her to sit to work, but since there was inadequate space for benches in the original experimental room, a room in another factory belonging to the same firm was used. Attention having been paid to the general work environment of the sweet dipper, motion study was applied to the actual movements of sweet dipping.

The experimenter observed that the action of sweet dipping involved straight movements, which were brought to a sudden standstill. New methods of moving the hand in curves to bring about even, circular movements were introduced and the more experienced workers in the department were examined to see if they already worked by the method suggested. The three whose output was greatest did, at times, use a similar method to the one the Board recommended. The new method was not imposed on workers who had grown accustomed for years to other methods, but it was decided to encourage younger departmental members to adopt it and a class was set up, away from those who used alternative methods. The new method was found not only to be easier but also to benefit output.

Other experiments were held in the sweet factories relating to the bottling of sweets and the covering and packing of chocolates. All of them, as well as experiments in other factories, were directed towards the worker's physiological and psychological well-being such as lessening fatigue, adapting motions to the worker's natural rhythm and, generally, showing concern for the human element in industry by helping the employee to feel more satisfied with his or her work. The experiments did not assume that workers were psychologically or physiologically equal and no attempts were made to standardise operations or to impose them. Rather, the importance of vocational guidance was appreciated so that the most suitable job might be found for each worker.[96]

Experiments in a firm of manufacturing chemists

In 1924, the Board published a report on the extent and effects of variety in repetitive work, following experiments in a number of industries including the boot and shoe industry, handkerchief manufacture, letter printing and bookbinding, and a firm of manufacturing chemists. The experiments were carried out because it was recognised that with the passing of the days of craftsmanship, when the worker made the complete article, modern industry increased the risk of boredom and monotony. Variety, on the other hand, was seen by the Board to offset monotony and this assumption was borne in mind when conducting the experiments. In the case of the manufacturing chemists, the particular process observed was the execution of orders for various kinds of tablets, the work usually including the cleaning, filling, padding, capping and labelling of small bottles. The various tasks were light but required dexterity and, on the whole, the work was varied since small orders for different articles were received from retail chemists.

Experiments were introduced which controlled the extent of variety in the making up of chemists' orders. On some days the female workers changed frequently from one aspect of the work to another and, on others days, the changes were restricted. A further modification in the usual methods of work entailed an entire absence of variety in the day's work, so that the girls had to repeat the same activity throughout the day. On the days of continuously repeated operations, the individual worker was able to increase her earnings but she disliked the uniformity. Indeed, during repetitive work, the girls showed signs of discomfort, especially in the latter part of the afternoon. They appeared to be physically uncomfortable and frequently changed their posture. The five-minute tea interval at 3.30 p.m. came as a great relief and the girls gathered at the same table enjoying the opportunity for general conversation. The report noted:

> As a congenial break in the ordinary routine the tea interval was undoubtedly most beneficial, and the operatives afterwards returned to work with renewed energy and greater powers of concentration. The

96. *Time and Motion Study*, pp. 5–47.

intermittent conversations carried on during work frequently acted as a mental relaxation on these days. Such conversations usually indicate a desire for change on the part of the operatives and tend to decrease the monotony of the task. The bored and strained expression which was sometimes noticeable after long-continued activity disappeared and gave place to a brighter and more cheerful attitude when conversation began. Thus in repetition work facilities for conversation act as a safeguard against the effects of monotony . . .[97]

The Board's experiments indicated that unvarying repetition created fatigue, boredom and monotony and was unpopular with the workers. And, although such repetition at times increased the workers' rapidity and dexterity, the cumulative effects of fatigue and monotony neutralised these advantages. The experiments also highlighted the fact that monotonous industrial work could be relieved by opportunities for social conversation, and the Board suggested that facilities for conversation were desirable in many cases to diminish the tendency for 'day-dreaming', or mind-wandering, in some modern industrial processes. Even in work which is not completely automatic and where a decrease in efficiency can result from the period of conversation, it was still recommended as a counteraction to uniformity and monotony and to maintain a regular output throughout the day.[98]

The foregoing two examples are illustrative of the many experiments conducted by the British Industrial Fatigue (Health) Research Board into the worker's well-being from 1918 to well beyond 1939 and they can be seen to continue the work begun by the Health of Munition Workers Committee.

National Institute of Industrial Psychology

In 1921, the National Institute of Industrial Psychology was formed in Britain as a voluntary organisation, financed initially by private donations.[99] Dr C. S. Myers resigned his appointment at the Psychological Laboratory, Cambridge in 1922 to work as full-time Principal of the new Institute [100] and Seebohm Rowntree became a committee member. From the beginning, the National Institute of

97. On the Extent and Effects of Variety in Repetitive Work, pp. 20-1.
98. Ibid., pp. iii-23.
99. As the importance of the Institute's activities became known, grants were made available from the Carnegie United Kingdom Trust and the Laura Spelman Rockefeller Memorial, in addition to private donations from British firms, such as Rowntree and Cadbury. See H. J. Welch and C. S. Myers, Ten Years of Industrial Psychology (London) 1932, pp. 5-7.
100. Myers had been an early investigator for the Industrial Fatigue Research Board, as has been noted, and he was primarily responsible for forming the National Institute of Industrial Psychology. Ibid., pp. 2-7, 130.

Industrial Psychology worked in close relation with the Industrial Fatigue Research Board and investigators were loaned or transferred between the two organisations. But, there were differences in the approaches to applied psychology by the two bodies. The Industrial Fatigue Research Board looked principally at *general* problems within a large number of industries and placed heavy emphasis on 'pure' research. Industry paid no fee for the Board's research and the results were withheld from the public often for many months until sufficient data had been collected and the reports had been agreed by the Board's committee system. The investigations by the National Institute of Industrial Psychology, on the other hand, were carried out at the request of *individual* industries or firms with the employer paying for the service and the results being made known more immediately. None the less, the two bodies joined together on some investigations and details of the experiments at the sweet factories, for example, are recorded in the literature of both organisations.[101]

In the field of industry,[102] psychology was seen by the National Institute of Industrial Psychology to have application in the four main areas of fatigue study, movement study, vocational guidance and management study. In the case of fatigue and movement studies, the investigations and laboratory experiments centred around similar issues commenced in Britain by the Health of Munition Workers Committee and the Industrial Fatigue Research Board. Monotony was still regarded as an essential factor in fatigue and Myers, in 1919, had shown professional interest in the relationship between monotony and industrial overstrain and mental illness, such as nervous breakdown.[103] Movement study was simply a more comprehensive approach to the type of motion study epitomised by the experiments in the sweet factories. The aim was to overcome fatigue by eradicating irrelevant movements, designing movements to relate to the worker's natural rhythm and, generally, making the employee comfortable. But, like the Industrial Fatigue Research Board, the National Institute of Industrial

101. C. S. Myers, *Industrial Psychology in Great Britain* (London) 1926. Revised edn 1933, pp. 19–23.
102. The activities of the National Institute of Industrial Psychology were not restricted solely to industrial and commercial organisations, but included some investigations for government departments, such as the Home Office, the Post Office, the War Office and the Ministry of Agriculture. For details, see H. J. Welch and C. S. Myers, *Ten Years of Industrial Psychology* pp. 76–92.
103. C. S. Myers, 'Industrial overstrain and unrest', *Lectures on Industrial Administration*, ed. by B. Muscio (London) 1920, pp. 172–84. Myers had qualified in medicine and was well equipped to study and make recommendations concerning the industrial worker's health. See L. S. Hearnshaw, *Short History*, p. 173.

Psychology did not believe in enforcing one method for all workers to adopt. On this point, Myers argued:

> To aim at pressing all workers into the same mould is not only to destroy individuality and to encourage needless monotony, but also to run counter to known psychological principles. It is the outcome of so-called 'scientific' management, mechanically formulated by the engineer, in which the mental factors of personality, sentiment and sympathy are sacrificed to purely physical considerations.[104]

American scientific management had gone far in developing apparatus for motion study, which was adapted to an extent by both the Industrial Fatigue Research Board and the National Institute of Industrial Psychology. However, although the British corporate bodies suggested comfortable methods of work based on motion study, they did not hold rigid views about their adoption. Taylor, by contrast, was emphatic that scientific laws could determine the 'one best way' to do a job and if, after proper teaching, a worker could not or would not work in accordance with the new methods and at high speed, he advocated that the worker should be discharged by management.[105] Furthermore, the National Institute of Industrial Psychology differed from Taylor inasmuch as it was careful to gain the co-operation of trade unions towards motion study and, in general, British trade unions raised no objections to the Institute's work. Indeed, in one of the early factory experiments, the workers thanked the Institute's investigator because they were returning home feeling so much less fatigued than before.

Concerning vocational guidance, the Institute devised and implemented tests for the purpose of determining the suitability of school-leavers and other applicants for certain industrial tasks 'to prevent the round peg getting into the square hole'. Management study, as the final sphere for the application of industrial psychology, included such matters as industrial discontent, restricted output and conditions affecting the happiness and well-being of the worker, such as anxiety and worry.[106] In fact, an important contribution by the National Institute of Industrial Psychology lies in this area of the study of emotions. Myers focused attention upon emotions in British industry as a result of his study of overstrain, which had involved the consideration of emotional reactions. On lines similar to Urwick's concern for creative expression, he pointed out that certain desires previously

104. C. S. Myers, *Mind and Work: The Psychological Factors in Industry and Commerce* (London) 1920, pp. 22–3.
105. F. W. Taylor, *Principles of Scientific Management*, p. 83.
106. See C. S. Myers, *Mind and Work, passim*, and H. J. Welch and C. S. Myers, *Ten Years of Industrial Psychology*, p. 3.

displayed in creativity are strongly repressed among workers in modern industry and, in some people, this repression leads to irritability, sensitivity and lack of confidence.[107]

In addition to Myers' own thinking, other spokesmen for the Institute set out their views on human emotions and the most important relate to individual self-assertion and behaviour in social groups. At the individual level, the instinct of craftsmanship was interpreted as being part of the general tendency towards self-assertion. Every man was understood to wish to assert himself in some degree and it was considered deeply wounding to his desire for self-assertion if he was treated as being of no consequence. Hence, the Institute's literature stressed that the manner in which orders are given, the attitude assumed by superior to inferiors and the way in which wages are paid all influence the impulse of self-assertion and can seriously affect the efficiency of factory work. In other words, the Institute was endorsing Wallas' argument about the worker's need for self-respect.[108]

However, an individual is also a member of social groups in society, the Institute pointed out, and his behaviour and feelings may alter in various ways within a social group. Certain social groups manifest a 'group spirit' which is 'the idea of the group with the sentiment of devotion to the group, developed in the minds of all its members'.[109] Social groups manifesting a group spirit directed towards rational purposes and ideals should be encouraged in industry, the Institute's spokesman maintained, but the formation of such groups requires three conditions: some continuity in the existence of the group; definite group self-consciousness; and the right type of organisation – that is, organisation preferably determined by the group itself rather than imposed from without or above.[110] Again, the National Institute of Industrial Psychology was supporting the views of individual con-

---

107. See C. S. Myers, 'Psychology and industry', *The British Journal of Psychology*, Vol X, March 1920, p. 181; C. S. Myers, 'Industrial overstrain and unrest', op. cit., pp. 172–84. and C. S. Myers, *Mind and Work*, pp. 164–9.

108. The study of human emotions and personality, including the employee's need for self-respect and self-actualization, has been developed more recently in the United States by A. H. Maslow, 'A theory of human motivation', *Psychological Review* Vol. 50, 1943, and reprinted in *Management and Motivation*, ed. by V. H. Vroom and E. L. Deci (London) 1970 pp. 31–3; C. Argyris, *Personality and Organization: The Conflict Between System and the Individual* (New York) 1957, particularly pp. 20–53, 76–122, and D. McGregor, *The Human Side of Enterprise* (New York) 1960, pp. 35–44.

109. C. S. Myers, ed., *Industrial Psychology* (London) 1930, p. 35.

110. Ibid., pp. 23–38.

tributors to the British Philosophy of Administration. Wallas and Urwick had noted the usefulness of group affiliations within industry while Haldane had proposed the creation of an *esprit de corps* in the Civil Service. It is not surprising, in view of this overlap between ethical idealism and the practical application of human relations by the National Institute of Industrial Psychology, that British administrative pioneers took a vital part in promoting the Institute's work. Haldane, for example, spoke at the first public meeting of the National Institute of Industrial Psychology in 1922 on the appropriateness of applied psychology in business and he, with Beveridge and Stamp, became officers of the Institute during the 1920s.[111]

The activities of this corporate body, therefore, were interwoven with the ethical ideals underlying the British Philosophy of Administration and the happiness and well-being of the worker was carried through as a main feature in the application of British human relations. This concern for happiness was confirmed by the Institute thus: 'This Institute . . . is . . . very directly concerned in largely increasing the commodity of "happiness". For it scientifically finds ways to avoid unnecessary worry, to avoid anxiety, and to see that the person who is qualified for a particular kind of work finds that work for which he or she is particularly qualified'.[112]

Two interesting parallels can be drawn between the work of the National Institute of Industrial Psychology in Britain and the Hawthorne studies in the United States. First, problems of industrial overstrain – to which Myers personally contributed a great deal of knowledge – became a matter of concern for the American investigators. In the Mica-splitting Test Room, set up in conjunction with the Relay Assembly Test Room experiments, two of the five female operatives were found to have an irregular work output and their records showed them to be 'nervous'. Both suffered from insufficient social contact due to family background and responded to the social relationships developed among the experimental group, although the output of the younger nervous girl fell again when faced with having to return home after living away. In the Interviewing Programme at the Hawthorne plant, similar cases were found of mental stress and illness which have been recorded by Elton Mayo.[113]

111. See H. J. Welch and C. S. Myers, *Ten Years of Industrial Psychology*, pp. 120–32.
112. Ibid., p. 121.
113. E. Mayo, *Human Problems*, pp. 101–9. As well as Myers, the Industrial Health (Fatigue) Research Board issued a report, 'The Nervous Temperament', (1930) and Mayo likened the Hawthorne findings to other schools of thought, including the British Industrial Health (Fatigue) Board.

The second parallel relates to the importance attached to social groups by the National Institute of Industrial Psychology and the Hawthorne investigators. It has been noted already that Wallas' thinking about the formation of groups was borne out by the Bank Wiring Assembly Room experiments.[114] The National Institute of Industrial Psychology examined at greater length the question of social groups, such as the sentiments they provoke and the organisation of groups, preferring groups organised within themselves rather than those formed deliberately by outsiders. But, despite this awareness of social groups, the British thinking on this subject was at a less accurate and less developed level than the American human relations discoveries at the Hawthorne Works. The Institute gave no concrete experimental evidence of informal group activity in industry, as in the case of the Bank Wiring Observation Room results, and its psychological views remained essentially at the level of seeking to promote social groups in industry for the purpose of realising purposes and ideals. Therefore, the conclusions by the National Institute of Industrial Psychology about social groups in organisations were not experimentally based and did little more than confirm the earlier thought of Wallas and Urwick. No depth-discussion followed, for example, about informal leadership in groups and only brief reference was made to the effect of group norms upon output.[115]

Conclusion to the ethical ideal of the happiness and well-being of the worker

The ethical ideal of the happiness and well-being of the worker was promoted by individual British administrative thinkers and extended through the work of corporate bodies. As a result of this ethical ideal and developments in psychology, the value of social groups, self-respect and non-economic incentives was recognised and new psychological methods, such as the interview and direct observation were introduced, which predate some aspects of the Hawthorne experiments begun in 1927 in the United States.

The development of psychology in Britain took account of 'instincts', but it cannot be dismissed simply as a passing phase in 'instinct' psychology. Graham Wallas (1914), for example, emphasised that he wished to steer psychology away from the pitfalls of instinct psychology as epitomised in the work of William McDougall. Wallas maintained

114. See this chapter, p. 144.
115. For the brief reference to the effect of group norms upon output, see C. S. Myers, *Mind and Work*, pp. 115–16.

that instinct psychology or 'anti-intellectualism' was part of a reaction against utilitarian 'intellectualism' and, also, a consequence of Darwin's study of human nature. He saw weaknesses in both 'intellectualism' and 'anti-intellectualism', for the former exaggerated the role of the intellect, or *reason*, in man's behaviour and the latter exaggerated the role of *instincts*. Both approaches fell into the trap of the 'two planes fallacy' in that they portrayed reason or instincts as if they operated on two separate planes of consciousness. Wallas rejected this dichotomy between instinct and intelligence and argued that both belong to *one* interconnecting series of dispositions ranging from the baser animal instincts at the bottom to the intellectual faculties at the top.[116] Certainly, Wallas promoted a concept of psychology which extended beyond the 'instinct' school but, at the same time, drew attention to the importance of human emotions in modern industrial life.

The ideal of happiness, therefore, focused upon the worker's emotions, partly because of an ethical climate which sought the well-being of the worker and partly because of advances in Britain in social and industrial psychology. As a result of this ethical–psychological awareness, Britain adopted a path midway between the two American movements of scientific management and psychology. Münsterberg (1913) lamented the fact that the two movements were progressing independently in the United States with the efficiency engineer rarely making excursions into the psychological laboratory, and he argued that 'the truth lies in the middle'.[117] Britain achieved the middle path by rejecting the worst elements of scientific management but borrowing some of its positive features, such as motion study and knowledge about fatigue and rest pauses, and using them in conjunction with industrial psychology. The result of this middle path was a combined interest in human relations *and* industrial output.

However, the lack of sophistication in the British studies is an important weakness. Although Wallas adopted the technique of the interview in his simple experiment of 1910 in the Boston factories, which later became a technique in both the Philadelphia enquiry and the Hawthorne experiments, his study was only a single pioneering experiment. It was conducted verbally among women of mixed races, many of whom were immigrants, and although it illustrated his hypothesis about the happiness of the worker it cannot compare to the lengthier, scientific studies undertaken at the Hawthorne plant. The benefit of Wallas' study was that it drew attention to non-economic

116. G. Wallas, *Great Society*, pp. 34–59.
117. H. Münsterberg, *Psychology and Industrial Efficiency*, pp. 49–56.

incentives and human needs which became the object of deeper studies by the Health of Munition Workers Committee, the Industrial Fatigue Research Board and the National Institute of Industrial Psychology.[118]

In Urwick's case, he held similar views to Wallas about the ideal of happiness, and laid equal stress on the importance of creative expression through craftsmanship or other outlets. Moreover, he suggested the same remedy as Wallas put forward to overcome the impersonality of modern industrial work – namely, the formation of groups. Yet, despite a strong similarity in the views of these two British administrative thinkers, Urwick made no acknowledgment of Wallas' earlier pioneering attempts in psychology and human relations.

While discussing craftsmanship, it is interesting to consider what relationship, if any, existed between the psychological stress on creative expression through craftsmanship and the special school of socialism – guild socialism – which prevailed in Britain early this century. This form of socialism laid stress on industrial self-government by means of workers' control rather than State management of industry. Guild socialists contended that the administration of socialised industries should be entrusted not to government departments but to self-governing guilds, and they supported the trade unions in the hope that from them the desired guilds might arise. Guild socialism passed through several phases, developing from 1906 to 1912 from a craftsmen's demand for the restoration of the medieval guild system to a demand for the creation of national guilds for the control of modern large-scale industry. Certain well-known Fabians became guild socialists,[119] but Graham Wallas, despite his Fabian background until 1904, saw a weakness in the late medieval guilds in that they tended to be narrow, restricting the entrance into the guilds of 'strangers'.[120] Urwick criticised the guild socialists, also, in relation to craftsmanship for being so dominated by the medieval idea, combined with the class-war bias, that they had lost their main thread.[121] No direct link existed, therefore, between the British Philosophy of Administration and guild socialism. Nevertheless, the doctrines shared a concern for the skills of craftsmanship and, no doubt, the literature of the guild socialists reinforced the interest in craftsmanship, confirming its validity in the

118. There is no evidence, however, that the British corporate bodies were aware of Wallas' earlier views.
119. For example, A. J. Penty and A. R. Orage were both guild socialists and former Fabians, see G. D. H. Cole, 'Guild socialism', *Encyclopaedia of the Social Sciences*, Vol. VII, 1932, 202–4.
120. G. Wallas, *Great Society*, pp. 327–8.
121. L. Urwick, 'Experimental psychology', op. cit., p. 30.

eyes of psychologists.

Turning to the broader aspects of psychology developed by the British corporate bodies, the National Institute of Industrial Psychology, in particular, gave high importance to laboratory experiments in its application of psychology. But, although the Institute had the support of British administrative thinkers, such as Haldane and Stamp, it represented a more scientific and less ethical approach to the happiness and well-being of the worker than the writings of the administrative thinkers themselves. Wallas, in fact, did not favour the laboratory approach of the applied psychologists and as early as 1914 wrote:

> ... the facts of human nature which are of the greatest importance to the social psychologist are just those to which laboratory methods are least applicable. It is almost impossible to arrange a series of identical experiments to illustrate the working of patriotism or . . . artistic and intellectual creativeness. In such matters the social psychologist must be content with the instances which arise in ordinary life, and must examine them by the older methods of introspection, personal evidence and analogy. In so doing, he knowingly lays himself open to the contempt of the experimentalist.[122]

Wallas pioneered the application of social psychology to administration this century, yet he held to the older philosophical tradition of psychology and criticised laboratory methods. Myers, by contrast, favoured experimental methods and noted, in 1920, that psychology was emancipating itself from the tutelage of philosophy and assuming more experimental methods. Therefore, although a strong link existed between ethical idealism and psychology, it can be seen that a difference of opinion prevailed as to the appropriate methods for determining the worker's happiness.[123]

The final weakness inherent in the ethical ideal of the happiness and well-being of the worker lies in the British approach to American scientific management. It has been argued that Britain took the middle path, rejecting large aspects of scientific management as being detrimental to the worker's well-being but modifying motion study to suit the British climate of ethics and psychology. Little credit was given to Taylor and Gilbreth, however, for their work on fatigue and motion study, because of the fear that British trade unions might equate the investigations in industrial psychology with American scientific management. The American movement had aroused the antagonism of

122. G. Wallas, *Great Society*, p. 32.
123. C. S. Myers, 'Psychology and industry' op. cit., pp. 177–78.

trade unions in both the United States and Britain, and great care was taken by the National Institute of Industrial Psychology to dissociate itself from American scientific management.[124] It would have been fairer to Taylor and Gilbreth if they had been praised or acknowledged more openly for those elements of American scientific management which were found acceptable to the British developments in industrial psychology, albeit in modified form. Accordingly, the scepticism demonstrated in Britain towards American scientific management, while 'genuine, was tinged with caution to appease British labour.

Conclusion

The conclusion to this chapter is divided into two parts. The first part summarises the major similarities and differences between the British and American developments in human well-being – or human relations – while the second part offers general conclusions about the ethical ideals underlying the British Philosophy of Administration.

A number of similarities can be seen between the two countries. Both began their practical investigations into human well-being with questions about fatigue and monotony. In the case of fatigue, British corporate bodies recognised that a wide range of industrial conditions had to be examined, and the extent of the British enquiries is reflected in the quantity of memoranda and reports issued about hours of work, ventilation and lighting, canteen facilities, healthy cloakrooms and other aspects of factory life. In neither country was fatigue treated as a simple matter, but rather as a convenient word to describe a variety of phenomena in industry. The Hawthorne experiments, likewise, began with a central concern for fatigue attributed to multiple causes.[125]

In one of its reports on monotony, the Industrial Fatigue Research Board stated that 'repetitive work is a thread of the total pattern, but is not the total pattern in the worker's day'.[126] This assertion implied that repetitive processes must be studied in their complete setting, which includes the repetitive work but takes into account other factors, such as the opinion of fellow workers and the authorities regarding that work,

---

124. For example, the name of the Institute was chosen carefully, in conjunction with trade union leaders, to avoid any association with 'human efficiency' or 'scientific management'. See H. J. Welch and C. S. Myers, *Ten Years of Industrial Psychology*, p. 3.
125. See E. Mayo, *Human Problems*, p. 56.
126. *Fourth Annual Report of the Industrial Fatigue Research Board*, see E. Mayo, *Human Problems*, pp. 35-7.

the physiological and emotional condition of the worker and the collective life of the factory. Not only did the Hawthorne findings confirm that human problems must be understood in the worker's total situation inside and outside the factory but, on several occasions, Elton Mayo quoted the British dictum that repetitive work is only a thread of the total pattern.[127]

Besides the discoveries concerning fatigue and monotony among workers, the study of social relations and group behaviour was prominent in both countries. This similarity has been discussed in some detail in the body of this chapter, but it is worth emphasising that while the Hawthorne experiments may have produced more information and evidence about informal group behaviour than the British Philosophy of Administration and the supporting corporate bodies, the British work predated that in America by some ten years. Another similarity relates to the improved personnel facilities which accompanied the discoveries about human needs in modern organisations. In Britain, the Ministry of Munitions widely extended the use of welfare supervisors in British industry. A parallel consequence of the Hawthorne findings was that they led to 'personnel counselling' at the plant for employees of both sexes.[128]

A final similarity centres on the subject of non-economic incentives. Contributors to the British Philosophy of Administration and the corporate bodies pointed out that the worker cannot be viewed as responding to economic incentives alone, but that non-economic incentives play a vital role. Wallas found evidence to support this assumption in the poorer factories of Boston and it was apparent during the First World War in Britain, when patriotism among munition workers acted as an incentive. Likewise, the Bank Wiring Observation Room experiment revealed that:

> ... the behavior of no one person in an industrial organization, from the very top to the very bottom, can be regarded as motivated by strictly economic or logical considerations ... This point of view is far from the one which is frequently expressed, namely, that man is essentially an economic being carrying around with him a few non-economic appendages. Rather the point of view which has been expressed here is that non-economic motives, interests, and processes, as well as economic, are fundamental in behavior in business ... [129]

The foregoing comparisons portray major similarities which existed

127. Ibid., pp. 35–40, 73–5, 169–70.
128. See F. J. Roethlisberger and W. J. Dickson, *Management and the Worker*, pp. 593–604.
129. Ibid., p. 557.

between the British and American developments in human relations. There were differences, however, between the approaches made in the two countries. The first difference was that the British concern for human well-being developed from a strong ethical and Christian motivation, whereas the American developments appear to have been founded on a purer scientific and academic basis. A closer analysis of the ethical ideals underlying the British Philosophy of Administration indicates that the *basis* of the ideals varied among pioneers, but the net result of their thinking was strikingly alike. Wallas gained his idealism from Greek philosophy, particularly Plato and Aristotle, and he was opposed to much orthodox religion. Haldane, similarly, rejected aspects of Christianity, holding instead the simple view that spirituality lies within man and calls for development, particularly through education. Quakerism also contributed to the ethical idealism among British administrative pioneers and was effective notably at the Rowntree Works. The Rowntree family had been Quakers for several generations and Seebohm, although somewhat unorthodox later in his life, learnt from his father what 'social Christianity' meant and continued in his turn to further it at the York factory.[130] Indeed, with Sheldon and Urwick at the York factory in the 1920s, the Rowntree Company offered a contribution to ethical idealism comparable to the impact of the Hawthorne plant in creating the American doctrine of human relations. Stamp was an orthodox Christian whose goal was to make his religion relevant to twentieth-century social and economic problems and this caused him to propound ethical ideals for administration, as well as for other spheres of life.

This merger of ethical idealism with practical experiments in human well-being did not prevail in the United States and, instead, the academic methodology consisted of more 'controlled' experiments into human relations and a more precise drawing together of conclusions. The British Industrial Fatigue Research Board and the National Institute of Industrial Psychology undertook some controlled work, but many of the British studies were based on observation of factory workers in their normal environment rather than in experimental rooms. Furthermore, as stated at the onset to this chapter, the British conclusions were not analysed and summarised with the precision adopted by American academics. Accordingly, once the initial impact of the British studies had died down, the ethical ideals underlying the British Philosophy of Administration and the corporate conclusions were neglected.

130. See A. Briggs, *Study of the Work of Seebohm Rowntree*, pp. 3–7.

A second difference between the developments in Britain and the United States was that in Britain more attention was paid to trade union attitudes. Mayo and the American human relations school have been charged with inattention to trade-union functions.[131] In contrast, contributors to the British Philosophy of Administration and the corporate bodies took into account the role of trade unions. For example, despite Sheldon's pointer that trade unions could be a force for good or evil, he was anxious that British management should become a partner with trade unions, since he believed they were both involved in the same task of labour administration. Sheldon, moreover, viewed trade-union association as part of the worker's desire for 'group-mindedness' – a factor to be enlisted into the corporate life of the factory by drawing trade unions into the factory instead of letting them be something apart.[132] Haldane also pointed out that trade unions had rendered valuable services to their members,[133] even though he and Sheldon were against sectional interests at the expense of community service. Urwick brought the role of trade unions into his discussion by arguing that since the trade unions' share in industrial responsibility was becoming more definite, they should adopt affirmative policy towards craftsmanship, which he saw as a supreme test of labour's ability to assume industrial control.[134] Of the corporate bodies, the National Institute of Industrial Psychology made a point of considering the views of trade unions and of seeking their co-operation towards its investigations. Two reasons account for this greater attention in Britain towards trade unions. First, it will be remembered that Britain was taking the 'middle path' between scientific management and psychology and trade-union leaders had to be sought out and convinced that the motion study inherent in industrial psychology had a different objective from American scientific management.

Second, British trade unions were more powerful after the First World War than American trade unions. British unions had been active from the early nineteenth century, whereas real unionism in the United

131. See J. Child, *British Management Thought*, p. 94. Child has argued that British management thinkers also ignored the role of trade unions in the 1930s, when the British trade union movement became less active after its period of rapid growth following the First World War. Certainly, more attention was given to the role of trade unions in Britain in the early 1920s than in the 1930s, but there is evidence, none the less, to suggest that British corporate bodies, such as the National Institute of Industrial Psychology, took trade union attitudes into account in their work, which extended into the 1930s. See H. J. Welch and C. S. Myers, *Ten Years of Industrial Psychology*, pp. 1–11, 55–75.
132. O. Sheldon, *Philosophy of Management*, pp. 186–92.
133. R. B. Haldane, 'An organized Civil Service', op. cit., 9.
134. L. Urwick, 'Experimental psychology', op. cit., p. 31.

States was kept at bay by a form of 'company unionism'. American employers encouraged 'company unionism' because it gave little power to the union bodies but simply provided cheap, friendly benefits. It was not until the 'New Deal' that 'company unionism' was overthrown in the United States and, although some real unionism had existed earlier, it was powerful only in a few industries and mostly among skilled workers. Therefore, a large number of workers within the great American industries of steel, cars, oil and others were not a part of a proper trade union until the late 1930s, which partly explains why trade unionism was excluded from the Hawthorne conclusions.[135]

Certain criticisms of the British and American developments into human well-being must now be discussed. Child (1969) has summarised these criticisms[136] which include the charge that the British developments conceived the factory as a psycho-therapeutic clinic rather than as a producer of economic goods at economic costs. It is true that the ethical ideals underlying the British Philosophy of Administration weighed in favour of communal service and the happiness and well-being of the worker, but the economics of production were not overlooked. From the worker's side, Sheldon pointed out that service to the community would work only if it was regarded as a *mutual* service to be rendered by both management and labour. For example, he argued that labour should not try to determine its own wages, for if it insisted on a wage disproportionate to the earnings of the industry, it might ruin the community.[137] From the side of management, the provision of amenities for the worker's well-being and happiness were costly, as Seebohm Rowntree acknowledged, but he believed that in the long run they would not increase the cost of production, since they would reduce labour unrest, including strikes, and lead to greater output.[138] Questions of economics were taken into account, therefore, but the intention was to balance the stress on material rewards with ethical and psychological factors.

Another criticism allied to the first was that human relations in general was a form of 'implied paternalism'. It is unlikely, because of the underlying ethical and Christian motivation, that the British efforts at individual welfare were either 'paternalistic' or a substitute for real

---

135. See G. D. H. Cole, *British Trade Unionism Today*, pp. 29–129, 527–32.
136. J. Child, *British Management Thought*, pp. 151–5. See also H. A. Landsberger, *Hawthorne Revisited: Management and the Worker, its Critics, and Developments in Human Relations in Industry* (Ithaca, New York) 1958. Third printing 1968.
137. O. Sheldon, *Philosophy of Management*, p. 161.
138. B. S. Rowntree, *Human Factor in Business*, pp. 172–3.

workers' control. Rowntree, for example, argued:

> The public conscience, powerfully stimulated by the trade union movement, is demanding that working conditions shall be humanised. This does not mean coddling the workers, or adopting a paternal attitude towards them. That would be almost as strongly resented by every worker of independent spirit as was the callous indifference displayed by the average employer in the early part of the nineteenth century. But though the workers refuse to be treated with benevolent paternalism, they demand that industry shall be so organised that proper consideration shall be given to their individual welfare.[139]

The British trade union movement grew quickly after the First World War[140] and there is evidence that the ethical ideals constituting the British Philosophy of Administration were *genuine* attempts to come to terms with this growing force. What is more likely than 'paternalism' is that there was some gulf between the social backgrounds of the contributors to the British Philosophy of Administration and the main stream of civil servants and industrial workers. Wallas, Sheldon and Urwick had received their higher education at Oxford University, while Haldane had benefited from a university education in Germany and Edinburgh. They approached ethical idealism from the experience of their educational backgrounds and, although they wished to see more workers receiving a good education, it was easier to *recommend* that the subordinate employee in his turn should serve the State, or community, than for the employee to *make* the sacrifices involved. But a possible gulf in education does not render the ethical idealism paternalistic nor does it suggest a type of 'social skill' incurring the manipulation of mass psychology, a criticism made of Mayo and his school. While the first two criticisms appear invalid, there is truth in a third criticism that Britain has been too eager to build on the results of the Hawthorne research, which took place in an American social setting. For, although there were many similar conclusions regarding human relations, it has been seen that there were also important differences. Therefore the third criticism is just, but the adoption of the American doctrine is understandable in view of the fragmentation of the British Philosophy of Administration.

The second part of the conclusion presents some general observations concerning the ethical idealism underlying the British Philosophy of Administration. It is clear that in the period after the

139. Ibid., pp. 171–2.
140. For an account of the reasons for the growth of the British trade-union movement immediately after the First World War, and its reduction again from the mid 1920s, see G. D. H. Cole, 'Trade Unions: United Kingdom and Irish Free State', *Encyclopaedia of the Social Sciences*, Vol. XV, 1935, pp. 7–12.

First World War, attempts at 'reconstruction' in Britain were not limited strictly to the Ministry of Reconstruction or the Haldane Committee's framework for the reorganisation of the Civil Service. Reconstruction was both a scientific and an ethical process; it related to organisational *structure* and to human *conduct*. It combined administrative thought about the formal organisation with concern for the informal organisation or social interaction in the sphere of work. This combination of scientific principles with ethical idealism led to a different concept of efficiency from that prevailing in the United States for most of the period 1900–39. In Britain, the Civil Service and industry were encouraged by pioneers of the British Philosophy of Administration to relate organisational goals to the attainment of virtue, excellence and the good life, as well as to efficient output and administration. The result was that efficiency assumed not a *quantitative* but a *qualitative* character, which was admired in the United States by academics such as White[141] and Dimock. For example, in 1936 Dimock observed:

> Efficiency is a matter of quality, and hence quantitative and mechanical methods of measurements must perforce be far from complete. Morale and satisfaction can be felt and enjoyed, but few people think seriously of attempting to codify or meter them. Efficiency, like happiness, is subtle. This qualitative view of the matter has been forcefully expounded by the late Lord Haldane. At the peak of his administrative career he observed that public service's 'real purpose must be the defined one of rendering the highest amount practicable of service to the state, and service of the highest quality'. Efficiency, he said, is the product of 'strong motive'.[142]

The qualitative concept of efficiency went hand-in-hand with an understanding of the organisation as a *living* phenomenon rather than a *mechanical* entity as inherent in the quantitative concept. Even Urwick, who has been linked by many later administrative thinkers exclusively with scientific and technical aspects of organisations, was concerned with the human or what he termed the 'dynamic' element.[143]

Another general observation relates to the forward-looking nature of the British Philosophy of Administration. By taking the 'middle path' which united the science of administration with ethical idealism and psycho-sociological factors, contributors to the British Philosophy of Administration, and the corporate bodies, promoted views

141. White drew attention to Sheldon's statement that industry cannot be rendered efficient until it is recognised as being primarily human. L. D. White, *Introduction to the Study of Public Administration* (New York) 1926 p. 206.
142. M. E. Dimock, 'Criteria and objectives of public administration', op. cit., p. 122.
143. L. Urwick, *Management of Tomorrow* (London) 1933, p. 23.

commonly associated in the United States with the late 1930s and beyond. For example, Stamp's writing on equilibrium was noted by C. I. Barnard (1938), who discussed the equilibrium of organisations in relation to their environment. Similarly, the views of Wallas, Urwick and Stamp regarding job satisfaction, such as the need to satisfy the employee's desire for self-respect and pride in craftsmanship, were advanced well ahead of the ideas on 'human motivation theory' expressed in the United States by Maslow (1943), Argyris (1957) and McGregor (1960).[144] However, the fragmented nature of the British Philosophy of Administration served to diminish the ongoing influence of the British doctrine and this fragmentation is now discussed.

The ethical ideals underlying the British Philosophy of Administration were dispersed at both the written and the practical levels. Haldane and Urwick wrote in article form only on this subject. Wallas, Sheldon and Stamp, on the other hand, documented their ethical idealism in book form, but they dealt at length with society, or the community at large, so that their administrative thought became fragmented. At the practical level, the conclusions of the several corporate bodies – the Ministry of Munitions, the Industrial Fatigue Research Board and the National Institute of Industrial Psychology – have remained largely distributed in a quantity of annual, and specialised, reports. Today, these reports are mainly a collection of individual pamphlets, instead of being a co-ordinated body of thought as in the case of the Hawthorne findings.

Finally, the gulf between the *ideal* and the *actual* must be discussed. Despite ethical ideals put forward within the British Philosophy of Administration, some gulf is inevitable between idealism and practice. In other words, to what extent did the Civil Service and industry adopt the goals of virtue, excellence and the good life as well as provisions for human relations? Certain practices have been noted already: the Rowntree 'model' factory and the example set by other Quaker industries; an increase in welfare facilities during the First World War; a wide number of investigations into the happiness and well-being of the worker and mechanisms for worker participation in both the Civil Service and industry. Other examples include a reappraisal of the general education system in an attempt to recruit into the Civil Service the kind of excellence Haldane envisaged. This reappraisal was carried out by the MacDonnell Royal Commission (1912–15) and, because of

144. A. H. Maslow, 'Theory of human motivation', op. cit., C. Argyris, *Personality and Organization*, and D. McGregor, *Human Side of Enterprise*.

the war, it was continued by the Tomlin Royal Commission (1929–31).[145] However, Haldane's ideal of equal opportunity in education leading to a broader basis of recruitment to the higher Civil Service was not introduced until the 1944 Education Act. Lastly, monotony in the Civil Service was seen to be a problem by the Tomlin Royal Commission and the mechanical duties performed by the lowest class – then 'the writing assistant class' were revised. This class was given more advanced clerical duties to make the day less monotonous and to provide an avenue for promotion.[146] Some progress, then, was made in the direction of translating ideals into practice, but idealism by its very nature remains to an extent in the realm of aspirations.

145. *Royal Commission on the Civil Service, Fourth Report of the Commissioners*, and *Report of the Royal Commission on the Civil Service 1929-31* (London) 1931.
146. *Report of the Royal Commission on the Civil Service 1929-31*, pp. 18–19.

Chapter 5

Bureaucracy
and the British Philosophy
of Administration

'Nobody is likely to deny that the necessities and emergencies of the Great War afforded a signal opportunity for departmental legislation and produced an enormous expansion in the annual output of rules, orders, and regulations. But the encroachments of bureaucracy began well before the war, and assuredly they have survived it'[1]

> The Rt. Hon. Lord Hewart of Bury

'... the civil servant is the product of the Civil Service in the sense that it is only by adapting himself to the rigid requirements of the system that he can hope to make headway'.[2]

> Sir S. Demetriadi

The main purpose of this book has been to delineate the doctrines of the British Philosophy of Administration 1900–39. However, within this period, Britain faced a mounting problem of 'bureaucracy' and this problem became entwined with the British doctrines. In this chapter, we discuss the several ways in which bureaucracy was relevant to the British Philosophy of Administration.

During the early twentieth century, the United States experienced the growth of an 'efficiency' drive. So widespread and pronounced was the emphasis on efficiency that the term 'craze' has been used to describe this phenomenon.[3] Efficiency became a goal stemming from, and attached to, the American administrative doctrines based on a science of administration.[4]

By contrast, the dominant concern in Britain in this period was not so much the question of 'efficiency' as of 'bureaucracy'. The British problem of bureaucracy had two aspects which related to the *power of officials* (with the emphasis on power) and *rule of the bureau*[5] (with the

1. The Rt. Hon. Lord Hewart of Bury, *The New Despotism* (London) 1929, p. 96.
2. Sir S. Demetriadi, *Inside a Government Office* (London) 1921, p. 21.
3. S. Haber, *Efficiency and Uplift* (Chicago) 1964, p. ix.
4. See Ch. 1, p. 6.
5. We have coined the phrase *rule of the bureau* used by C. J. Friedrich and T. Cole in the 1930s, because it is a neat expression to characterise the disadvantages of red-tape and established routine in administration. C. J. Friedrich and T. Cole, *Responsible Bureaucracy: A Study of the Swiss Civil Service* (Cambridge, Mass.) 1932, p. 1.

emphasis on red-tape). Allegations about the *power of officials* were lodged by constitutional experts and lawyers – notable among whom was Lord Hewart, then the Lord Chief Justice of England. Hewart set out his criticisms in a controversial treatise, in which he likened executive power to despotism. Accompanying this first form of criticism were the charges of *rule of the bureau*. In this instance, the critics were businessmen who had returned to their commercial environment after temporary employment in the British Civil Service during the First World War and drew unfavourable comparisons between public and business administration. The most renowned of the business critics was Sir Stephen Demetriadi, who wrote two books on the subject of rigidity in the Civil Service and other administrative faults commonly associated with red-tape. This twofold problem of bureaucracy assumed the proportions of a national outcry in Britain, with critics challenging the power of public officials and the swathes of red-tape which engulfed Civil Service administration. This concern about bureaucracy was relevant to the British Philosophy of Administration in three ways, which are now identified.

Firstly, there was a link between the first form of bureaucracy – *power of officials* – and the individuality of contributors to the British Philosophy of Administration. In Chapter 1, we suggested that the pioneers of the British Philosophy of Administration – and the radical reformers Sidney and Beatrice Webb and Harold Laski – possessed some highly individualistic views about administration as well as sharing some common opinions and interests.[6] Bureaucracy as *power of officials* was an area of administrative thought which demonstrated these different opinions. Haldane and Beveridge tended to *underrate* the danger of power by officials, being content to describe the fusion of policy-making and administration without envisaging in detail any adverse consequences of the public administrator's growing legislative and judicial powers. Conversely, the radical reformers Sidney and Beatrice Webb went to the other extreme of *overrating* the risk of tyranny by officials and proposing a complicated system of checks and balances against this danger.[7] Within the British Philosophy of Administration, Josiah Stamp's views were the most astute, since he was aware of both dangers and merits concerning the increased *power of officials*. Similarly, the radical reformer Harold Laski took a helpful approach to the subject. He was less extreme than the Webbs regarding the risk of tyranny but, in several works, he indicated possible dangers

6. See Ch. 1, p. 31.
7. See Ch. 2, pp. 37–54.

of the growing *power of officials*.[8] Indeed, Laski was appointed a member of the Committee on Ministers' Powers which was set up to investigate the allegations of executive power. Thus, on the question of bureaucracy as *power of officials*, the individuality of contributors to the British Philosophy of Administration – and the radical reformers – was to the fore.

Secondly, it has been argued in previous chapters that fragmentation was a major weakness of the British doctrines. This fragmentation, coupled with the slow, partial implementation of the Haldane Report, had implications for the second form of bureaucracy – *rule of the bureau*. The business critics were scornful about delays and confusion in government departments and the complicated written communi-cations issued by civil servants. These inadequacies of public administration received serious study by several contributors to the British Philosophy of Administration including Graham Wallas, Richard Haldane, William Beveridge and Josiah Stamp. Accordingly, common thought rather than individuality prevailed among these administrative pioneers towards the problem of red-tape.[9] In fact, many of the criticisms lodged by businessmen could have been avoided if the British Philosophy of Administration had been less fragmented and implemented more extensively into the Civil Service by the early 1920s, particularly the scientific principles of 'organisation' and 'communication'. Hence, the way in which bureaucracy as *rule of the bureau* was relevant to the British Philosophy of Administration derived from the fragmented nature of the doctrines.

Thirdly, the British Philosophy of Administration was forward-looking in many respects, but another of its limitations was the neglect of theory by its pioneers. Stamp, for example, offered valuable information about the functions of bureaucracy in the case of both the *power of officials* and *rule of the bureau*. But he failed to relate his views to previous theories, such as Weber's 'ideal' type, and concentrated instead on the practical aspects of bureaucracy prevalent in Britain.[10] Once the British problem had subsided, Stamp's views

8. H. J. Laski's works include *Authority in the Modern State* (New Haven, Conn.) 1919; *A Grammar of Politics* (London) 1925. Reprinted edn 1926; 'The growth of administrative discretion', *Journal of Public Administration* Vol. I, 1923, 92–100 and 'Bureaucracy', *Encyclopaedia of the Social Sciences*, Vol. III, 1930, 70–4.

9. The possible exception to this common thought was Stamp's reference to advantages, as well as disadvantages, of red-tape. See this chapter pp. 221–3.

10. Stamp made brief reference to Greek city states but, on the whole, he restricted his thinking about bureaucracy to the British problem. See J. Stamp, 'The contrast between the administration of business and public affairs', *Journal of Public Administration*, Vol. I, 1923, 158–71, and 'Recent tendencies towards the devolution of legislative functions to the administration', *Journal of Public Administration*, Vol. II, 1924, 23–38.

were lost from sight. Even Haldane, who was a German scholar, made no reference to Weber's work. This is surprising, since in the United States Friedrich and Cole (1932) approached their study of bureaucracy in the Swiss Civil Service by first discussing the characteristics listed by Weber.[11] Therefore, the British problem produced *empirical* evidence about the functions and dysfunctions[12] of bureaucracy, but none of the contributors to the British Philosophy of Administration constructed any *theoretical* framework to delimit the subject of bureaucracy or to facilitate its future study.[13] Accordingly, the subject is associated today with scholars such as M. Weber (1922), C. J. Friedrich (1932 and 1952), R. K. Merton (1936 and 1952), A. W. Gouldner (1952), M. Crozier (1964), P. Self (1965), A. Downs (1967), H. Parris (1969) and M. Albrow (1970),[14] while the British contributions made earlier this century have been overlooked. This chapter seeks to portray the main features of the British bureaucracy problem, from the viewpoint of these three ways in which it was relevant to the British Philosophy of Administration.

To begin, however, the twofold problem of bureaucracy must be defined. We have indicated that each form of bureaucracy had its own professional following, with constitutional and legal experts complain-

11. Friedrich and Cole were impressed by Weber's writing and decided to create a new description of bureaucracy incorporating some of his ideas. Their intention was to avoid attaching value judgments to bureaucracy in terms of pejorative or praiseworthy characteristics and instead they sought to devise a measure to assess the validity of such value judgments. They applied their measure to the Swiss Civil Service, see C. J. Friedrich and T. Cole, *Responsible Bureaucracy*. Later Friedrich was more critical of Weber's study of bureaucracy, see C. J. Friedrich, 'Some observations on Weber's analysis of bureaucracy', in *Reader in Bureaucracy*, ed. by R. K. Merton et al. (New York) 1952, pp. 27–33.

12. The term 'dysfunctions' was established by the American scholar R. K. Merton to describe the imperfections of bureaucracy. See R. K. Merton, 'Bureaucratic structure and personality', in *Reader in Bureaucracy*, p. 364. Although the words 'defects' or 'evils' were used in Britain between 1900 and 1939, rather than 'dysfunctions', we adopt the latter term because of its wide use today.

13. Laski came nearest to providing a theoretical framework for the study of bureaucracy, see H. J. Laski, 'Bureaucracy', op. cit. In this essay, he included the origin and characteristics of bureaucracy and, unlike contributors to the British Philosophy of Administration, Laski cited Weber's work in his bibliography. However, his definition of bureaucracy was confusing, as we shall see shortly.

14. See M. Weber, *Wirtschaft und Gesellschaft* (Grundriss der Sozialökonomik) Vols. i–ix (Tubingen) 1914–29, Vol. iii, 1922; C. J. Friedrich and T. Cole, *Responsible Bureaucracy*, and C. J. Friedrich, 'Some observations', op. cit.; R. K. Merton, 'The unanticipated consequences of purposive social action' *American Sociological Review*, Vol. 1, 1936, 894–904 and *Reader in Bureaucracy*; A. W. Gouldner, *Patterns of Industrial Bureaucracy* (Glencoe, Illinois) 1954; M. Crozier, *The Bureaucratic Phenomenon* (Chicago) 1964; P. Self, *Bureaucracy or Management?* (London) 1965; A. Downs, *Inside Bureaucracy* (Boston, Mass.) 1967; H. Parris, *Constitutional Bureaucracy* (London) 1969; and M. Albrow, *Bureaucracy* (London) 1970.

ing about the *power of officials* and businessmen deriding *rule of the bureau*. Because these two sets of criticisms were delivered almost simultaneously in the interwar period, they became blurred into a single charge of 'bureaucracy'. Thus, the term assumed ambiguity.[15] Despite his familiarity with the problem, Harold Laski epitomised this ambiguity by combining the *two* separate criticisms into *one* definition:

> Bureaucracy is the term usually applied to a system of government the control of which is so completely in the hands of officials that their power jeopardizes the liberties of ordinary citizens. The characteristics of such a regime are a passion for routine in administration, and sacrifice of flexibility to rule, delay in the making of decisions and a refusal to embark upon experiment. In extreme cases the members of a bureaucracy may become a hereditary caste manipulating government to their own advantage.[16]

In the United States, Laski's definition puzzled Friedrich and Cole, who questioned why he laid stress on the *power of officials* when much of his essay related to fixed rules and established routine in administration. Laski had in mind, of course, the accusations emanating from British constitutional and legal experts, such as Hewart, about power by officials. But, by amalgamating this form of bureaucracy with the disadvantages of red-tape, he did not meet the approval of Friedrich and Cole. They preferred to emphasise bureaucracy as *rule of the bureau*,[17] which is understandable when the United States was not suffering from the same allegations of the misuse of power by officials, despite some increase in the discretionary powers of federal civil servants.[18]

We propose that it is less confusing – and more applicable to the British problem – to recognise two definitions of bureaucracy[19]

15. This ambiguity is evident from the writing of the Rt. Hon. Sir J. Anderson, 'Bureaucracy', *Public Administration*, Vol. VII, 1923,3. and C. J. Friedrich and T. Cole, *Responsible Bureaucracy*, p. 1.
16. H. J. Laski, 'Bureaucracy', op. cit., 70.
17. Although Friedrich and Cole tried to avoid making value judgments about bureaucracy they, nevertheless, began their study by quoting Laski's definition. They criticised his definition, arguing that normally emphasis was placed on *rule of the bureau* and not on the *power of officials*. See C. J. Friedrich and T. Cole, *Responsible Bureaucracy*, p. 1.
18. The United States was not suffering from allegations of bureaucracy as *power of officials* at this time partly because Acts of Congress put more detail into legislation, which limited the discretion of administrators. See J. Willis, *The Parliamentary Powers of English Government Departments* (Cambridge, Mass.) 1933, p. 8.
19. Other definitions of bureaucracy exist. For example, P. Self, *Bureaucracy or Management?*, p. 7 adopted a neutral definition of bureaucracy concerned with large-scale organisation. Later, M. Albrow recognised seven definitions of bureaucracy,

representing the two forms of criticism manifest in Britain. The first definition of *power of officials* is taken from Hewart's book *The New Despotism*. Hewart insisted that he was not attacking the British Civil Service itself but the mischiefs of bureaucracy or 'the new despotism' which he defined as:

> ... a persistent and well-contrived system, intended to produce, and in practice producing, a despotic power which at one and the same time places Government departments above the Sovereignty of Parliament and beyond the jurisdiction of the Courts. If it appears that this system springs from and depends upon a deep-seated official conviction ... that this . . . is the best and most scientific way of ruling the country, the consequences, unless they are checked, must be in the highest degree formidable.[20]

This definition of the *power of officials* can be expanded by reference to Hewart's 'creed' of the ardent bureaucrat. The creed summarises the faith of the new despot and is composed of nine points, which may be regarded as the characteristics of bureaucracy:

1. The Business of the Executive is to govern.
2. The only persons fit to govern are experts.
3. The experts in the art of government are the permanent officials, who, exhibiting an ancient and too much neglected virtue 'think themselves worthy of great things, being worthy'.
4. But the expert must deal with things as they are. The 'foursquare man' makes the best of the circumstances in which he finds himself.
5. Two main obstacles hamper the beneficent work of the expert. One is the Sovereignty of Parliament, and the other is the Rule of Law.
6. A kind of fetish-worship, prevalent among an ignorant public, prevents the destruction of these obstacles. The expert, therefore, must make use of the first in order to frustrate the second.
7. To this end let him, under Parliamentary forms, clothe himself with despotic power, and then, because the forms are Parliamentary, defy the Law Courts.
8. This course will prove tolerably simple if he can:

   (a) get legislation passed in skeleton form;
   (b) fill up the gaps with his own rules, orders, and regulations;
   (c) make it difficult or impossible for Parliament to check the said rules, orders and regulations;
   (d) secure for them the force of statute;
   (e) make his own decision final;
   (f) arrange that the fact of his decision shall be conclusive proof of its legality;

including those relating to power; red-tape and large-scale organisation. See M. Albrow, *Bureaucracy*, pp. 84–105.
20. Lord Hewart of Bury, *New Despotism*, p. 14.

     (g) take power to modify the provisions of statutes and

     (h) prevent and avoid any sort of appeal to a Court of Law.'

  9. If the expert can get rid of the Lord Chancellor, reduce the judges to a branch of the Civil Service, compel them to give opinions beforehand on hypothetical cases, and appoint them himself through a business man to be called 'Minister of Justice',[21] the coping-stone will be laid and the music will be the fuller.[22]

The second definition of bureaucracy as *rule of the bureau* is extracted from Demetriadi's criticism of the Civil Service. He did not use the word 'bureaucracy', but his allegations were conceived in these terms. Accordingly, bureaucracy is:

> . . . a habit of mind which is so general amongst officials as to constitute a part of the system . . . the official becomes so accustomed to the ways of the system that he ceases to realise that the system itself is the means and not the end. It is probably to this fact that we can trace the amazing complications which invariably envelop the efforts of the official mind.'[23]

The concept of *rule of the bureau* cannot be enlarged by a 'creed', since Demetriadi did not offer one. However, he attributed numerous bad habits to the public official and to the Civil Service 'system'. From his descriptions, seven characteristics of the bureaucratic system can be isolated:

1. The system fulfils its own ends almost mechanically and it is only by adapting to its rigid requirements that the civil servant can make progress.
2. The system subjects the Minister to precedent. If he tries to reform his department, he risks something akin to civil war, because the permanent officials are more concerned with the system than with the success or failure of the Minister, who is temporary.
3. The system renders personal responsibility impossible due to the fact that many minds are involved in Civil Service work.
4. Paperwork is of prime importance to the system.

21. Hewart was attacking the idea of a Ministry of Justice, which was a recommendation of the Haldane Committee (1918) and a personal ambition of Haldane. See Ch. 3, p. 103. As Lord Chief Justice of England, Hewart was opposed to a Minister of Justice on the grounds that this office would be on the same plane as other political posts in the government (unlike the special judicial nature of the Lord Chancellor's Office) and open to general competition among rising politicians. His criticism of the public official, therefore, contained a genuine fear of lay control over the judiciary by civil servants under a new Minister of Justice. See Lord Hewart of Bury, op. cit., pp. 104–10.
22. Ibid., pp. 20–1.
23. Sir S. Demetriadi, *Inside a Government Office*, p. 47.

5. The system operates in a vacuum without concern for the changing environment outside it.
6. The system encourages lack of competition within departments but fierce competition between departments.
7. The system is extremely complicated.[24]

Two distinct complaints about the Civil Service – of depotism and red-tape – have been defined. In both cases, the stress was upon detrimental characteristics, so discrediting the word 'bureaucracy'.[25] The three ways in which this problem of bureaucracy was linked to the British Philosophy of Administration will now be elaborated.

1. The individuality of contributors to the British Philosophy of Administration and its relevance to bureaucracy

We have argued that the individuality of contributors to the British Philosophy of Administration had significance for the first form of bureaucracy – *power of officials*. Chapter 2 of this book has outlined the British Philosophy of Administration doctrine of a fusion between policy-making and administration. In connection with this doctrine, Haldane and Beveridge described the realistic fusion of constitutional and policy-making matters with administration, but they saw little danger in the *power of officials*. Indeed, the Haldane Committee proposed further structural arrangements in the Civil Service to assist public administrators in their policy-making tasks. By contrast, the radical reformers Sidney and Beatrice Webb, who took an institutional approach to the study of government, devised a set of new institutions for the socialist commonwealth of Great Britain which incorporated several precautions against tyranny by officials.[26] Although the Webb's

24. Ibid., pp. 21–54.
25. 'Bureaucracy' had been used earlier in the pejorative sense, see M. Albrow, *Bureaucracy*, pp. 16–32. However, in Britain between 1900 and 1939, the word was discredited with renewed vigour.
26. Four specific precautions against executive power can be discerned from the Webbs' proposals for the socialist commonwealth of Great Britain. First, there was the division of powers between two Parliaments and their executives–the Political Parliament and its Executive and the Social Parliament and its Executive. Second, within the Social Executive, duplicate departments were envisaged – one of control and one of administration – relating to each major function of government. Third, within the Social Executive, detailed publicity to each nationalised industry or service was scheduled. Finally, in both Parliaments, a series of standing committees to oversee public administration was intended. S. and B. Webb, *A Constitution for the Socialist Commonwealth of Great Britain* (London) 1920, pp. 97–202. See also Ch. 2, pp. 45–54.

plan sought to expand the civil servant's role by nationalising more industries and services, they were suspicious about the *power of officials*. The bureaucracy problem was centred between these two extremes of insufficient attention being paid by Haldane and Beveridge to possible dangers in the exercise of power by officials and the Webbs' scheme to alter radically the institutions of British government. The problem arose because Hewart and other constitutional and legal experts discerned potential abuses in the exercise of power by officials.[27] But, in many cases, they voiced these potential abuses as actual abuses of power – power which they claimed was being delegated to civil servants on an alarming scale.

The critics, therefore, emphasised the *devolutionary* causes of the *power of officials*. Josiah Stamp linked the British Philosophy of Administration to this problem by providing an alternative explanation for executive power, which focused on *evolutionary* causes. By concentrating on evolution instead of devolution,[28] he threw a creditable light on bureaucracy, which mitigated its evils. Thus, the individuality of contributors to the British Philosophy of Administration is evident as much from the omission of the problem of the *power of officials* by Haldane and Beveridge as from Stamp's evolutionary stand. This section will contrast the devolutionary causes of bureaucracy cited by the critics with Stamp's evolutionary causes.

We begin by presenting the devolutionary causes of bureaucracy as *power of officials*. Hewart was the most vociferous of the critics of the *power of officials*, but he did not originate the criticisms. However, his accusations created such consternation that the Committee on Ministers' Powers was set up in 1929[29] to review the charges. One of the

27. The constitutional and legal experts included A. V. Dicey, 'The development of administrative law in England', *Law Quarterly Review* Vol. XXXI, 1915, 148–53; C. T. Carr, *Delegated Legislation* (London) 1921; C. K. Allen, *Law in the Making* (London) 1927 and Lord Hewart of Bury, *New Despotism*. See *Committee on Ministers' Powers Report* (London) 1932. Reprinted edn 1972, pp. 1–2.

28. No clear distinction was made at this time between 'devolution', 'delegation' and 'decentralisation'. Stamp argued about the *power of officials*: 'We may come to think of the problem as one of evolution rather than devolution . . . As to "devolution" – well, one finds "delegation" used as a synonymous alternative, and I do not waste time drawing you a subtle distinction.' J. Stamp, 'Recent tendencies', op. cit., 23–4.

29. The Committee (1929–32) was composed of seventeen members, including two civil servants of distinction – Sir W. Fisher and Sir J. Anderson; three professors including H. J. Laski and numerous King's Counsel and politicians. See R. V. Vernon and N. Mansergh *Advisory Bodies: A Study of their Uses in Relation to Central Government, 1919–1939* (London) 1940, p. 45. The Chairman of the Committee was originally the Rt. Hon. the Earl of Donoughmore, K. P., but he resigned in April 1931 for reasons of ill-health and his place was taken by the Rt. Hon. Sir Leslie Scott, K. C. See *Committee on Ministers' Powers Report*, pp. v–1.

Committee's initial tasks was to summarise the critics' views, which fell into two categories relating to the legislative and judicial *power of officials*.[30] These categories corresponded to the principal causes of bureaucracy – namely, the subordination of Parliament and the evasion of the courts of law. Since Hewart was a primary critic, his views are selected as typifying these devolutionary causes of bureaucracy.

The subordination of Parliament as a cause of the power of officials

Hewart insisted that Parliament was being outmanoeuvred by the process of delegated legislation – a process which increased the legislative *power of officials*. The process of delegated legislation took three main forms. First, Parliament tended to pass Acts expressing its intention in general terms only, leaving the implementation of that intention to be settled by rules and regulations made by the executive department charged with its supervision. Second, departments were often given the power to make orders having the force of law with reference to the subject-matter of the statute. Finally, in some cases, departments were empowered, within limits, to repeal or vary the provisions of the Act conferring the powers. The Rating and Valuation Act, 1925, was, in Hewart's view, the crucial proof of bureaucracy because it granted comprehensive powers to the Minister to 'do any thing' he thought expedient for the purpose named and empowered him also to make orders which 'may modify the provisions' of the Act of Parliament itself. Although such powers were often granted to the Minister, Hewart regarded this as only an expression meaning that departmental officials would be responsible for exercising the powers and he was against regulations having the force of statute being made by civil servants, under conditions which gave little safeguard against abuse.

Safeguards against abuse of power by officials were intended to exist, but Hewart found weaknesses in them. One safeguard was the provision inserted into some statutes conferring legislative powers, that before the powers can be exercised, interested persons should be given the

30. The Committee's terms of reference were: '... to consider the powers exercised by or under the direction of (or by persons or bodies appointed especially by) Ministers of the Crown by way of (a) delegated legislation and (b) judicial or quasi-judicial decision, and to report what safeguards are desirable or necessary to secure the constitutional principles of the sovereignty of Parliament and the supremacy of the Law'.
Committee on Ministers' Powers Report, pp. 1–4.

opportunity to object. Section I of the Rules Publication Act, 1893, laid down, for example, that advance publication of proposals to make statutory rules should be published in the *London Gazette*. However, Hewart observed six loopholes in section I which rendered its provisions inadequate, such as: 'First, they apply only to statutory rules made in pursuance of an Act which directs that they are to be laid before Parliament, and it is only in a comparatively small number of the statutes giving power to make statutory rules that there is any such direction.'[31]

Much inaccuracy abounded, in Hewart's view, concerning safeguards for delegated legislation and he maintained that this trend was favoured by the proponents of the new despotism. Furthermore, many statutes were framed in obscure language, which showed itself in ill-considered amendments and ambiguous terminology. Hewart's argument was that civil servants were deliberately attempting to make regulations behind the back of Parliament, which came into force without the knowledge or assent of Parliament. This demand for power was facilitated by the inadequate safeguards attached to delegated legislative powers and by the unintelligible language of delegated legislation.[32]

Evasion of the courts of law as a cause of the power of officials

Hewart discussed the growing judicial *power of officials* under the nomenclature of 'administrative lawlessness', which denoted the civil servant's evasion of the courts of law and constituted the second cause of bureaucracy. The Rule of Law had been a major feature of the British constitution since the eleventh century and it means that the predominant basis of justice is law and not arbitrary power. Under the system of the Rule of Law all citizens, including civil servants, are equal before the ordinary law of the land which is administered by the normal courts. Accordingly, British civil servants are subject to the common law and can be brought before the courts in the same way as any other citizen. Hewart contrasted this British system with continental *droit administratif* (Administrative law) whereby the rights and obligations of all public servants are governed by special rules which are administered by special tribunals. In contrast to the British system, the ordinary courts of justice have no jurisdiction over disputes affecting the government or its servants, since they are dealt with by administrative courts, such as the Conseil d'Etat in France. *Droit*

31. Lord Hewart of Bury, *New Despotism*, p. 84.
32. Ibid., pp. 1–164.

administratif differs, then, from the ordinary law of a country, but it is based none the less on legal principles and it forms a recognised branch of law, although one which Britain has never favoured. Hewart proposed that Britain was moving to a situation midway between the traditional Rule of Law and continental *droit administratif* – a trend which he termed 'administrative lawlessness'.

Administrative lawlessness had been developing in Britain, he claimed, because a large number of statutes had been conferring judicial and quasi-judicial powers on Ministers, or directly upon the departments of government, with the result that the courts of law which normally administer justice and protect the liberty of the citizen, were being bypassed. Instead of resting with the ordinary courts, the power to decide judicial questions was passing in many cases to Ministers and inevitably to public officials who were rarely bound by a particular course of procedure or rules of evidence. Hewart insisted that the Rule of Law in Britain was being replaced by a pseudo-form of continental *droit administratif*, which lacked the special rules and proper apparatus of the continental system. Indeed, the British trend amounted to no more than the exercise of lawless power by public officials.[33]

Hewart wrote passionately about administrative lawlessness, but he failed to refer to earlier, similar criticisms. For example, Dicey was one of the first this century to indicate the move in England towards a form of continental *droit administratif*. In an article of 1915[34], Dicey succinctly described the decline in the Rule of Law in the strict sense and its replacement by growing judicial and quasi-judicial powers in the hands of officials. He illustrated his argument with two cases involving the exercise of judicial powers by government departments, which were (1) the *Board of Education* v. *Rice* (1911) and (2) the *Local Government Board* v. *Arlidge* (1915). In the second case, the statute had conferred judicial powers on the government department without laying down any rule about how these powers should be exercised and, consequently, the department was not bound to follow the rules of procedure adopted by

33. Ibid., pp. 23–58.
34. A. V. Dicey, 'The development of administrative law in England' op. cit. See also A. V. Dicey, *Introduction to the Study of the Law of the Constitution* (London) 1885. Eighth edn 1915 and Ninth edn 1939, reprinted 1956. It is interesting to note Dicey's evolving views regarding the British constitution. In the early editions of his famous text, he identified the sovereignty of Parliament and the Rule of Law as fundamental principles of the British constitution. However, by 1915, in his article and in a lengthy introduction to the Eighth edn of his text, he referred to the decline in the Rule of Law and the growing trend for statutes to confer judicial and quasi-judicial powers on government departments. Hence, Dicey moved from a firm conviction about the constitutional principle of the Rule of Law in 1885 to a modified view about this principle by 1915.

the English courts.[35] From Dicey onwards, a series of warnings and criticisms about the growth of both legislative and judicial powers in the hands of officials had been stated,[36] but they culminated in Hewart's provocative attack.

In contrast to the critics' devolutionary arguments, Stamp's evolutionary causes of bureaucracy are now discussed. Several years before Hewart's overt claim of despotism, Stamp made it clear to the Institute of Public Administration that he was displeased about the sinister allegations of power by officials. Referring specifically to delegated legislation – or the official's legislative powers – he observed:

> On occasions when this subject is mentioned, we usually find it expressed as 'the *encroachment* of the administration upon legislative functions', or 'the *usurpation* of Parliamentary functions by the departments', or some such phrase . . . it behoves us to be up and doing, and to check this nefarious tendency before its momentum becomes too great for us, and it takes us to constitutional perdition. If you want to import into the matter still more definite implications, you will deal with it in the best style of a press stunt, and refer to it as 'the growing grip of bureaucracy'.[37]

35. Although Haldane did not write in detail about the *power of officials*, he did comment on the Arlidge case, arguing that ministerial responsibility was a check on administrative irregularities. Dicey, by contrast, considered ministerial responsibility to be a poor guarantee as compared with review by the courts. See A. V. Dicey, op. cit. Ninth edn, p. xci.

36. For example, besides the critics mentioned in this chapter, p. 206, *Public Administration* had carried a number of printed discussions about executive power, including the views of H. J. Laski and J. Stamp. W. Ivor Jennings, a specialist in English law at the University of London, made the following comment:
'Among the learned journals, *Public Administration* has naturally devoted the closest attention to the problem; see in particular the following: "Growth of Administrative Discretion", by H. J. Laski (April 1923); "Recent Tendencies towards the Devolution of Legislative Functions to the Administration", by Sir Josiah Stamp (January 1924); "The Appellate Jurisdiction of Central Government Departments", by F. H. C. Wiltshire (October 1924); "Appellate Jurisdiction", by I. G. Gibbon (October, 1924); "The Expert and the Layman", by Sir R. V. N. Hopkins (January, 1925); "The Principles of Regulation" by Garnham Roper (October, 1926); "The Principles of Regulation" by W. Tetley Stephenson (October, 1926); "Some Aspects of English Administrative Law", by K. B. Smellie (July, 1927); "The Powers of Public Departments to make Rules having the Force of Law", by I. G. Gibbon (October, 1927); "The Powers of Public Departments to make Rules having the Force of Law", by M. L. Gwyer (October, 1927); "The Powers of Public Departments to make Rules having the Force of Law", by Poul Anderson (October, 1927); "Legislative Powers of Public Authorities", by Harold Potter (January, 1928); "Local Inquiries", by E. H. Rhodes (January, 1928); "Bureaucracy", by the Rt. Hon. Sir John Anderson (January, 1929) . . . Most of these were published before the Lord Chief Justice's book, and none of them is quoted by him . . .'
See W. I. Jennings, 'The Report on Ministers' powers' *Public Administration*, Vol. X, 1932, 333.

37. J. Stamp, 'Recent tendencies', op. cit., 23.

To check this abusive tendency, Stamp suggested that the problem should be viewed in evolutionary rather than devolutionary terms. He identified two evolutionary causes of delegated legislation – the vast extension of State activities and the exceptional circumstances of the First World War. In discussing these evolutionary causes, he shifted emphasis away from the dysfunctions of bureaucracy to its functions.

The vast extension of State activities as a cause of the power of officials

In the nineteenth century, Stamp pointed out, the State had been concerned with preserving internal order and repelling the enemy from without. By the 1920s, this policeman image had been replaced by the State 'as nurse, doctor, chemist, and benefactor, guide, philosopher and friend from cradle to grave'.[38] These extensive and new functions meant that it was useful to delegate or devolve powers to administrators for the following reasons:

1. Local variety and detail,
2. Unknown future conditions,
3. Complex and technical affairs,
4. Urgency,
5. Political feeling.

In the first case, the variety and detail of legislation had become so great and less obvious to the legislator that he no longer had the time or the ability to deal with it adequately. Accordingly, delegation to local areas or individuals familiar with local knowledge and able to apply general rules is desirable, Stamp advised, particularly in local government affairs. Second, legislation may be passed but, because of the problem of an unknown future, changes may occur subsequent to legislation which require its alteration. For example, conditions may change completely and require a new attitude, or conditions may not change but they may be quite unexplored until the administrative machinery of a statute studies them closely. Third, the subject-matter of legislation is so complicated and technical that only experts can handle it and expert administrators are in a better position to deal with these details than Members of Parliament. Fourth, in some cases, immediate action may be needed and it might be inexpedient to summon Parliament, or if Parliament is sitting to interrupt its considerations of other matters. For example, it is more convenient in the case of an

38. Ibid., p. 25.

epidemic or outbreak of foot and mouth disease for an official body to issue orders under statutory powers, even if the action requires subsequent ratification.

Lastly, Stamp declared, it may be inadvisable to make details of administration part of the programme of party strife, for if a general principal had been carried by a majority of the House after strong opposition, precise instances of practical difficulty could rekindle the controversy and repeatedly raise all the heated arguments of the original debate. Consequently, the general principle might never get a fair chance of establishment if it is discredited on instances of application.

The exceptional circumstances of the First World War as a cause of the power of officials

Public officials had been acquiring extended powers prior to the First World War, Stamp confirmed. But the exceptional and emergency conditions of war meant that Parliament, faced with the main burden of war, had to delegate more powers to State departments than in normal circumstances, without reserving the power of confirmation or revision.[39] However, since the Armistice, modification of these powers had occurred with endeavours by Parliament to retain a check over them.[40]

Stamp sought to counter the critics' views of bureaucracy as an evil, arguing that the *power of officials* was an evolutionary trend caused by the twentieth-century desire for more government and the emergencies of war rather than coercive demands for power. Moreover, he considered that the development of delegated legislation could be continued to advantage, although he did not deny that it was open to abuse and required safeguards. Accordingly, Stamp suggested certain safeguards to ensure that the original intention of the legislating authority would be carried out continuously. For example, he urged that the limits within which the delegated power is to be exercised should be laid down.[41]

39. Stamp observed that the Defence of the Realm Act (D.O.R.A.) was one case of an Act which had widely increased the *power of officials* and this Act was quoted by many critics.
40. J. Stamp, 'Recent tendencies', op. cit.
41. In all, Stamp recommended five safeguards for the exercise of delegated legislative powers, taken from C. T. Carr's earlier work, *Delegated Legislation*.

Conclusion to the individuality of contributors to the British Philosophy of Administration and its relevance to bureaucracy

Before the individuality of contributors to the British Philosophy of Administration can be discussed fully in relation to bureaucracy as *power of officials*, it is appropriate to record the verdict of the Committee on Ministers' Powers. The Committee took lengthy written and oral evidence from a variety of sources[42] about the legislative and judicial powers of British civil servants. Regarding legislative powers exercised by officials, the Committee concluded, after reviewing the criticisms:

> Each of these criticisms is important, but they do not destroy the case for delegated legislation. Their true bearing is rather that there are dangers in the practice; that it is liable to abuse; and that safeguards are required. Nor do we think that either the published criticisms or the evidence we have received justifies an alarmist view of the constitutional situation. What the system lacks is coherence and uniformity in operation. Its defects, as we have sought to show, are the inevitable consequence of its haphazard *evolution* . . . For the most part the dangers are potential rather than actual; and the problem which the critics raise is essentially one of devising the best safeguards.[43]

Concerning judicial powers exercised by officials, the Committee agreed with the critics that the Rule of Law had declined and ought to be reinforced. Furthermore, the Committee disapproved of a system of *droit administratif* for England and rejected a detailed proposal for the adoption of a true system.[44] In several instances, therefore, the Committee concurred with the critics, but its findings failed to verify administrative lawlessness on the scale suggested by Hewart's new despotism.[45] The charges were found to be less threatening than the critics alleged and were caused, as Stamp had noted, by evolutionary trends rather than sinister demands for power.[46] Even though the

42. Having read Hewart's book, the Committee invited the Lord Chief Justice to give evidence, but his reply was that 'he had at present nothing further to add'. *Committee on Ministers' Powers Report*, p. 3.

43. *Committee on Ministers' Powers Report*, p. 54 (author's italics).

44. The proposal was put forward by Mr. W. A. Robson, then Barrister at Law and Lecturer in Industrial and Administrative Law at the London School of Economics and Political Science. Ibid., pp. 3, 110–12.

45. Ibid., pp. 6–7, 113–15.

46. However, Stamp's earlier recognition of the evolutionary causes of the *power of officials* differed from the Committee's verdict because he stated more emphatically the functions of the *power of officials*. By contrast, the Committee's Report left the impression, despite its conclusions, that delegated legislation was a necessary evil to be watched with misgiving. Owing to this negative impression, two members of the Committee, including Harold Laski, appended notes to the Report to eradicate the dysfunctional residue which lingered concerning the *power of officials*. See *Committee on Ministers' Powers Report*, pp. 137–8.

problem of bureaucracy was not as serious as the critics proclaimed, the Committee on Ministers' Powers agreed that safeguards were necessary to protect delegated legislative and judicial powers in the hands of officials. Among its recommendations to safeguard legislative powers, the Committee proposed that the Rules Publication Act, 1893, should be amended [47] and that procedures for delegated legislation should be standardised, so that ambiguous expressions like 'rule', 'order' and 'regulation' acquired a definite usage and understanding. Also, the Committee repeated Stamp's earlier proposal that precise limits of the law-making power conferred by Parliament on a Minister should be expressed by the statute conferring it in clear language. With respect to safeguarding judicial powers in the hands of officials, the Committee drew a distinction between judicial and quasi-judicial decisions, maintaining that the former should be entrusted to the ordinary courts of law and the latter to Ministers.[48]

The first conclusion concerns Stamp's individuality towards the problem of bureaucracy as *power of officials*. Instead of describing the realistic fusion of constitutional and policy-making issues with administration, like Haldane and Beveridge, he approached constitutional matters by coming to grips with the bureaucracy problem. He recognised the threat of constitutional perdition posed by the abusive criticisms of power by officials, which both Haldane and Beveridge overlooked. In the light of the later Committee on Ministers' Powers, it can be understood why Haldane and Beveridge paid little attention to the *power of officials*, since the problem was one of *procedures* rather than *power*. In other words, there was no bid for despotism by Whitehall officials, although it was a potental risk. Instead, the growth of the positive State had carried with it a haphazard evolution of procedures with respect to the executive's legislative and judicial powers. Nevertheless, there was a degree of neglect by Haldane and Beveridge towards the civil servant's growing powers in the era of the positive State. Bureaucracy as *power of officials*, then, was a problem

47. Later, the Rules Publication Act was replaced by the more comprehensive Statutory Instruments Act, 1940. See H. W. R. Wade, *Administrative Law* (London) Second edn 1967, pp. 308–9.
48. The Committee distinguished a quasi-judicial decision from a purely judicial one by indicating that the former had *some* but not all the attributes of a judicial decision. An important legal element missing from the quasi-judicial decision is that the Minister is left free to take what administrative action he may think fit, whereas a judicial decision carries a statutory obligation to apply the law of the land to the facts and to act accordingly. In other words, the quasi-judicial decision allows for considerations of public policy to be borne in mind. *Committee on Ministers' Powers Report*, pp. 64–118.

interpreted individualistically by contributors to the British Philosophy of Administration.

The second conclusion relates to the adoption of Stamp's evolutionary views in the United States. His ideas were taken up – albeit incognito – by Marshall Dimock in the 1930s.[49] Although the United States experienced no outcry of power by officials akin to the British problem, Congress was leaving more details to administrative discretion. Dimock agreed with this trend, explaining it in terms of the same evolutionary causes propounded by Stamp:

> The principal reasons which account for and justify administrative discretion are the limits of time and limits of aptitude of the legislative body, plus the fact that its procedure is slow and it is not always in session; then, too, administrative discretion takes care of urgent matters such as quarantine, provides opportunity for local variety and detail, makes leeway for unknown future conditions, affords the indispensable means of handling complex and technical affairs, and tends to obtain freedom from party strife.[50]

Therefore, Stamp's evolutionary causes of the *power of officials* were heeded in the United States. However, there were two weaknesses in his views. He dealt only with delegated legislation – or delegated *legislative* powers – without discussing the *judicial* aspects of the British problem, such as the decline of the Rule of Law. And, although he came to grips with the bureaucracy problem, he did not write in a profound manner on this subject. Rather, he presented his evolutionary and functional causes of the *power of officials* as a lecture and relied upon depth studies by other British scholars to give substance to his arguments.

2. The fragmentation of the British Philosophy of Administration and its relevance to bureaucracy

The fragmented nature of the British Philosophy of Administration had relevance for the second form of bureaucracy – *rule of the bureau.* In this section, we show how the British Philosophy of Administration could have minimised the problem of red-tape, if it had been less fragmented and if the Haldane Report had been applied more

---

49. M. E. Dimock, 'The role of discretion in modern administration', in *The Frontiers of Public Administration*, ed. by J. M. Gaus et al. (Chicago) 1936, pp. 45–100.
50. Ibid., p. 58.

comprehensively. This section begins with an outline of the dysfunctional causes of *rule of the bureau* stressed by the business critics.[51] Next, remedies for these causes of bureaucracy will be seen to lie within the doctrines of the British Philosophy of Administration. Finally, an important alternative and functional cause of bureaucracy, which the business critics failed to consider, will be identified.

Of the business critics, Demetriadi documented his complaints most clearly and they are taken as being representative of the criticisms of *rule of the bureau*.[52] Demetriadi worked in the Ministry of Pensions during the First World War but, on leaving, he published his views about inadequacies in British public administration. From his criticisms of the Civil Service, two dysfunctional causes of bureaucracy can be discerned, which are rigidity in the system and deficiencies in personnel administration.

Rigidity in the system as a cause of rule of the bureau

Demetriadi was critical of rigidity in the Civil Service, such as the system's failure to take account of outside circumstances and the mechanical pursuance of its own goals. He argued that this rigidity was created partly because the machinery of government was unable to adapt itself quickly enough to the problem of war. He explained how British public administration is converted into rigidity. A permanent official, saturated in tradition and precedent, possesses only one idea of how to cope with an emergency – to do the customary thing more frequently than usual. The official, having adhered strictly to certain procedure for the duration of his career, and never having been permitted to ask himself whether that procedure is the best or most economical, when faced with sudden emergencies such as war, has neither the inclination nor the ability to 'swerve from the beaten track'. Demetriadi continued:

> Were fifty clerks previously employed in doing this work? Is there now ten times the amount of work to be done? Then requisition an additional 450 clerks, take some great hotel in which to house them, and do the

51. There were obviously numerous business critics, for there were repeated references in literature to 'the critics' or 'the businessmen' but, with the exception of Demetriadi, they were rarely named individually. For example, see M. Murby, 'Routine and the civil servant', *The Development of the Civil Service* (London) 1922, p. 136, and E. F. Wise, 'The Civil Service in its relation to industry and commerce', in *The Civil Servant and His Profession* (London) 1920, p. 80.
52. Stamp referred to Demetriadi's opinion as 'the most representative criticism', see J. Stamp, 'The contrast between the administration of business and public affairs', op. cit., 171.

same thing ten times where it was previously done once. What could be more simple? Here we have the true explanation of bloated staffs and exasperating delays. To all criticism the official has but one answer, that permanent officials were few and that the new staff could not be 'assimilated' with sufficient rapidity to cope with the work. This explanation for want of a better has been generally accepted. I am inclined to think, however, that the real source of the weakness i. to be found in the attempt to supply extraordinary demands with ordinary machinery rotating at ordinary speed.[53]

Demetriadi launched an energetic attack on the Civil Service[54] but, like Hewart, he failed to acknowledge earlier criticisms. Yet, Muir (1910) in a detailed study had identified similar inefficiencies associated with rigidity in the system, including 'the Sin of Red-Tape'.[55] In fact, a number of criticisms had been circulating about the Service since the last century, such as suspicions left by novelists like Anthony Trollope in *The Three Clerks* about time-wasting by civil servants.[56] Rigidity in the system, then, was not a new discovery by Demetriadi or other businessmen who infiltrated the Civil Service between 1914 and 1918, but it received renewed publicity by them.

Deficiencies in personnel administration as a cause of rule of the bureau

Demetriadi considered that the method of recruiting civil servants by competitive examination was good, having the advantages of securing an educated staff for departments, reducing patronage and selecting the most competent applicants from a given number – in other words, enlisting the best brains into the Service. However, in practice, he claimed that these advantages were outweighed by the disadvantages of the system which ruined the good material rather than making full use of it. For example, the system inhibits initiative since the intelligent recruit finds that unless he displays flagrant misconduct, he will gain the maximum pay of his class within a given number of years and,

53. Sir S. Demetriadi, *Inside a Government Office*, pp. 28–9.
54. Ibid., pp. 7–63.
55. Muir recognised four defects of bureaucracy, which were the Sins of Red-Tape; Mystery Mongering; Jack-in-Office and Gentlemanly Malingering. R. Muir, *Peers and Bureaucrats* (London) 1910, pp. 48–52.
56. Several references were made earlier this century to Trollope's novel *The Three Clerks* and the unsatisfactory impressions it had left about civil servants such as they 'play like fountains in Trafalgar Square from ten to four'. See Ministry of Reconstruction, *The Business of Government* (London) 1919, p. 2. For a recent account of Trollope's novels and his views about the British Civil Service, see R. A. W. Rhodes, 'Anthony Trollope and the nineteenth century Civil Service', *Public Administration*, Vol. 51, Summer 1973, 207–19.

subsequently, retire on pension. The higher official, therefore, has a predetermined career because promotion is based principally on seniority. Another cause of bureaucracy as *rule of the bureau*, therefore, was inherent in the Civil Service recruitment and promotion procedures, which Demetriadi argued ought to be: '. . . far more willing to admit, far less willing to promote. At the present moment there is no continuous weeding out, owing to the large part played by seniority and . . . every official must be provided with work of some sort even to the exclusion of better men.'[57]

His attack on the Civil Service exalted the business system while, at the same time, criticising public administration.[58] But, again, Demetriadi's comparisons were not unique, for Muir's earlier work had compared public and business administration and he had recorded the ill-effects on civil servants of security of tenure. Furthermore, Muir had noted specific dangers in the competitive examination as well as in the permanent career. He maintained that the competitive examination lent a bias in favour of Oxford and Cambridge by being too 'purely academic' and he urged that in the selection of administrators greater marking value in the examination should be accorded to subjects taught in the modern universities, such as history, law and economics.[59] From 1910 onwards, bureaucracy as *rule of the bureau* was seen to be caused by rigidity in the Civil Service system and deficiencies in personnel administration. But, by the beginning of the 1920s, accusations to this effect were being heaped on the Service by businessmen and, most markedly, by Sir Stephen Demetriadi.

The businessmen's attack gained momentum after the First World War because the Press charged the Civil Service with ineptitude and encouraged the public to think of the Service in terms of red-tape and monetary extravagance.[60] As well as being prompted by the Press, the public was resentful of what some called 'State interference',[61] while a distrust of officialdom still lingered from the nineteenth-century criticisms of malingering. No official committee was set up to investigate bureaucracy as *rule of the bureau*, although demands by the Press and the general public led to the creation of the Geddes Committee (1921–22) to enquire into government spending. The

57. Sir S. Demetriadi, *Inside a Government Office*, p. 54.
58. Ibid., pp. 21–63.
59. R. Muir, *Peers and Bureaucrats*, pp. 52–66.
60. See H. J. Laski, 'Civil Service and Parliament', *The Development of the Civil Service* (London) 1922, pp. 21–2.
61. See H. H. Ellis, 'The relations between state departments and the nation', *Journal of Public Administration*, Vol. IV, 1926, 98–106.

Committee suggested substantial economies with respect to naval and military expenditure and proposed reductions of expenditure on certain services. However, regarding the number of civil servants employed and the salaries paid, the Committee's recommendations were of relatively minor importance, so reducing the suspicion that British civil servants were underworked and overpaid.[62] None the less, the dysfunctions of *rule of the bureau* were a definite problem and rigidity in the system and deficiencies in personnel methods accounted for some of these defects. Demetriadi offered his own remedies for the problem which repeated – in more critical tone – some of the ideas contained within the British Philosophy of Administration. To overcome rigidity in the system, his proposals for the reallocation of functions between departments and the simplification of public administration by more verbal discussion reiterated the SLOCUS scientific principles of 'organisation' and 'communication'.[63]

The doctrines of the British Philosophy of Administration were still emerging in the early 1920s but, nevertheless, Wallas and Haldane had formulated scientific principles of administration from the turn of the century. As Chapter 3 demonstrated, Haldane was dedicated to the principle of 'organisation' and his views were embodied in the Haldane Report of 1918. The Haldane Committee recommended the organisation of government departments according to major function, after detecting severe overlapping of functions between departments and consequent obscurity and confusion. In practice, the ten executive departments proposed by the Committee were not implemented in the immediate post-war period.[64] This failure by the government to apply the Haldane Report speedily and fully was in part responsible for the problem of *rule of the bureau*. If departments had possessed a clearer objective corresponding to the current needs of the community, they would have been less out of touch with the outside world and less inclined to revolve mechanically. Furthermore, competition between departments to undertake certain functions would have been reduced. This point was confirmed by William Beveridge, who defended civil servants against the prevailing criticisms. In 1920, he endorsed the recommendations of the Haldane Committee, remarking: 'It is hardly

62. See H. J. Laski, 'The Civil Service and Parliament', op. cit., p. 21. H. H. Ellis, 'Relations between State departments', op. cit. p. 102, and G. K. Fry, *Statesmen in Disguise: The Changing Role of the Administrative Class of the British Home Civil Service 1853–1966* (London) 1969, pp. 75–83.
63. Sir S. Demetriadi, *Inside a Government Office*, pp. 57–63, and *A Reform for the Civil Service* (London) 1921, pp. 31–42.
64. See Ch. 3, pp. 100–15.

likely that the theoretically perfect scheme of departmental grouping suggested by that committee will be adopted in any reasonably near future. Some of the reforms are urgent . . . the more acute cases of overlapping functions should be removed; they are the main reason for those departmental disputes of which so much is heard.'[65]

Therefore, the scientific principle of 'organisation' as expounded in the Haldane Report could have overcome some of the defects of rigidity in the Civil Service system. Similarly, the scientific principle of 'communication' could have curtailed the businessmen's complaint of excessive paperwork, which reinforced rigidity. Prior to the First World War, both Wallas and Haldane had indicated the limitations of red-tape. As early as 1908, Wallas drew attention to the civil servant's tendency to adopt 'official' habits of thought, such as narrowness and rigidity, and to develop a sense of corporate interest contrary to the public interest. He advocated that the official should do more of his work by oral communication as an alternative to writing, so that he would not acquire the type of adverse characteristics described later by Demetriadi.[66]

Likewise, Haldane – as War Minister – had been alerted by the Esher Committee to the dangers of superfluous paperwork. Shortly before he took up his post as Minister, the War Office had faced the problem of complex regulations which produced a mass of unnecessary correspondence. The consequences of red-tape led Haldane to support a similar argument to Graham Wallas concerning oral communication. Despite this awareness by Wallas and Haldane – and later by Beveridge – of the dangers of rigidity and red-tape, the scientific principles of 'organisation' and 'communication' were not co-ordinated into a recognisable body of thought, as we have argued in Chapter 3.

Regarding deficiencies in personnel administration, these had been observed by contributors to the British Philosophy of Administration. Demetriadi referred to the competitive examination as being good, yet the examination had been under review before and during the First World War because it was recognised that improvements could be made. As a member of the MacDonnell Royal Commission (1912–15), Wallas queried the apportionment of marks to subjects and the undue

---

65. W. Beveridge, *The Public Service in War and in Peace* (London) 1920, p. 52. The Ministry of Reconstruction also confirmed that the reorganisation of government departments, according to the Haldane Report, would overcome some of the 'ailments' of bureaucracy. See *Business of Government*, pp. 11–14.

66. See Ch. 3, pp. 115–25. See also G. Wallas, *Human Nature in Politics*, 1908. Republished (London) 1962, pp. 276–81, *The Art of Thought* (London) 1926, pp. 136–7.

advantage which 'Oxbridge' appeared to have over newer universities. Haldane, although favouring classics as a suitable background for higher civil servants, agreed none the less with Wallas, in evidence to the Royal Commission, that the marking of subjects for the Class I examination needed rethinking.[67] Accordingly, the MacDonnell Commission made a strong case for reforming the competitive examination, but its Report was paralysed to a large extent by the onset of the First World War. In 1916, the Leathes Committee was set up to enquire into the competitive examination system and, as a result of the Committee's investigation, the interview test was introduced. However, in the interwar years, the interview was suspected of being a vehicle of social prejudice and came under question by the Tomlin Royal Commission (1929–31).[68] Although these developments in the Class I examination were taking place, Demetriadi made no reference to any of them, but simply assumed that the examination was satisfactory.

Haldane's primary interest in recruitment was for a reform of the entire educational system, so that a greater section of the population would benefit from university education and the range of applicants for the Civil Service would be extended. His views form part of the ethical ideal of 'service to the community' described in Chapter 4. Furthermore, the Haldane Committee recommended that a separate division specialising in 'establishment' work should be set up in the Treasury to study personnel matters throughout the Service.[69] Beveridge (1920) also made a series of recommendations to improve personnel methods, which included rearranging the rules of superannuation to shorten the average tenure of a civil servant's office, without diminishing its attractiveness.[70] Thus, pioneers of the British Philosophy of Administration were alive to rigidity in the Civil Service system and deficiencies in personnel administration and put forward remedies to treat these causes of *rule of the bureau*. But, by reason of the fragmentation of the British Philosophy of Administration and the slow reception to the Haldane Report, their remedies failed to prevent the worst defects of *rule of the bureau*.

Josiah Stamp defended a certain amount of red-tape in public administration by revealing alternative and, in some cases, functional

67. See *Royal Commission on the Civil Service: Appendix to First Report of the Commissioners* (London) 1912, pp. 78–93.
68. See G. K. Fry, *Statesmen in Disguise*, pp. 75–83. See also *Report of the Royal Commission on the Civil Service 1929–31* (London) 1931, pp. 68–70.
69. See Ch. 3, pp. 80–1.
70. W. Beveridge, *The Public Service*, pp. 24–63.

causes of bureaucracy. The most important cause he identified, besides ministerial responsibility and its subsequent risk of questions in the House of Commons, was the need for consistency in public administration.

The need for consistency in public administration as a cause of rule of the bureau

The administration of an Act of Parliament requires a consistency by government departments which does not exist in business, Stamp explained. Its detailed application to individuals involves the exercise of discretion in varying degrees by officials and this discretion needs to be consistent, not erratic. He specified four dimensions of consistency relevant to public administration:

1. Consistency over the whole range of possible action.
2. Consistency over the whole geographical area of the United Kingdom.
3. Consistency of time.
4. Consistency of punishment according to the seriousness of the crime.

The first dimension of consistency deals with the question of *degree*. Although there are two extreme points, most cases with which public administrators deal lie at positions between these two extremes. For example, the administration of the Stamp Acts involves penalties for infringements ranging over a continuous line from nothing up to £10 for the different degrees of offence. If the department puts a penalty of 3 shillings on a document that was three days overdue and then a penalty of £7 on a document that was four days overdue, consistency would be lacking and a question would probably be raised about it in the House of Commons next day.

In the case of the second dimension, consistency between the extremes of 'nothing' and £10 must be carried forward unbroken over a given *area* (i.e. the whole area to which the Act applies). The administrative machinery must permit consistency to be effected over that whole area. A much more invidious question would arise in the House, Stamp observed, if treatment by administrators varied in Caernarvon, London and Aberdeen. Thirdly, it would be irritating if in the month of January discretion about penalising a document was very severe and in June it was very light or if discretion varied from year to year. Inconsistency of *time* would give rise to public criticism. Finally, statutory penalties vary tremendously according to the different *kinds* of crime. This is a problem for the legislator more than the administrator, but consistency ought to result in the sense of making the punishment fit the crime. From these four dimensions, he concluded that consistency is a necessary factor in public administration but not in business administration.

Stamp sought to counteract the mutual reviling which was growing up between civil servants and businessmen by reviewing the reasons for different methods in public and business administration.[71] In so doing, he pointed to advantages of rules and regulations in public administration, such as the consistency they grant to different classes of people.[72]

Conclusion to the fragmentation of the British Philosophy of Administration and its relevance to bureaucracy

The first conclusion concerns the morale of civil servants during the early 1920s. They were 'stung' by the criticisms of red-tape and retaliated by hitting back at business methods, so creating antagonism between public and business administrators.[73] This blow to the morale of civil servants could have been reduced if the British Philosophy of Administration had been less fragmented and implemented more positively. For, dangers associated with red-tape had been foreseen by contributors to the British Philosophy of Administration, particularly in the context of the scientific principles of 'organisation' and 'communication'.

The second conclusion relates to the strengths and weaknesses of the business critics. In Demetriadi's case, several weaknesses were inherent in his arguments. He exaggerated the inefficiencies of public administration, making sweeping statements based on his personal experience in wartime without referring to earlier criticisms of bureaucracy or noting accurately recent developments in Civil Service

---

71. Stamp was well placed to speak on behalf of public and business administration because he was on the council of both the Institute of Public Administration and the Institute of Industrial Administration. See Ch. 1, p. 28.
72. J. Stamp, 'The contrast', op. cit., 158–71.
73. Civil servants, and ex-civil servants, who defended a degree of red-tape in public administration or hit back at business methods, included W. Beveridge, *The Public Service*, pp. vii–63; H. H. Ellis 'Relations between state departments', op. cit., pp. 95–106; J. Lee, 'The psychology of the civil servant' in *The Civil Servant and his Profession*, (London) 1920, pp. 101–2 and M. Murby 'Routine and the civil servant', op. cit., pp. 132–63.

administration, such as developments in the competitive examination or reforms in the Treasury. The latter reforms included the reinstatement of one permanent head of the Treasury, instead of three Permanent Secretaries as prevailed during the war,[74] and the setting up of a special 'establishment' division in the Treasury to deal with personnel matters throughout the Service, as proposed by the Haldane Committee.[75] In the interest of war, departments had gained comparative freedom to make their own arrangements and this lack of cohesion exacerbated the problem of the overlapping of functions between departments. However, when Warren Fisher became the one permanent head of the Treasury in 1919, he actively fostered unification of the Service *vis-à-vis* departmentalism.[76] Thus, Demetriadi's account of the Civil Service was exaggerated and, to some extent, inaccurate in relation to peacetime conditions. H. E. Dale, who later recorded his own experience in the Civil Service, referred to the business critics' inaccuracy:

> The war of 1914–18 . . . changed the great Departments and their inmates on a scale beyond wonder: and after 1918 they changed back again on an almost equal scale. It is no disparagement of the writers who have turned to professional account their experience as temporary civil servants between 1914 and 1920 to say that that experience and its results in print (however witty and amusing these last may be) have little relevance to the Civil Service as it was either before 1914 or before 1939.[77]

Demetriadi was reproached by Stamp for another weakness, his failure to consider the political and constitutional environment of public administration. Demetriadi expected public administration to be conducted in the same manner as business administration, but he overlooked the special conditions of government, such as ministerial

74. See Sir H. P. Hamilton, 'Sir Warren Fisher and the Public Service', *Public Administration*, Vol. 29, 1951, 9–12.
75. See this chapter, p. 221. This same proposal for the creation of an 'establishment' division of the Treasury was made by the MacDonnell Royal Commission (1912–15) and the Bradbury Committee on Staffs (1918–19). See *Royal Commission on the Civil Service 1912–15, Fourth Report of the Commissioners* (London) 1914, Majority Report, pp. 84–7, and P. and G. Ford, *A Breviate of Parliamentary Papers 1917–1939* (Shannon) 1969, pp. 22–3.
76. See Sir H. P. Hamilton, 'Sir Warren Fisher', op. cit., 14–15.
77. H. E. Dale, *The Higher Civil Service of Great Britain* (London) 1941, p. 63. Both the numbers and the composition of the Civil Service changed during the First World War. The number of non-industrial civil servants increased from 289,000 in August 1914 to 426,000 in November 1918. The composition of the Service also changed because large numbers of civil servants joined the forces and the balance of Civil Service staff was made up temporarily of businessmen, solicitors, lecturers and – of course – women. See W. Beveridge, *The Public Service*, pp. 11–16. However, the greater part of the women were employed on routine or subordinate duties.

responsibility.[78] Third, Demetriadi attributed the defects of *rule of the bureau* exclusively to the Civil Service, suggesting that business administration was free from fault. More realistically, Stamp pointed out later that red-tape can apply to any large-scale organisation, whether public or private.[79] But the business critics had points in their favour. They directed attention towards reforms needed in the Civil Service, including the reallocation of functions between departments, the limitations of excessive paperwork and remaining deficiencies in personnel methods, such as the method of superannuation. Accordingly, the business critics – in more forceful tone – confirmed and reinforced aspects of the British Philosophy of Administration.

3. The lack of theory within the British Philosophy of Administration and its relevance to bureaucracy

Before, and in response to the twofold problem of bureaucracy, contributors to the British Philosophy of Administration raised issues corresponding to elements in Max Weber's 'ideal' type and to ideas promoted later by the American writer, R. K. Merton. However, the lack of attention paid to theory by these British administrative pioneers resulted in an absence of any theoretical framework in which to set the study of bureaucracy. Moreover, when the British problem reached its peak in the 1920s and early 1930s, Weber's work was virtually unknown[80] and the advances made to his 'pure' type by contributors to the British Philosophy of Administration have passed unnoticed. This section will indicate these advances to the understanding of bureaucracy.

It is useful, at this stage, to summarise the Weberian characteristics and causes of bureaucracy. The relevant characteristics of bureaucracy are those which Weber associated with the exercise of legal authority in modern organisations. By legal authority, he had in mind a system of abstract rules applied to particular cases and he argued that the 'purest' exercise of legal authority featured a bureaucratic administrative staff. Weber attributed ten characteristics to the bureaucratic administrative

---

78. J. Stamp, 'The contrast', op. cit., 170–1.
79. See J. Stamp, 'Note to the address by the Rt. Hon. Sir J. Anderson, *Public Administration*, Vol. VII, 1929, pp. 14–15. Laski also associated red-tape with all large-scale organisations, see H. J. Laski, 'Bureaucracy', op. cit., 72.
80. It should be remembered, however, that Laski referred to Weber's work, see this chapter, p. 201.

staff – or bureaucracy – which included a clear hierarchy of offices, a career structure with promotion based on seniority or merit, a money salary together, usually, with pension rights, and selection on the basis of professional qualification, ideally substantiated by a diploma acquired by examination. The bureaucratic administrative staff was deemed capable of attaining the highest degree of efficiency, whether operating within the church, armies, economic institutions or other types of modern corporate groups. Indeed, Weber considered it to be the most *rational* method of administering authority over individuals and superior to other forms in precision, stability, discipline and reliability. The factor making this type of bureaucracy rational was the exercise of control on the basis of knowledge – both the technical knowledge gained through examination and the knowledge growing out of experience.[81]

In addition to the foregoing characteristics, Weber recognised three causes of the legal–rational type of bureaucracy – the development of the money economy as a presupposition of bureaucracy; the quantitative development of administrative tasks; and the qualitative enlargement of administrative tasks. The qualitative increase in tasks related to the growing sophistication of a State expressed in increased wealth, as well as by growing demands on culture, which call for bureaucratic provision unknown previously, or supplied locally or by a private economy.[82] These Weberian ideas about the legal–rational type of bureaucracy will be expanded by reference to views put forward by pioneers of the British Philosophy of Administration during the British problem.

Although contributors to the British Philosophy of Administration did not discuss Weber's work directly, their views can be seen to develop his legal–rational type of bureaucracy in two ways. In the first case, Weber concentrated on the *functions* of bureaucracy and expounded the advantages of the expert application of general rules to particular cases. Josiah Stamp extended this thought by making the functional approach relevant to British public administration.[83] He pointed out, in connection with the problem of the *power of officials*, that expert

81. For an account of Weber's study of bureaucracy, see M. Albrow, *Bureaucracy*, pp. 40–9 and A. M. Henderson and T. Parsons, eds., *Max Weber: The Theory of Social and Economic Organization*, 1947: Republished (New York) 1964, pp. 324–41.
82. M. Weber, 'The presuppositions and causes of bureaucracy', *Reader in Bureaucracy*, pp. 60–8.
83. Laski also promoted the functional approach to bureaucracy, as demonstrated by the note he appended to the *Committee on Ministers' Powers Report*, see this chapter, p. 213, f.n. 46.

officials are able to deal more effectively with complicated and technical legislation than Members of Parliament. In fact, he argued that general rules which leave the detailed formulation of legal authority to expert officials are advantageous for a number of reasons – reasons of local variety and detail, unknown future conditions, complexity, urgency and to avoid party political entanglement. Similarly, with respect to the problem of *rule of the bureau,* Stamp stressed the merits to be obtained from the public official's consistent application of rules to particular cases. Stamp also provided evidence to support Weber's ideas about the causes of bureaucracy. Weber noted the qualitative and quantitative enlargement of administrative tasks as causes of the growth of the legal–rational type of bureaucracy. By identifying evolutionary, rather than devolutionary, causes of the *power of officials,* Stamp gave practical expression to Weber's ideas. For, he recognised the growth of the positive State in Britain and the emergencies of the First World War as having caused the nation's administrative tasks to increase qualitatively and quantitatively.[84]

The second way contributors to the British Philosophy of Administration – and the vociferous critics – developed Weber's legal–rational type of bureaucracy was by indicating some of its *dysfunctions.* Weber paid little attention to the limitations of his 'pure' type, yet the characteristics he isolated were capable of creating disadvantages as well as advantages. For example, Weber associated legal authority with written documents. But, Wallas and Haldane pointed out weaknesses of excessive written communications and their views were borne out by the British problem of *rule of the bureau.* Again, the Weberian characteristics of a continuous career structure, linked to pension rights, carried risks of inefficiency deriving from the methods of promotion and superannuation. Before Demetriadi's attack on the British Civil Service, Beveridge had observed that in peacetime some men were kept on routine work in the Service until the age of forty or fifty, which denied them responsibility early enough in life. Beveridge attributed this fault to the career structure, which was based on almost lifelong service. He urged that pension arrangements should be more flexible, so that officials could move from the Civil Service to other work without losing their accrued rights, and vice versa.[85] Thus,

---

84. Later, R. A. Chapman reached a similar conclusion about the causes of bureaucracy. However, he argued that the real cause of bureaucracy 'is found in the social pressure, or will, which has demanded the new regulations, inspections, or welfare provisions of twentieth century government'. See R. A. Chapman, 'The real cause of bureaucracy', *Administration*, Vol. 12, 1964, 55–60.
85. W. Beveridge, *The Public Service,* pp. 41–5.

pioneers of the British Philosophy of Administration produced information about dysfunctions of bureaucracy. This information, coupled with the critics' allegations of the *power of officials* and *rule of the bureau*, created a wealth of knowledge in Britain about dysfunctions of bureaucracy. This knowledge preceded the famous work of R. K. Merton in the United States. Merton reviewed the negative habits of officials, including rigidity and the bureaucrat's tendency to displace goals by converting means into ends in themselves. The American scholar supported his arguments about 'dysfunctions' of bureaucracy with full academic references and structured his work systematically, ending with a selection of problems for research. [86] Although the same kind of dysfunctional habits had been discussed earlier in Britain by Wallas, Haldane and Beveridge and were highlighted during the problem of *rule of the bureau*, contributors to the British Philosophy of Administration failed to analyse bureaucracy with the same academic rigour as Merton. For example, Merton cited the early British work by Muir (1910), but pioneers of the British Philosophy of Administration did not draw upon Muir's work. Consequently, Merton's study of the dysfunctions of bureaucracy carries wide significance today, while the British information has receded in importance.

Conclusion to the lack of theory within the British Philosophy of Administration and its relevance to bureaucracy

The dual problem of bureaucracy in Britain revealed more knowledge about dysfunctions of bureaucracy than functions. This empirical information could have been used more usefully by contributors to the British Philosophy of Administration. For, although this section has shown that their views advanced Weber's 'ideal' type in two ways, these British administrative pioneers made no attempt to expand existing theories of bureaucracy in the period ending in 1939. Indeed, Weberian thought could have been enlarged in yet a third way by utilising more extensively the empirical information about the *power of officials*. This problem shed light on the nature of legal authority, which was the basis of Weber's concept of modern bureaucracy. But, with the exception of Stamp, pioneers of the British Philosophy of Administration did not examine the *power of officials* in detail and they certainly did not relate it to Weberian concepts. This lack of attention to theory within the British Philosophy of Administration is disappointing, since it has meant that valuable information about bureaucracy and legal authority

86. R. K. Merton, 'Bureaucratic structure', op. cit., pp. 361–71.

has been overlooked.

Consider, for example, the Report of the Committee on Ministers' Powers. This document contained a variety of opinions about the nature of legal authority and its exercise by officials. First, the Committee concluded that it was misleading to interpret legal authority indiscriminately as 'rules', 'regulations' and 'orders'. Instead, the Committee proposed that, with regard to delegated legislation, legal terminology should be standardised, so that it can be understood clearly by all concerned. Second, the Report drew attention to the fact that, however expert the official applying legal authority may be, limits on administrative discretion need to be stated in order that the official does not overstep his duties. Third, the Committee recommended that 'rules' or other forms of legislation must be drafted skilfully to avoid the obscurity about which Hewart complained.[87] If contributors to the British Philosophy of Administration had analysed some of this empirical information more thoroughly and related it to theories of bureaucracy, their views would have been more likely to have endured after the British problem subsided.

Conclusion

Two separate criticisms of bureaucracy have been portrayed in this chapter in terms of how they relate to the British Philosophy of Administration. Several additional conclusions about this relationship will be discussed briefly. To begin, it is clear that the empirical evidence about bureaucracy validated the doctrines of the British Philosophy of Administration, but it was not used systematically for this purpose. For example, the problem of the *power of officials* confirmed the doctrine of a fusion between constitutional matters and administration. The Committee on Ministers' Powers stated early in its Report: 'In the British Constitution there is no such thing as the absolute separation of legislative, executive, and judicial powers; in practice it is inevitable that they should overlap. In such constitutions as those of France and the United States of America, attempts to keep them rigidly apart have been made, but have proved unsuccessful.'[88]

The Committee acknowledged that British civil servants exercised certain legislative and quasi-judicial powers and agreed, although somewhat grudgingly, that they should continue to do so. Thus, the

87. See this chapter, p. 208. See also *Committee on Ministers' Powers Report*, pp. 54–70.
88. *Committee on Ministers' Powers Report*, p. 4.

Committee upheld the British Philosophy of Administration doctrine of a *fusion* between the processes of government rather than the Webbs' doctrine of *separation*.[89] Similarly, the problem of *rule of the bureau* reinforced the importance of scientific principles of administration, particularly the principles of 'organisation' and 'communication'. Greater utilisation of this empirical information by contributors to the British Philosophy of Administration would have verified and enriched the British doctrines. But, despite wide coverage of the bureaucracy problem in the journal *Public Administration*, including constructive lectures by Stamp on the subject, the lack of conceptual framework within the British Philosophy of Administration resulted in the twofold problem of bureaucracy being little more than a collection of individual papers.

Nevertheless, the British views about bureaucracy were transported to the United States. This chapter has shown already that Stamp's thinking was adopted by Dimock.[90] In addition, the conclusions of the Committee on Ministers' Powers were integrated into the Report of the President's Committee on Administrative Management (1937). The United States had the reverse problem to Britain. Instead of too much executive power in the United States, the rule-making, or legislative, power had become dispersed among the multiplicity of regulatory boards and commissions. Accordingly, the President's Committee suggested co-ordinating the rule-making power in the President. This action was the direct antithesis to the British fear of power by officials. A reason for the American confidence in the *power of officials* was the verdict of the British Committee on Ministers' Powers that the problem was one of safeguards rather than power itself. Therefore the President's Committee accompanied its recommendations for increasing the President's rule-making power by a set of safeguards based on the Report of the British Committee. The President's Committee focused attention, for example, on avoiding haphazard methods in connection with legal authority and improving draftsmanship.[91]

The second conclusion relates to other interesting administrative

89. Although the Committee on Ministers' Powers upheld the British Philosophy of Administration doctrine by confirming a *fusion* between the processes of government, it distinguished between judicial and quasi-judicial decisions and was criticised for attempting to make this separation. See W. I. Jennings, 'Reviews: Ministers' powers', *Public Administration*, Vol. XI, 1933, 111–13. See also this chapter, p. 214.
90. See this ch., p. 215.
91. Administrative Management in the United States: Studies on Administrative Management No. 5, 'The Exercise of Rule-Making Power' by J. Hart (Washington) 1937, pp. 3–45.

factors which emerged from the British bureaucracy problem. For example, Stamp and others responded to the allegations of *rule of the bureau* by discussing essential differences between public and business administration – a topic which has continued to be of interest in the post-Second World War era.[92] Another point to stem from the problem of *rule of the bureau* was the lack of authoritative books on the British Civil Service. After the First World War, some members of the British public held a distorted image of the Civil Service, based on nineteenth-century novels, the partially inaccurate views of the business critics and press reports. These views concentrated on the evils of bureaucracy and were not offset by accurate texts on the Civil Service. This absence of literature was noted by the Ministry of Reconstruction:

> ... the influence of Trollope on the public mind has successfully (and in some respects disastrously) survived the facts of a whole generation of Civil Service reform. Quite an appreciable proportion of the public still think vaguely of the Civil Service as composed largely of young men with powerful connections, who are 'jobbed into lucrative billets in the Tape and Sealing Wax Department', where they have little else to do than read the leading articles in the 'Thunderer' . . . There has, however, been published in the last year a Report by a Reconstruction Committee on the general question of the Machinery of Government, which should be read by all those who take any practical interest in the eminently practical issues of this difficult subject.[93]

The absence of detailed texts on the British Civil Service continued into the late 1930s, leading H. E. Dale to make a similar claim: '. . . so far as I know no one, either assailant or defender, has attempted in fiction or otherwise to delineate with any fulness the idiosyncrasy of the high permanent official in our time and country . . .'[94]

Dale wrote his own account, *The Higher Civil Service of Great Britain*, to fill this apparent gap. However, although the gap was real in the sense of consolidated texts about the British Civil Service, or British public administration, this book has demonstrated that distinctive administrative doctrines prevailed in Britain in the period 1900–39.

92. Modern writers who have examined differences between public and private organisations include P. Self, *Bureaucracy or Management?* p. 9 and A. Dunsire, *Administration: The Word and the Science* (London) 1973, pp. 166–79. However, it should be noted that, although differences between public and business administration were discussed in the period 1900–39, Urwick differed from Stamp by believing that these differences were overstressed. Urwick preferred to emphasise the similarities, rather than the differences, between the two types of administration. See L. Urwick, 'Organization as a technical problem', in *Papers on the Science of Administration*, ed. by L. Gulick and L. Urwick (New York) 1937, p. 49.
93. *Business of Government*, pp. 2–3.
94. H. E. Dale, *The Higher Civil Service*, p. 65.

Yet, their fragmented nature and their insufficient attention to theory meant that no one authoritative text dealing with public administration could be distinguished.

Another conclusion concerns the role of the critics. On the side of their weaknesses, the two major critics of bureaucracy – Hewart and Demetriadi – did not put forward original ideas. Instead, they repeated, with some harshness and exaggeration, dangers in British public administration which had been noted earlier this century. Furthermore, they were so intent on stressing dysfunctional causes of bureaucracy that they failed to consider functional reasons for entrusting legislative and judicial powers to officials or applying rules methodically and consistently in public administration. On the side of their strengths, however, the critics rendered a service to public administration. The Committee on Ministers' Powers expressed its thanks to the constitutional and legal experts, including Hewart, for drawing attention to the need for safeguards against potential abuses of power by officials.[95] Likewise, Demetriadi and other business critics provided a service to public administration in the sense that they confirmed aspects of the British Philosophy of Administration and brought to the surface for attention other administrative factors, such as differences between public and business administration.

A fourth conclusion centres on the absence, during the British problem, of any direct association (as distinct from a natural confusion) between the two forms of bureaucracy. Some common ground existed between bureaucracy as *power of officials* and *rule of the bureau* because both types referred to complexity in public administration. In the case of the *power of officials*, the complexity related to the haphazard procedures for delegating legislative and judicial powers to the executive, while *rule of the bureau* involved complex written communications issued by civil servants. Apart from this limited common ground,[96] the *power of officials* and *rule of the bureau* were separate allegations as this chapter has attempted to show. What is interesting is that red-tape was not identified clearly by the constitutional and legal experts as a form of manipulative control – that is, another power weapon in addition to delegated powers. Hewart hinted at this association when he argued that delegated legislation was

95. *Committee on Ministers' Powers Report*, p. 7. Despite the importance of the *Committee on Ministers' Powers Report*, many of its recommendations did not receive legislative sanction. See R. V. Vernon, and N. Mansergh, *Advisory Bodies*, pp. 77–9.
96. It was this common ground, no doubt, which led Laski to combine the two forms of bureaucracy into one definition, see this chapter, pp. 201–2.

framed intentionally in obscure language to prosper the new despotism, but he did not connect his accusations to the detailed attack on red-tape made a few years before by businessmen, the public and the Press. Later, however, the French scholar Crozier (1964) pointed out that rigid behaviour by officials, or ritualism, constitutes a useful instrument in the struggle for power and control and he provided a lengthy study to support his thesis.[97]

Finally, what of bureaucracy today? New empirical evidence is accumulating about the *power of officials* and *rule of the bureau*, which reflects the earlier criticisms. For example, the Royal Commission on the Constitution (Memorandum of Dissent) restated the warnings of the 1920s about the *power of officials*, without apparently being aware of them:

> There is some reason to believe that the day-to-day burden on Ministers is now so great that they are unable to control adequately the full range of departmental business. If this is true the new balance of power gives bureaucracy an edge over democracy . . . governments today increasingly by-pass the House of Commons in the policy-making process.[98]

Another example is the recent complaint about the Price Commission's 'draconian powers'. Under the Counter-Inflation Act, 1973, the Price Commission was given powers to fight inflation, quickly and fairly, but the powers have been challenged in a mode similar to that adopted by Hewart. And, without reference to Hewart, his phrase 'excluding or ousting the jurisdiction of the court' has been brought into the debate, although cautiously.[99] Hewart's warning, then, is repeated in the 1970s. Safeguards against potential abuses of power should be reviewed and, if necessary, new safeguards applicable to our time should be applied to the system of British government, before the critics attack more vigorously. Alternatively, the functional causes of delegated powers should be stated, so that it is understood by all concerned, including the public, why civil servants are required to exercise these powers in the last quarter of the twentieth century.

In the case of *rule of the bureau*, the critics are already active. In 1975, the morale of civil servants was reported to be waning under a 'malicious campaign'[100] of abuse against them. This time the attack is alleged to be conducted by politicians and the Press and, again,

97. M. Crozier, *Bureaucratic Phenomenon*, particularly p. 199.
98. *Royal Commission on the Constitution 1969–1973*, Vol. II, *Memorandum of Dissent*, by Lord Crowther-Hunt and Professor A. T. Peacock (London) 1973, p. 4.
99. *The Times*, 23 Nov. 1974.
100. Ibid., 22 Nov. 1975.

deficiencies in personnel administration are a cause of the problem. This modern attack on the Civil Service criticises the growing number of public officials and their ample pay and pension arrangements. Once more it is vital to examine functional, as well as dysfunctional, causes of bureaucracy. To counter these criticisms, civil servants have recently been roused to put forward the same cause of bureaucracy which Weber and, later, Stamp identified – the enlargement of administrative tasks.[101] If there was wider understanding of the development of British administrative thought and practice this century, civil servants might be affected less by the present abuse, knowing that similar criticisms arose earlier this century when administrative tasks expanded and there was concern about 'State interference'.

101. Ibid.

Chapter 6

Conclusion
to the British Philosophy
of Administration

'... the American political environment is so different from the British that American public administration theory is not at all adequate for the British situation'.[1]

R. J. S. Baker

This book has identified the central doctrines characterising the development of British administrative thought between 1900 and 1939. These doctrines, which we have called the British Philosophy of Administration, are associated primarily with six administrative pioneers – Wallas, Haldane, Beveridge, Sheldon, Urwick and Stamp. In the course of describing these doctrines, comparisons have been made with traditional American administrative doctrines and with the alternative, and more radical, views put forward in Britain by Sidney and Beatrice Webb and Harold Laski. Final analyses have been considered at the relevant points in each individual chapter and it is considered unnecessary to summarise these analyses in this concluding chapter. It is more appropriate now to review some of the national developments which account for contrasts – and similarities – between the development of administrative doctrines in Britain and the United States. Finally, in the second part of this chapter, we shall examine the relationship between the British Philosophy of Administration and current administrative trends. This examination will reveal the continuing significance today of certain aspects of the British Philosophy of Administration and the tendency for administrative themes to recur,·despite the increasing complexity of modern public and business administration.

---

1. R. J. S. Baker, *Administrative Theory and Public Administration* (London) 1972. p. 186.

1. A review of national developments in Britain and the United States which helped to mould the respective administrative doctrines

In Britain at the turn of the century, there was a strong ethical, and moral,[2] approach to society and this is evident from the many public and private enquiries into the place of labour in society and into health and social security matters, such as the Royal Commission on the Poor Law and Relief of Distress (1905–09). In addition to these efforts at social reform, novelists like H. G. Wells and J. Galsworthy focused attention on evils in our society. It has been recorded about Britain in the period from 1900 to 1916 that: '... streams of thought from different sources converged to produce and strengthen an ethical quality in political thinking, a desire to see individual activity in harmony with social good.[3]

The emergence of the British Philosophy of Administration went hand-in-hand with this general concern for the social good. Rowntree's influence on British administrative thought and practice has been acknowledged in these chapters, but he was a keen reformer of larger societal problems, such as poverty.[4] Similarly, Beveridge – when a young civil servant in 1909 – published his famous studies on unemployment.[5] Thus, the spread of ethical thought in Britain was captured in the doctrines of the British Philosophy of Administration.

The United States was influenced at this time more by the importance of science than of ethics – a development which has been called 'the second phase of the industrial revolution'.[6] This optimism towards science became translated into the American administrative doctrines. F. W. Taylor, and other pioneers of scientific management, gained a band of enthusiastic followers in the United States, whereas Britain responded to scientific management with caution and scepticism. The *philosophical* approach to administration in Britain, which combined science with ethics, placed less faith in pure science. A consequence of these different approaches to administration is discernible from the contrasting developments in training for the public service. Waldo has noted, with respect to the United States, that

2. See the distinction between ethics and morality in Ch. 4, pp. 140–1.
3. P. and G. Ford, *A Breviate of Parliamentary Papers 1900–1916* (Oxford) 1957, pp. ix–xiv. Quotation p. xiii.
4. See Ch. 4, p. 163.
5. W. Beveridge, *Power and Influence* (London) 1953, pp. 9–71.
6. D. Waldo, *The Administrative State* (New York) 1948, pp. 8–21.

there was no ideal of 'State service' as in Britain,[7] and those interested in training were rootless. It was, therefore, principally the cult of science which stimulated training for administration in the United States, leading to a demand for 'specialists'[8] rather than the traditional British 'generalist'. The American science of administration was strengthened, also, by reforms in the governmental process. While in the nineteenth century Britain had moved away substantially from patronage appointments to the Civil Service to the competitive examination system, the American 'reform movement' remained active during the first decades of this century. More party political appointments were made in American public administration and many able young men were not attracted to a career in the public service because of the taint of corruption. Instead, they chose a career in business, finance or law. Accordingly, American reform institutions, universities and private foundations became involved in raising standards of public administration. These organisations encouraged both training for, and research about, the public service – for example, the New York Bureau of Municipal Research, the Maxwell School of Citizenship and Public Affairs established in 1924, the Rockefeller Foundation and the Spelman Fund.[9] The reform movement and the emphasis on science in the United States led to an academic, as well as an analytical, focus on the subject of administration. This analytical approach was adopted, for example, in the case of the Hawthorne studies, which were undertaken later by the Harvard Business School.

Britain, with a larger percentage of permanent higher civil servants selected by competitive examination directly from university, had less need to rely on outside training for public administration. Rather, the British 'generalist' once recruited into the Civil Service acquired training on-the-job. The London School of Economics offered courses in public and business administration and other British universities, like Oxford and Cambridge, provided analogous courses in economics and politics.[10] But, although the London School of Economics aided the study of administration, the universities in Britain, in general, took a lesser role than those in the United States in developing the study of public administration. Indeed, the doctrines of the British Philosophy

7. For reference to the ideal of service to the State within the British Philosophy of Administration, see Ch. 4, pp. 156–9.
8. D. Waldo, op. cit., pp. 29–31.
9. See L. Urwick, 'George Maxwell had a dream: An historical note with a comment on the future', *Maxwell News and Notes*, Vol. 9, No. 2, Special Issue Fall 1974, 5–7, commemorating the fiftieth anniversary of the Maxwell School.
10. F. Merson. 'Public administration: a science', *Journal of Public Administration*, Vol. I, 1923, p. 221.

of Administration were shaped as much by the Institute of Public Administration and the Institute of Industrial Administration as by the universities. The Institute of Public Administration, for example, provided a meeting ground for public officials and academics and sponsored national and regional lectures and conferences. With the exception of Sheldon, all contributors to the British Philosophy of Administration participated in the Institute's activities. The result, however, was a practitioner-cum-academic approach to administration. Much wisdom, including portions of the doctrines of the British Philosophy of Administration, was accumulated in the form of lectures delivered to practising civil servants and published in the Institute's journal, *Public Administration*. These lectures were illuminating, discussing traditions and embodying the speaker's personality, such as his sense of humour. But, virtually no academic texts on administration emerged in Britain as noted in Chapter 5. Moreover, British central government has given, and continues to give, little positive encouragement to the academic study of public administration – an important point which will be discussed in detail later.

Another significant national development in Britain, which contrasted with the American experience, was the growth of trade unionism. The trade-union movement was stronger in Britain after the First World War than in the United States – one of the factors which caused Britain to take the 'middle path' between scientific management and psychology[11]. Haldane, Sheldon and Urwick bore in mind trade unionism when expounding their administrative thought, particularly their ethical ideals. Also, the British corporate bodies – notably the National Institute of Industrial Psychology – modified aspects of American scientific management to suit its psychological interests *and* to meet the approval of trade-union officials. In the United States, many of the great industries were not part of a proper trade-union movement until the late 1930s. Therefore, the influence of trade unionism figured slightly less in American thought and practice.

A number of national developments in Britain and the United States have been seen to shape the emergence of administrative thought – and practice – in *different* ways. Briefly, some of the *similarities* between administrative developments in the two countries will now be recalled. Both British and American administrative thought this century was influenced by war. The British Philosophy of Administration embodied within it many lessons from war administration. Wallas drew upon

11. See Ch. 4, pp. 161–2, 192–3.

decisions taken in wartime to illustrate his ideas about group decision-making;[12] Haldane was War Minister and developed his early thought in the context of administration for war and Urwick served in the First World War, finding the experience valuable when he returned to business.[13] Likewise, Waldo's study records the effect of war on American administrative thought and practice.[14]

In addition to war, both countries shared a common desire to move away from nineteenth-century rule-of-thumb attitudes towards administration, particularly in the sphere of business, and to identify scientific principles. With respect to scientific principles of administration, there was also common ground between British and American government reports. Chapter 3 has revealed that the British Haldane Report (1918) bore similarities to the American Brownlow Report (1937), even though the acronym SLOCUS is more relevant than POSDCORB to describe the principles underlying the British Philosophy of Administration. Again, both Britain and the United States were influenced by Germanic thought. Woodrow Wilson's argument for a science of administration in the United States, akin to the German science, helped to mould the American doctrines,[15] as did Haldane's admiration of German writings on administration.[16] Finally, similarities existed between the British and American discoveries about human well-being in organisations. In fact, the lengthy experiments conducted at the Hawthorne plant in the United States verified some of the earlier less co-ordinated British ideas.

Although not classifying as a national development, it is applicable to mention another similarity between British and American administrative thought in the period 1900–39. The views of the American, Mary Parker Follett, had much in common with the British Philosophy of Administration. She contributed to some of the Rowntree conferences and, additionally, shared similar viewpoints with Wallas, Haldane and Urwick. Haldane wrote the introduction to a later impression of her book *The New State* (1926) and they both regarded organisations as being dynamic and self-developing. They were firm believers in democracy and favoured the idea of a creative, or inspired, democracy.[17] Like Wallas and Urwick, Miss Follett had studied 'the new

12. See Ch. 2, pp. 56–8.
13. See Ch. 3, pp. 88–92.
14. D. Waldo, *Administrative State*, pp. 10–12.
15. See Ch. 1, pp. 10–11.
16. See Ch. 3, pp. 88–9.
17. See M. P. Follett, *The New State* (New York) 1918. Fifth impression 1926, pp. vi–p. 15.

psychology'[18] and integrated psychological ideas into her administrative thought. It is not surprising, then, that Urwick paid tribute to Miss Follett before an audience of the Institute of Public Administration, following her death in Boston in the 1930s.[19] Her views have been included with some difficulty within the traditional American doctrine of the science of administration. Indeed, sometimes, her thinking has been omitted because of her early stress on psychology, which she propounded often in lecture form – again both characteristics of the British Philosophy of Administration.

2. The relevance of the British Philosophy of Administration today

This section begins by observing the continuing effect on the study of administration in Britain of the practitioner-cum-academic approach. The British Philosophy of Administration emerged from a less academic background than the American doctrines and this factor still influences the study of administration today. British academics in the 1970s are uncertain whether public and business administration are academic disciplines in their own right and, if so, where they should be located in the university structure? Although the British Civil Service has had its Civil Service College for the training of public officials since 1970, Britain continues to lag behind the United States with respect to schools of administration. One comparatively new British 'graduate school' was launched in 1963 by the Institute of Local Government Studies at the University of Birmingham.[20] In addition to the graduate school, this Institute offers management training for British local government officers and undertakes numerous research activities. On the whole, however, British dons are still seeking to develop the academic disciplines of public and business administration and to establish 'university-linked' schools of administration on the lines of

18. In connection with 'the new psychology' Miss Follett mentioned specifically W. McDougall's work, *Social Psychology*, and Wallas' books, *Human Nature in Politics* and *The Great Society*. However, Wallas had indicated a fundamental weakness in McDougall's thinking, see Ch. 4, pp. 185–6.

19. L. Urwick, 'A republic of administration', *Public Administration*, Vol. XIII, 1935, pp. 263–70. Urwick also co-edited Miss Follett's papers, see L. Urwick and H. C. Metcalf, *Dynamic Administration: The Collected Papers of Mary Parker Follett* (London) 1941. Reprinted edn 1965. Urwick paid tribute again to Miss Follett in L. Urwick and E. F. L. Brech, *The Making of Scientific Management* (London) Vol. I, 1945. Reprinted edn 1966, pp. 48–57.

20. See R. A. W. Rhodes, 'The state of public administration: An evaluation and a response', *Public Administration Bulletin*, No. 16, June 1974, pp. 27–39.

the American schools.[21]

It is the academic study of business administration which appears to be progressing more favourably in Britain than public administration. The recent Chapman Report shows that central government has given generous grants to the British Institute of Management to further management studies for industry and commerce. Yet, the study of public administration has received scant recognition by central government.[22] The Report suggests a complacency within the Civil Service towards the academic discipline of public administration and a misunderstanding about the nature and content of such courses. Examples of the complacency are a lack of significant reward within the Civil Service promotion system to diplomas and degrees in public administration, and the failure to implement the idea of a committee to examine the study of public administration in the British universities and colleges in relation to the needs of the public services. Lastly, another example is the meagre secondment of civil servants to the universities – despite participation by a high proportion of university lecturers at the Civil Service College.[23] Until more official encouragement is given in Britain to the academic study of public administration, there will be inadequate demand for the university-linked schools or for the latest proposal of a British Brookings Institution for research in government and the social sciences generally.[24]

A more positive effect of the British Philosophy of Administration today is the renewed interest in a *philosophy* of administration. In the United States, there is evidence of a disenchantment with the single science of administration, which predominated again in the 1960s and, this time, influenced more substantially the theory and practice of British administration. There is now a fresh revival of ethics. This development has been called 'the new public administration' in the United States. Yet, its message reflects many of the ideas of the earlier British Philosophy of Administration. There is alarm about a 'runaway technology' and a call for organisations to reduce social and psychic

21. See F. F. Ridley, 'Public administration: cause for discontent', *Public Administration*, Vol. 50, Spring 1972, 71–7. Besides the Maxwell School at Syracuse, the American graduate schools include the Harvard Business School and the Kennedy School of Government at Harvard, the Wilson School at Princeton and the Pittsburgh Graduate School of Public Affairs.

22. By contrast, British local government has given greater reward and encouragement to its personnel to gain qualifications in administration.

23. R. A. Chapman, *Teaching Public Administration* (London) 1973.

24. Professor R. Dahrendorf, Director of the London School of Economics has recommended that a research organisation should be established in Britain similar to the American Brookings Institution. See H. Keast, 'Brookings Institution for Britain', *Local Government Chronicle*, 28 Jan. 1977, 83–6.

suffering and to enhance life opportunities for workers inside and outside the organisation. Second thoughts are being given to scientific techniques, such as PPBS, and vigorous attempts are being made to define ethical guidelines and to examine the teaching of ethics of administration.[25]

In Britain, following corruption in local government which had ramifications for central government, a Royal Commission on Standards of Conduct in Public Life reported in 1976.[26] Similar fears to those in the United States are being expressed about scientific advances – and scientific techniques, including cost–benefit analysis, are being evaluated more critically.[27] However, we can learn from the British Philosophy of Administration the importance of a *balance* between science and ethics and we should avoid oscillating between the two extremes.

Besides a general interest in a philosophy of administration, individual components of the British Philosophy of Administration are still relevant in the 1970s. R. Klein (1974) has urged, in similar vein to Sheldon, the development of policy-making studies. While Sheldon suggested that the conditions and purposes of policy-making should be analysed,[28] Klein has proposed that a typology of policy situations should be established.[29] The Haldane Report (1918) recommended the use of committees[30] and, today, the concept of committees as co-ordinating and communicating devices is a major corner-stone of the reorganised British National Health Service.[31] But, some disadvantages of committees were noted by Urwick in the earlier doctrines and we should do well to reconsider these, and other, disadvantages of committees.

In view of the current interest in ethics of administration, what ethical ideals can be carried forward from the period ending 1939 to the present day? The ideal of service to the community underlying the

25. See F. Marini ed., *Toward a New Public Administration: The Minnowbrook Perspective* (USA) 1971. See also J. A. Rohr, 'The study of ethics in the P. A. curriculum', *Public Administration Review*, Vol. 36, No. 4, July/Aug. 1976, 398–406.
26. *Report of the Royal Commission on Standards of Conduct in Public Life 1974–1976* (London) July 1976. Chairman: The Rt. Hon. Lord Salmon.
27. For example, see P. Self, *Econocrats and the Policy Process: The Politics and Philosophy of Cost-Benefit Analysis* (London) 1975.
28. Ch. 2, pp. 60–7.
29. R. Klein, 'Policy problems and policy perceptions in the National Health Service', *Policy and Politics*, Vol. 2, No. 3, 1974 234–6.
30. Ch. 3, pp. 120–1.
31. See Department of Health and Social Security publication, *Management Arrangements for the Reorganised National Health Service* (London) 1972.

British Philosophy of Administration reminds us of the need to attach an ethical, as well as an economic, cost to goods which are produced. The ideal sought, also, to promote communal over sectional interests. Sheldon warned of dangers to the community if labour tried to determine its own wages and, in Britain now, we are experiencing some of these dangers. Variety, instead of monotony, in work is another ethical factor which continues to be pertinent. The European Commission has proposed abolishing the assembly-line operation because of the psychological harm it causes workers in such industries as car manufacture.[32] But, ample opportunities exist in other types of organisations to enquire into monotony in work. Although the details and examples of the British Philosophy of Administration often are outmoded today, a wealth of wisdom, which is still valid, can be drawn from the doctrines.

32. See 'An escape from the machine', *The Times*, 24 Apr. 1973.

Appendix

Profiles and selected bibliographies relating to the six contributors to the British Philosophy of Administration 1900-1939

A profile and bibliography relating to each contributor to the British Philosophy of Administration is included in this Appendix. The six administrative pioneers are listed in chronological order according to their dates of birth. The profile of each contributor is brief because in all cases, with the exception of Sheldon and Urwick, a detailed autobiography or biography exists.

The bibliographies concerning the six pioneers are selective rather than comprehensive. From the varied writings of each man, we have selected those sources which represent the development of the British Philosophy of Administration. These selected bibliographies have formed the backbone to this book, but they are supported, nevertheless, with texts by numerous other writers, which are listed in the final bibliography.

Richard Burdon Haldane

Rt. Hon. Richard Burdon Haldane, 1st Viscount of Cloan created 1911, F.R.S., K.T., O.M. b. 30 July 1856 s. of Robert Haldane Cloanden and Mary Elizabeth Burdon Sanderson. Educ. Edinburgh Academy, Edinburgh and Göttingen Universities. M.A. First-class Honours in Philosophy, Edinburgh University. Barrister 1879; Q.C. 1890; M.P. (Liberal) Haddingtonshire, Scotland 1885–1911; Secretary of State for War 1905–12; Lord High Chancellor of Great Britain 1912–15 and 1924. Also, Chairman: Machinery of Government Committee 1917–18; Judicial Committee of Privy Council; Rector of Edinburgh University 1905–8; President of the Institute of Public Administration 1922–27; Vice-President of the National Institute of Industrial Psychology 1925–28; Chancellor, University of Bristol; Chancellor St Andrews University, 1928. d. 19 August 1928.

Richard Burdon Haldane was gifted in many spheres; as a lawyer, philosopher and politician. As Secretary of State for War from 1905, he

244

was directly responsible to Parliament for the administration of the War Office and for preparing the Army for war. It was in this capacity that he developed his talent for identifying scientific principles of administration. At this stage, Haldane was engaged in practical aspects of administration and it was not until later, in *Richard Burdon Haldane: An Autobiography*, that he reflected upon his belief in, and search for, principles of administration. Accordingly, his autobiography provides a useful background to his administrative thinking. Haldane carried forward his respect for underlying principles of administration into his role as Chairman of the Machinery of Government Committee, so influencing the findings of the Ministry of Reconstruction *Report of the Machinery of Government Committee* (1918), which perpetuates some of the administrative ideas he implemented as War Minister.

In addition to the foregoing texts, Haldane added to his administrative thought in numerous lectures and addresses. For example, he expressed his ethical idealism about the British Civil Service in his address 'An organized Civil Service' published in the *Journal of Public Administration* (1923). Of equal significance was his speech stressing the constitutional implications for administration, published subsequently as 'The constitutional evolution of the Civil Service' in the *Journal of Public Administration* (1924).

Haldane will be remembered primarily as an investigator of scientific principles of administration – principles which he implemented as Secretary of State for War. But, his ethical idealism and his constitutional awareness should not be underestimated, since they constituted his overall *philosophy* of administration.

Selected bibliography

Books/articles and other writings by Haldane, R. B.

'An organized Civil Service', *Journal of Public Administration*, Vol. I, 1923. Being the President's inaugural address to the Institute of Public Administration.

Ministry of Reconstruction, *Report of the Machinery of Government Committee* (London) HMSO, Cd 9230, 1918. Chairman: R. B. Haldane.

'Preface' to *The Development of the Civil Service* (London) P. S. King, 1922. A series of lectures delivered to the Society of Civil Servants, 1920–21.

Richard Burdon Haldane: An Autobiography (London), Hodder &

Stoughton, 1929. Published posthumously by his sister, Elizabeth.

Royal Commission on the Civil Service: Appendix to First Report of the Commissioners 1 Vol. (London), HMSO, Cd 6210, 1912. R. B. Haldane is cross-examined by Commissioner G. Wallas.

Royal Commission on the Civil Service: Appendix to Sixth Report of the Commissioners (London) HMSO, Cd 8130, 1915. Haldane is cross-examined regarding his proposal for a separate Department of Justice to absorb the administrative work of the Lord Chancellor.

'The constitutional evolution of the Civil Service', *Journal of Public Administration*, Vol. II, 1924. Being the Presidential address to the Institute of Public Administration, Oct. 1923.

'The machinery of government', *The Civil Servant and His Profession* (London), Pitman. A lecture delivered to the Society of Civil Servants, Mar. 1920.

Commentaries on Haldane, R. B.

'Haldane and defence', by C. Falls, published in *Public Administration*, Vol. 35, 1957.

'Haldane, Rt. Hon. Richard Burdon Haldane', *Who Was Who 1916–1928*, Vol. 2 (London), A. & C. Black, 1929.

'Lord Haldane', by Rt. Hon. Viscount Grey of Fallodon, published in *Public Administration*, Vol. VI, 1928.

'Lord Haldane as Lord Chancellor', by Sir C. Schuster, published in *Public Administration*, Vol. VI, 1928.

'Lord Haldane at the War Office', by Sir C. Harris, published in *Public Administration*, Vol. VI, 1928.

'Lord Haldane, his influence on higher education and on administration', by Sir H. F. Heath, published in *Public Administration*, Vol. VI, 1928.

Graham Wallas

Graham Wallas b. Sunderland 31 May 1858 s. of Rev. G. I. Wallas, afterwards Rector of Shobrooke, Devon and Ada Radford. Educ. Shrewsbury School 1871–77; Corpus Christi College 1877–1881,

classical scholar; second-class *Literae Humaniores* 1881. School-
master 1881–90; University Extension Lecturer 1890; Lecturer at
London School of Economics 1895–1923; University Professor of
Political Science 1914–23; Professor Emeritus 1923. Also,
member of Fabian Society 1886–1904; London School Board
1894–1904; member of Technical Education Board of London
County Council 1898–1904; member of London County Council
1904–7; member of Royal Commission on the Civil Service
1912–15; Lowell Lecturer (Boston USA) 1914 and Dodge
Lecturer (Yale) 1919. d. 9 August 1932.

Graham Wallas' name is associated usually with *Human Nature in
Politics* (1908); the first book he published after his early study of *The
Life of Francis Place* (1897). Place had been both a disciple and a
personal friend of Jeremy Bentham and in the course of writing Place's
biography, Wallas came to question seriously Bentham's interpretation
of human nature. From his doubts about Bentham's views on
psychology, Wallas developed his own thoughts for his book *Human
Nature in Politics*. He believed that an understanding of human nature
was the key to successful society and government and the main thread
which runs through Wallas' works is his desire to promote a greater
knowledge of the human processes of government, particularly
decision-making.

From a purely administrative viewpoint, Wallas' book *The Great
Society* (1914) stands out as his most important work. Indeed, if the
sections on administration had been approached more systematically,
rather than emerging from his views on psychology, sociology and
philosophy, this book could have acted as 'the administrator's bible'. It
is rich in insights about administration – for example, it contains
Wallas' criticisms of American scientific management and his ideas
about human well-being and happiness in organisations. Two works of
secondary importance for administration are, firstly, *Our Social
Heritage* (1921), which includes two case-studies of group decision-
making extracted from the First Report of the British Dardanelles
Commission (1917) and the Report of the Mesopotamia Commission
(1917). Secondly, *Social Judgment* represents the first part only of a
new book Wallas was working on when he died in 1932, and which was
published posthumously by his daughter May. In this last work, Wallas
used ideas similar to those found later in C. I. Barnard's book *The
Functions of the Executive* (1938) about logical and non-logical thought

processes in decision-making.

Wallas' contributions to administrative thought are stated principally in book form; his articles and other writings simply providing more information about himself, his life and his opinions without offering any substantial extension to his books. A detailed background to Wallas' life has been provided by M. J. Wiener *Between Two Worlds: The Political Thought of Graham Wallas* and this study enhances our appreciation of Wallas – the man – although some of Wiener's conclusions with respect to Wallas' political thought can be challenged from an administrative viewpoint. For example, Wiener tends to see Wallas as an isolated thinker between the two worlds of science and ethics – or evangelism. But, seen in the context of British administrative thought this century, Wallas had much in common with other British thinkers, such as Haldane, Stamp and Sheldon, all of whom were seeking to unite the two worlds of science and ethics into a *philosophy* to underlie society and administration.

Selected bibliography

Books/articles and other writings by Wallas, G.

Human Nature in Politics. First published (London) A. Constance, 1908. Republished (London) Constable, 1962.

Royal Commission on the Civil Service: Appendix to First Report of the Commissioners 1 Vol. (London) HMSO Cd 6210, 1912. G. Wallas cross-examines witness R. B. Haldane.

Social Judgment (London) G. Allen & Unwin, 1934.

'Socialism and the Fabian Society.' First published as an essay in 1916. Reprinted posthumously in *Men and Ideas: Essays by Graham Wallas*, ed. by M. Wallas (London) G. Allen & Unwin, 1940.

The Art of Thought (London) Cape, 1926.

The Great Society: A Psychological Analysis (London) Macmillan, 1914.

Our Social Heritage (New Haven) Yale University Press, 1921.

Commentaries on Wallas, G.

Between Two Worlds: The Political Thought of Graham Wallas, by

M. J. Wiener (London) Oxford University Press, 1971.

'Graham Wallas', by H. J. Laski, published in *The New Statesman and Nation*, 20 Aug. 1932.

'Graham Wallas', by J. Stamp, published in *Economica*, Vol. XII, Nos. 35–8, 1932.

'Wallas Graham', *Who Was Who 1929–1940*, Vol. 3 (London) A. & C. Black, 1941.

William Henry Beveridge

William Henry Beveridge, Baron Beveridge b. 1879 s. of Henry Beveridge and his second wife Annette Akroyd. Educ. Charterhouse and Balliol College, Oxford; first-class *Literae Humaniores*; Stowell civil law fellowship at University College Oxford 1902–9; Subwarden of Toynbee Hall, Whitechapel 1903–5; civil servant 1908–19; Director of London School of Economics 1919–37; Master of University College Oxford 1937–44. Also, assistant inquirer Royal Commission on the Poor Laws 1905–9; Chairman of the Interdepartmental Committee on Social Insurance and Allied Services 1941 leading to the Beveridge Report; 1944–45 (Liberal) MP for Berwick-on-Tweed. Later Chairman Aycliffe and Peterlee 'new towns'. d. 16 March 1963

The two studies normally associated with William Beveridge concern unemployment and social security and they are *Unemployment: A Problem of Industry* (1909) and the *Beveridge Report* (1942). But, Beveridge also published his views on administration, drawing on his experience as a civil servant. Beveridge entered the Board of Trade in 1908, transferred to the new Ministry of Munitions in 1915 and progressed to the Ministry of Food to become Permanent Secretary in 1919. It was this latter experience which motivated his administrative thought; in particular his thinking about the influential, albeit anonymous, role of the Permanent Secretary in policy-making which Beveridge portrayed in *The Public Service in War and in Peace* (1920). This public lecture was an attempt to give a first-hand account – or inside view – of the higher Civil Service, which Beveridge was able to do freely in his new capacity as Director of the London School of Economics without contravening the regulations preventing civil servants from saying or writing anything in public about their work or position.

Some Experiences of Economic Control in War-Time (1940) is the published version of another lecture Beveridge delivered and it provides a brilliant small book on public administration based on his direct, practical experience as a civil servant. It contains two excellent case-studies – the first concerned with some lessons in food control, focusing upon the Ministry of Food, while the second case-study illustrates bottle-necks in the Ministry of Munitions. Although Graham Wallas' writing included two case-studies on decision-making, British administrative thinkers between 1900 and 1939 did not promote case-studies actively as a teaching method as in the United States. Therefore, it is useful to be able to identify some case-study material within the British Philosophy of Administration.

Beveridge did not document his administrative thought in many publications and, therefore, his autobiography *Power and Influence* (1953) affords further insights into his practical work as a civil servant. Another significant piece of administrative writing by Beveridge is his lecture to the Society of Civil Servants entitled 'The civil servant of the future', published in *The Development of the Civil Service* (1922). Like *The Public Service in War and in Peace*, this lecture attempts to reveal the true working of the British Civil Service and to remove the myths which had grown up around its working.

Selected bibliography

Books/articles and other writings by Beveridge, W.

Power and Influence: An Autobiography (London) Hodder & Stoughton, 1953.

Some Experiences of Economic Control in War-Time (London) Oxford University Press, 1940. Sidney Ball lecture delivered Feb. 1940, Oxford.

'The civil servant of the future', *The Development of the Civil Service* (London) P. S. King, 1922. A lecture delivered to the Society of Civil Servants, 1920–21.

The London School of Economics and Its Problems 1919–1937 (London) G. Allen & Unwin, 1960.

The Public Service in War and in Peace (London) Constable, 1920. This is a longer printed version of Beveridge's public lecture delivered in 1919 as Director of the London School of Economics.

Commentaries on Beveridge, W.

An Epic of Clare Market; Birth and Early Days of The London School of Economics, by J. Beveridge (London) G. Bell, 1960. Janet Mair married W. Beveridge in Dec. 1942.

'Beveridge, William Henry', *International Encyclopaedia of the Social Sciences*, Vol. 2 (USA) Crowell, Collier and Macmillan, 1968.

Josiah Charles Stamp

Josiah Charles Stamp, First Baron of Shortlands created 1938; G.C.B. cr. 1935; G.B.E. cr. 1924; K.B.E. cr. 1920. b. 21 June 1880 s. of Charles Stamp and Clara Jane Evans. Educ. London University (External student, faculty of Economics and Political Science) B.Sc. First-class Honours 1911; D.Sc. 1916. Civil servant 1896–1919; industrialist 1919–26; President of the Council and Chairman Elect of the Board of the LMS Railway 1926–41. Also, Director of the Bank of England; member of Royal Commission on Income Tax 1919; British representative on the Reparation Commission's (Dawes) Committee on German Currency and Finance 1924, Vice-President of the National Institute of Industrial Psychology 1928 onwards; President of the Institute of Public Administration 1937–41; Chairman of the London School of Economics. d. 16/17 April 1941.

Josiah Stamp's life as a civil servant and industrialist fails to suggest the immense variety of work to which he dedicated himself inside and outside his fixed hours of duty. The above biographical paragraph states only a fraction of his achievements, which range from being patron of innumerable welfare organisations to the holder of honorary degrees from over twenty-five universities. A study of Josiah Stamp's administrative thought, therefore, should begin with *Josiah Stamp Public Servant: The Life of the First Baron Stamp of Shortlands* (1964). This biography by J. Harry Jones traces Stamp's life from before his entry into the Inland Revenue Department of the British Civil Service as a boy clerk in 1896, through his external studies at London University, to his work as Chairman and President of the LMS Railway in 1926. Finally, Stamp's death in his own home in 1941 from an enemy bomb is recorded.

From the administrative perspective, two of Stamp's most

interesting books are, firstly, *Motive and Method in a Christian Order* (1936) which seeks to identify non-economic incentives which could be used in society and in organisations to replace the emphasis on monetary incentives. The second book is *The Science of Social Adjustment* (1937) in which Stamp pointed to the necessity of obtaining equilibrium between scientific and ethical developments in modern society and his views apply to administration as well as to other aspects of society.

In addition to his books, Stamp, like Haldane and Beveridge, put forward his administrative ideas in addresses and lectures. For example, his views about bureaucracy are of great value, but they were delivered verbally to the Institute of Public Administration. These addresses were published as 'The contrast between the administration of business and public affairs', *Journal of Public Administration* (1923) and 'Recent tendencies towards the devolution of legislative functions to the administration', *Journal of Public Administration* (1924). Stamp's main contribution to British administrative thought, therefore, lies in the sphere of ethics and in connection with the problem of bureaucracy.

Selected bibliography

Books/articles and other writings by Stamp, J.

Ideals of a Student (London) E. Benn, 1933. A collection of addresses which Stamp gave internationally in the early 1930s.

Motive and Method in a Christian Order (London) Epworth Press, 1936.

'Note to the address by the Rt. Hon. Sir J. Anderson (on bureaucracy), *Public Administration*, Vol. VII, 1929.

'Recent tendencies towards the devolution of legislative functions to the administration', *Journal of Public Administration*, Vol. II, 1924. Being the inaugural lecture delivered to the Manchester Regional Group of the Institute of Public Administration.

'The administrator and a planned society', *Public Administration*, Vol. XVI, 1938. The President's address given at the inaugural meeting of the Institute of Public Administration, 1937.

'The contrast between the administration of business and public affairs', *Journal of Public Administration* Vol. I, 1923. An address delivered to the Society of Civil Servants at the London School of Economics.

The Science of Social Adjustment (London) MacMillan, 1937.

Commentaries on Stamp, J.

'Stamp, Josiah Charles Stamp', *Who Was Who 1941–1950*, Vol. 4 (London) A. & C. Black, 1952.

Josiah Stamp Public Servant: The Life of the First Baron Stamp of Shortlands, by J. H. Jones (London) Pitman, 1964.

Lyndall Urwick

Lyndall Urwick, Lt-Col., O.B.E., M.C., M.A., F.B.I.M., M.I.P.E., C.I.Mech.E., b. 3 March 1891 s. of Sir Henry Urwick. Educ. New College, Oxford. Organising Secretary Rowntree & Co. Ltd 1922–28; Director International Management Institute, Geneva 1928–33; Chairman Urwick, Orr & Partners Ltd (management consultants) 1934–63. Also, Consultant HM Treasury 1940–42; Chairman Committee on Education for Management 1947; Vice-Chairman British Institute of Management 1947, Hon. D.Sc. (Univ. of Aston) 1969. Currently resident in NSW, Australia.

Lyndall Urwick was the most prolific writer of the six contributors to the British Philosophy of Administration. However, his ability to record his own administrative thought and to restate the views of other pioneers, such as Henri Fayol, has certain disadvantages. For example, faced with an array of Urwick's writing on administration, the tendency has been to concentrate on a few of his better-known works, such as *Papers on the Science of Administration* (1937), and to neglect his other equally valuable administrative ideas.

Urwick's lesser-known administrative ideas include his book *Committees in Organisation* (1930s), which indicates his original thought about committees and increases our knowledge of the principle of 'communication'. Another concise book dedicated to administrative thought is *The Meaning of Rationalisation* (1929). This publication gives Urwick's account of why Britain was cautious towards American scientific management and it defines and explains the growth of the European 'rationalisation' movement, which took place in the interwar years. This book supplements the accounts of American scientific management found in the writings of Graham Wallas and Oliver Sheldon. Urwick followed up *The Meaning of Rationalisation* by other books on American administrative developments – the most useful being *The Making of Scientific Management*, Volumes, I, II and III.

He did not restrict his administrative writing to books, but published many articles as well. Urwick's most revealing article is 'Experimental psychology and the creative impulse', *Psyche* (1922) which shows his early administrative thought before he gave increased attention to scientific principles of administration. Indeed, this article confirms his ethical approach to administration; his concern for creative expression in work and the need to develop our understanding of psychology. The article provides a more rounded picture of Lyndall Urwick before he became rather impatient with Britain's slowness to implement scientific principles and with the misconceptions about American scientific management, which he sought to rectify.

Selected bibliography

Books/articles and other writings by Urwick, L.

'A republic of administration', *Public Administration*, Vol. XIII, 1935. A luncheon talk to the Institute of Public Administration, Jan. 1935, as a tribute to the late Mary Parker Follett.

Committees in Organisation (Reprinted from the *British Management Review* (London) by Management Journals, late 1930s.

'Executive decentralisation with functional co-ordination', *Public Administration*, Vol. XIII, 1935.

'Experimental psychology and the creative impulse', *Psyche*, Vol. III, No. 1 (New Series) July 1922.

Management of Tomorrow, (London) Nisbet, 1933.

'Organization as a technical problem', *Papers on the Science of Administration*, ed. by L. Gulick and L. Urwick (New York) Institute of Public Administration, 1937. Based on a paper read to the British Association for the Advancement of Science, Sept. 1933, Leicester.

Papers on the Science of Administration (New York) Institute of Public Administration, 1937. Co-editor L. Gulick.

The Development of Scientific Management in Great Britain (London) Management Journals, late 1930s.

'The function of administration: with special reference to the work of

Henri Fayol', *Papers on the Science of Administration*, ed. by L. Gulick and L. Urwick (New York) Institute of Public Administration 1937. A lecture delivered to the Institute of Industrial Administration, Nov. 1934.

The Making of Scientific Management (London) Management Publications Trust, Vols. I, II and III, 1945–48. Co-author E. F. L. Brech.

The Meaning of Rationalisation (London) Nisbet, 1929.

L. Urwick, 'The nature of line and staff', *Management: A Book of Readings*, ed. by H. Koontz and C. O'Donnell (New York) McGraw-Hill, Inc, 1964.

Commentaries on Urwick, L.

Information supplied by Rowntree Mackintosh Ltd, York dated 5 Feb. 1975.

Personal correspondence and notes to the author from Lt-Col. Urwick dated 28 Feb. 1975 and 1 Apr. 1975 and Sept. 1976.

'Urwick, Lt. Col. Lyndall', *International Who's Who* (London) Europa Publications, thirty-sixth edn 1972–73.

Oliver Sheldon

Oliver Sheldon b. 13 July 1894. Educ. King's College School, Wimbledon and Merton College, Oxford, B.A. Officer in the East Surreys 1914–18 War. Joined Rowntree & Co. Ltd 1919 as Personal Assistant to Mr B. S. Rowntree; appointed in 1931 to the general Board of Directors at the Rowntree Co. Member of the National Liberal Club; Honorary Fellow of the Mercer's Company of London and Fellow of the Institute of Industrial Administration. d. 7 Aug. 1951.

Far less is known about Oliver Sheldon than the other contributors to the British Philosophy of Administration, despite the esteem his book *The Philosophy of Management* (1923) gained in Britain and the United States. Sheldon does not appear in the appropriate volume of *Who Was Who*, but his service to industry and to British administrative thought and practice is remembered warmly today by present employees at the Rowntree Mackintosh Co. Ltd, York.

Sheldon's greatest contribution to British administrative thought is his major work *The Philosophy of Management*, which epitomises his views about the ethical role business administration should play in modern British life. However, his administrative thought did not rest with ethics of administration. He advocated, in connection with business administration, scientific principles which rival in importance those delineated in the Haldane Report with respect to public administration. Sheldon recognised the similar development being made in the spheres of public and business administration and his book contains a useful appendix which draws attention to the parallel conclusions about scientific principles. Although he wrote no more books on his own, Sheldon provided a well-structured chapter in a joint publication by personnel at the Rowntree Company entitled *Factory Organization* (1928). This joint work was one of the earliest British attempts this century to define systematically what an organisation is and how it expands. Therefore, Sheldon's chapter forms a vital complement to his sections on scientific principles in his book *The Philosophy of Management*.

Sheldon extended his contribution to British administrative thought by writing articles, which he published in the United States. The two most interesting articles are, firstly, 'The art of management: from a British point of view', *Bulletin of the Taylor Society* (1923) which explains Britain's cautiousness towards, and rejection of, American scientific management. The second significant article is 'Policy and policy-making', published in the *Harvard Business Review* (1925). He was astute in recognising the need to develop the study of policy-making, as well as administration, so that the two interrelating aspects of industry might progress together.

Sheldon worked actively in industrial administration, but he took time aside to reflect and write about the subject. He had an original mind; a colourful writing style – although somewhat emotive – and since he wrote sparingly, each of his writings is worthy of attention.

Selected bibliography

Books/articles and other writings by Sheldon, O.

Factory Organization (London) Pitman, 1928. Co-authors were C. H. Northcott, J. W. Wardropper and L. Urwick.

'Policy and policy-making' *Harvard Business Review*, Vol. IV, No. 1, Oct. 1925.

'Taylor the creative leader', *Bulletin of the Taylor Society*, Vol. IX, No. 1, Feb. 1924.

'The art of management: from a British point of view', *Bulletin of the Taylor Society*, Vol. VIII, No. 6, Dec. 1923.

The Philosophy of Management (London) Pitman. First published 1923; reprinted edn 1930.

'The significance of rationalization', *Harvard Business Review*, Vol. VI, No. 3, Apr. 1928.

Commentaries on Sheldon, O.

Information supplied by Rowntree-Mackintosh Ltd, York dated 5 Feb. 1975.

Bibliography

Additional sources to the selected texts relating to the contributors to the British Philosophy of Administration

Books/articles and press sources

Albrow, M. *Bureaucracy* (London) Macmillan, 1970.

Allen, C. K. *Law in the Making* (London) Oxford University Press, 1927.

Anderson. Rt. Hon. Sir J. 'Bureaucracy', *Public Administration*, Vol. VII, 1929.

Appleby, P. *Policy and Administration* (Alabama) University of Alabama Press. First published 1949; reprinted edn 1965.

Argyris, C. *Personality and Organization: The Conflict Between System and the Individual* (New York) Harper & Bros., 1957.

Baker, R. J. S. *Administrative Theory and Public Administration* (London) Hutchinson, 1972.

Banfield, E. C. ed. *Urban Government: A Reader in Administration and Politics* (New York) The Free Press. First published 1961; revised edn 1969.

Barnard, C. I. *The Functions of the Executive* (Cambridge, Mass.) Harvard University Press. First published 1938; thirtieth edn 1968.

Bentham, J. *An Introduction to The Principles of Morals and Legislation*. First published 1789; republished (Darien, Conn.) Hafner, 1948.

Bentham, J. 'Constitutional Code', *The Works of Jeremy Bentham*, Vol. IX, ed. by J. Bowring (Edinburgh), W. Tait, 1843.

Bridges, Rt. Hon. Lord. 'Haldane and the Machinery of Government Committee', *Public Administration*, Vol. 35, 1957.

Briggs, A. *A Study of the Works of Seebohm Rowntree 1877–1954* (London) Longmans, 1961.

Bunbury, Sir H. N. 'Notes: The Summer Conference of 1932', *Public Administration*, Vol. X, 1932.

Bunbury, Sir H. N. 'Rationalisation and the processes of administration', *Public Administration*, Vol. VIII, 1930.

Bunbury, Sir H. N. 'The Institute of Public Administration: A critical survey', *Public Administration*, Vol. XI, 1933.

Bunbury, Sir H. N. 'The problem of government in the United States', *Public Administration*, Vol. XVII, 1939.

Cadbury, E. *Experiments in Industrial Organization* (London) Longmans, 1912.

Carr, C. T. *Delegated Legislation* (London) Cambridge University Press, 1921.

Catlin, G. E. G. *The Science and Method of Politics* (New York) A. A. Knopf, 1927; republished edn (Hamden, Conn.) Archon Books, 1964.

Chapman, R. A. *The Higher Civil Service in Britain* (London) Constable, 1970.

Chapman, R. A. 'The real cause of bureaucracy', *Administration*, Vol. 12, 1964.

Chapman, R. A. *Teaching Public Administration* (London) Royal Institute of Public Administration, 1973. A Report submitted to the Public Administration Committee of the Joint University Council for Social and Public Administration.

Chester, D. N., ed., and Willson, F. M. G. *The Organization of British Central Government 1914–1964* (London) G. Allen & Unwin. First published 1957; second edn 1968.

Child, J. *British Management Thought: A Critical Analysis* (London) G. Allen & Unwin, 1969.

Cole, G. D. H. *British Trade Unionism Today: A Survey* (London) V. Gollancz, 1939.
Cole, G. D. H. 'Guild socialism', *Encyclopaedia of the Social Sciences*, Vol. VII, 1932.
Cole, G. D. H. 'Trade unions: United Kingdom and Irish Free State', *Encyclopaedia of the Social Sciences*, Vol. XV, 1935.
Corner, H. G. 'The aims of the Institute of Public Administration', *Journal of Public Administration*, Vol. I, 1923.
Crozier, M. *The Bureaucratic Phenomenon* (Chicago) University of Chicago Press, 1964. Fifth Impression 1971.
Dale, H. E. *The Higher Civil Service of Great Britain* (London) Oxford University Press, 1941.
Davis, K. *Human Relations at Work: The Dynamics of Organizational Behavior* (New York) McGraw-Hill. First published 1957; third ed. 1967.
Deane, H. A. 'Laski, Harold J.' *International Encyclopaedia of the Social Sciences*, Vol. 9, 1968.
Demetriadi, Sir S. *A Reform for the Civil Service* Cassell, 1921.
Demetriadi, Sir S. *Inside a Government Office* (London) Cassell, 1921.
Dicey, A. V. *Introduction to the Study of the Law of the Constitution*. First published (London) Macmillan, 1885. Eighth edn 1915 and ninth ed. 1939; reprinted 1956.
Dicey, A. V. 'The development of administrative law in England', *Law Quarterly Review*, Vol. XXXI, 1915.
Dimock, M. E. *A Philosophy of Administration* (New York) Harper & Row, 1958.
Dimock, M. E. 'Public administration: The potential incentives of public employment', *The American Political Science Review*, Vol. XXVII, 1933.
Dimock. M. E. 'Scientific method and the future of political science' in *Essays in Political Science in Honor of Westel Woodbury Willoughby* ed. by J. M. Mathews and J. Hart (Baltimore), The John Hopkins Press, 1937.
Dimock, M. E. 'The criteria and objectives of public administration', in *The Frontiers of Public Administration* ed. by J. M. Gaus et al. (Chicago) University of Chicago Press, 1936.
Dimock, M. E. 'The role of discretion in modern administration', in *The Frontiers of Public Administration* ed. by J. M. Gaus et al. (Chicago) University of Chicago Press, 1936.
Downs, A. *Inside Bureaucracy* (Boston, Mass.) Little, Brown, 1967.
Dror, Y. *Public Policymaking Reexamined* (San Francisco) Chandler Publishing Co., 1968.
Dunsire, A. *Administration: The Word and the Science* (London) Robertson, 1973.
Easton, D. *The Political System: An Inquiry into the State of Political Science* (New York) A. A. Knopf. First published 1953; reprinted edn 1965.
Ellis, H. H. 'The relations between State departments and the nation', *Journal of Public Administration*, Vol. IV, 1926.
Emery, F. E. ed. *Systems Thinking* (London) Penguin Books Ltd. 1969.
Fayol, H. *General and Industrial Management*. First published 1916; republished (London) Pitman, 1969.
Fayol, H. 'The administrative theory in the State', in *Papers on the Science of Administration*, ed. by L. Gulick and L. Urwick (New York) Institute of Public Administration, 1937.
Finer, H. *The British Civil Service* (London) The Fabian Society and G. Allen & Unwin 1937.
Finer, S. E. *Comparative Government* (London) Penguin Press, 1970.
Follett, M. P. *Dynamic Administration: The Collected Papers of Mary Parker Follett*, ed. by H. C. Metcalf and L. Urwick (London) Pitman. First published 1941; reprinted edn 1965.
Follett, M. P. *Freedom and Coordination* (London) Management Publications Trust, 1949.
Follett, M. P. *The New State* (New York) Longmans, 1918. Fifth impression 1926.

Ford, P. and G. *A Breviate of Parliamentary Papers 1900–1916* (Oxford) Blackwell & Mott, 1957.

Ford, P. and G. *A Breviate of Parliamentary Papers 1917–1939* (Shannon) Irish University Press, 1969.

Friedrich, C. J. and Cole, T. *Responsible Bureaucracy: A Study of the Swiss Civil Service* (Cambridge, Mass.) Harvard University Press, 1932.

Friedrich, C. J. 'Some observations on Weber's analysis of bureaucracy', in *Reader in Bureaucracy*, ed. by R. K. Merton (New York) The Free Press, 1952.

Fry, G. K. 'Policy-planning units in British central government', *Public Administration*, Vol. 50, Summer 1972.

Fry, G. K. *Statesman in Disguise: The Changing Role of the Administrative Class of the British Home Civil Service 1853–1966* (London) Macmillan, 1969.

Gardiner, G. and Martin, A. eds *Law Reform Now* (London) V. Gollancz, 1974.

Gilbreth, F. B. *Primer of Scientific Management* (London) Constable, 1912.

Goodnow, F. J. *Politics and Administration: A Study in Government* (New York) Macmillan, 1900.

Gordon, H. *The War Office* (London) Putnam, 1935. The Whitehall Series.

Gouldner, A. W. *Patterns of Industrial Bureaucracy* (Glencoe, Illinois) The Free Press, 1954.

Graicunas, V. A. 'Relationship in organization', in *Papers on the Science of Administration*, ed. by L. Gulick and L. Urwick (New York) Institute of Public Administration, 1937.

Gulick, L. 'George Maxwell had a dream: An historical note with a comment on the future', *Maxwell News and Notes*, Vol. 9, No. 2, Special Issue Fall 1974, commemorating the fiftieth anniversary of the Maxwell School.

Gulick, L. 'Notes on the theory of organization: with special reference to government in the United States', in *Papers on the Science of Administration*, ed. by L. Gulick and L. Urwick (New York) Institute of Public Administration, 1937.

Gulick, L. 'Research in public administration' *Public Administration*, Vol. IX, 1931.

Gulick, L. 'The place of finance departments, committees and officers in administrative control', *Public Administration*, Vol. V, 1927.

Haber, S. *Efficiency and Uplift* (Chicago) University of Chicago Press, 1964.

Hamilton, Sir H. P. 'Sir Warren Fisher and the public service', *Public Administration*, Vol. 29, 1951.

Hamilton, Gen. Sir I. *The Soul and Body of an Army* (London) Arnold, 1921.

Harcourt-Smith, Sir C. 'Opening address', *The Civil Servant and His Profession* (London) Pitman, 1920.

Hearnshaw, L. S. *A Short History of British Psychology 1840–1940* (London) Methuen, 1964.

Henderson, A. M. and Parsons, T. eds. *Max Weber: The Theory of Social and Economic Organization*. First published 1947; republished (New York) The Free Press, 1964.

Hewart of Bury, The Rt. Hon. Lord *The New Despotism* (London) Benn, 1929.

Hill, M. J. *The Sociology of Public Administration* (London) Weidenfeld & Nicolson, 1972.

Hobbes, T. *Leviathan*. First published 1651; republished (London) Penguin Books, 1968.

Jennings, W. I. 'Reviews: Ministers' powers', *Public Administration*, Vol. XI, 1933.

Jennings, W. I. 'The Report on Ministers' powers' *Public Administration*, Vol. X, 1932.

Katz, D. and Kahn, R. L. *The Social Psychology of Organizations* (New York) Wiley, 1966.

Keast, H. 'Brookings Institution for Britain', *Local Government Chronicle*, 28 Jan. 1977.

Kelly, E. T. ed. *Welfare Work in Industry* (London) Pitman, 1925.

Klein, R. 'Policy problems and policy perspectives in the National Health Service', *Policy and Politics* Vol. 2, No. 3, 1974.

Landsberger, H. A. *Hawthorne Revisited: Management and the Worker, its Critics and*

Developments in Human Relations in Industry (Ithaca, New York) Cornell University 1958; third printing 1968.

Laski, H. J. *A Grammar of Politics* (London) G. Allen & Unwin. First published 1925; reprinted edn 1926.

Laski, H. J. *An Introduction to Politics* (London) G. Allen & Unwin, 1931.

Laski, H. J. *Authority in the Modern State* (New Haven, Conn.) Yale University Press, 1919.

Laski, H. J. 'Bureaucracy', *Encyclopaedia of the Social Sciences*, Vol. III, 1930.

Laski, H. J. 'Government', *Encyclopaedia of the Social Sciences*, Vol. VII, 1932.

Laski, H. J. *The American Presidency* (New York) Harper & Bros., 1940.

Laski, H. J. 'The Civil Service and Parliament', *The Development of the Civil Service* (London) P. S. King, 1922.

Laski, H. J. 'The growth of administrative discretion', *Journal of Public Administration*, Vol. I, 1923.

Laski, H. J. 'The Price–Laski debate on the Presidential system', *Selected Readings for Government 1a* (USA) Harvard,University Printing Office, 1961.

Laski, H. J. 'The Tomlin Report on the Civil Service', *The Political Quarterly*, Vol. II, No. 4, Oct.–Dec. 1931.

Lasswell, H. D. *Politics: Who Gets What, When, How* First published (New York) McGraw-Hill 1936; reprinted (New York) World Publishing Co., 1972.

Lee, J. 'The psychology of the civil servant', in *The Civil Servant and His Profession* (London) Pitman, 1920.

Lindblom, C. E. 'The Science of "muddling through"', *Public Administration Review*, Vol. 19, Spring 1959.

McGregor, D. *The Human Side of Enterprise* (New York) McGraw-Hill, 1960.

March, J. G. and **Simon, H. A.** *Organizations* (New York) J. Wiley & Sons, 1958.

Marini, F. ed. *Toward a New Public Administration: The Minnowbrook Perspective* (New York) Chandler Pub. Co, 1971.

Martin, K. *Harold Laski (1893–1950): A Biographical Memoir* (London) V. Gollancz, 1953.

Maslow, A. H. 'A theory of human motivation', in *Management and Motivation*, ed. by V. H. Vroom and E. L. Deci (London) Penguin Books, 1970.

Mayo, E. 'The basis of industrial psychology' *Bulletin of the Taylor Society* Vol. IX, No. 6 December 1924.

Mayo, E. *The Human Problems of An Industrial Civilization* (New York) Macmillan, 1933.

Mayo, E. *The Social Problems of An Industrial Civilization* (London) Routledge & Kegan Paul, 1949.

Merson, F. 'Public administration: a science', *Journal of Public Administration*, Vol. I, 1923.

Merton, R. K. 'Bureaucratic structure and personality', in *Reader in Bureaucracy*, ed. by R. K. Merton (New York) The Free Press, 1952.

Merton, R. K., ed. *Reader in Bureaucracy* (New York) The Free Press, 1952.

Merton, R. K. 'The latent functions of the machine', in *Urban Government: A Reader in Administration and Politics*, ed. by E. C. Banfield (New York) The Free Press. First published 1961; revised edn 1969.

Merton, R. K. 'The unanticipated consequences of purposive social action', *American Sociological Review*, Vol. I, 1936.

Mooney, J. D. and **Reiley, A. C.** *Onward Industry! The Principles of Organization and their Significance to Modern Industry* (New York) Harper & Bros., 1931.

Mooney, J. D. 'The principles of organization', in *Papers on the Science of Administration*, ed. by L. Gulick and L. Urwick (New York) Institute of Public Administration, 1937.

Mooney, J. D. *The Principles of Organization* (New York) Harper and Row, 1947. Revised edn.

Mosher, F. C. et al. *Watergate: Implications for Responsible Government.* A Report for the Senate Select Committee on Presidential Campaign Activities by a Panel of the National Academy of Public Administration (New York) Basic Books, 1974.

Muir, R. *Peers and Bureaucrats* (London) Constable, 1910.

Münsterberg, H. *Psychology and Industrial Efficiency* (USA) Houghton Mifflin, 1913.

Murby, M. 'Routine and the civil servant', *The Development of the Civil Service* (London) P. S. King, 1922.

Myers, C. S. 'Industrial overstrain and unrest', Lecture No. 8 in *Lectures on Industrial Administration*, ed. by B. Muscio (London) Pitman, 1920.

Myers, C. S., ed. *Industrial Psychology* (London) T. Butterworth. First published 1929; reprinted edn 1930.

Myers, C. S. *Industrial Psychology in Great Britain* (London) J. Cape. First published 1926; revised edn 1933.

Myers, C. S. *Mind and Work: The Psychological Factors in Industry and Commerce* (London) University of London Press, 1920.

Myers, C. S. 'Psychology and industry', *The British Journal of Psychology*, Vol.X, Mar. 1920.

Newman, B. *Yours for Action* (London) H. Jenkins, 1953.

Novick, D. 'Brief history of program budgeting', in *Current Practice in Program Budgeting* (PPBS), ed. D. Novick (London), Heinemann Educ. Books, 1973.

Parris, H. *Constitutional Bureaucracy* (London) G. Allen & Unwin, 1969.

Person, H. S. 'Scientific management', *Encyclopaedia of the Social Sciences*, Vol. XIII, 1934.

Person, H. S. 'The origin and nature of scientific management', in *Scientific Management in American Industry* ed. by H. S. Person (New York) Harper & Bros. 1929.

Price, D. K. 'Administrative co-ordination in Great Britain and the United States', *Public Administration*, Vol. XIII, 1935.

Price, D. K. 'The Price–Laski debate on the Presidential system', *Selected Readings for Government 1a* (USA) Harvard University Printing Office, 1961.

Rhodes, R. A. W. *An Introduction to Organisation Theory* (London) Joint Committee of Student Societies of the Institute of Municipal Treasurers and Accountants, 1972.

Rhodes, R. A. W. 'Anthony Trollope and the Nineteenth Century Civil Service', *Public Administration*, Vol. 51, Summer 1973.

Rhodes, R. A. W. 'The state of public administration: An evaluation and a response', *Public Administration Bulletin*, No. 16, June 1974.

Ridley, F. F. 'Public administration: cause for discontent', *Public Administration*, Vol. 50, Spring 1972.

Ridley, F. F. *The Study of Government: Political Science and Public Administration* (London) G. Allen & Unwin, 1975.

Riggs, F. W. *Administration in Developing Countries: The Theory of Prismatic Society* (Boston) Houghton Mifflin, 1964.

Roberts, L. 'Committees, legislative', *Encyclopaedia of the Social Sciences*, Vol. IV, 1931.

Robson, W. A. 'Harold Laski', *Public Administration*, Vol. 28, 1950.

Roethlisberger, F. J. and **Dickson, W. J.** *Management and the Worker* (Cambridge, Mass.) Harvard University Press. First published 1939; reprinted edn 1964.

Rohr, J. A. 'The study of ethics in the P. A. curriculum', *Public Administration Review*, Vol. 36, No. 4, July/Aug. 1976.

Rowntree, B. S. *The Human Factor in Business* (London) Longmans. First published 1921; second edn 1925.

Ruggiero, G. de 'Idealism', *Encyclopaedia of the Social Sciences*, Vol. VII, 1932.

Seidman, H. *Politics, Position, and Power: The Dynamics of Federal Organization* (New York) Oxford University Press Inc, 1970.

Self, P. *Administrative Theories and Politics* (London) G. Allen & Unwin, 1972.

Self, P. *Bureaucracy or management?* (London) G. Bell, 1965.

Self, P. 'The organization of government', Letter to the Editor, *The Times* 17 Jan. 1974.

Self, P. *Econocrats and the Policy Process: The Politics and Philosophy of Cost–Benefit Analysis* (London) Macmillan, 1975.

Simon, H. A. *Administrative Behavior: A Study of Decision-Making Processes in Administrative Organization:* First published 1945. Republished (New York) by The Free Press, paperback edn 1965.

Simon, H. A., Smithburg, D. W. and Thompson, V. A. *Public Administration* (New York) A. A. Knopf. First published 1950; twelfth edn 1968.

Slichter, S. H. 'Efficiency', *Encyclopaedia of the Social Sciences*, Vol. V, 1931.

Smith, T. V. 'Ethics', *Encyclopaedia of the Social Sciences*, Vol. V, 1931.

Spriegel, W. R. and Myers, C. E., eds. *The Writings of the Gilbreths* (Homewood, Illinois) R. D. Irwin, 1953.

Subramaniam, V. 'The classical organization theory and its critics', *Public Administration*, Vol. 44, Winter 1966.

Taylor, F. W. *Shop Management* (New York) Harper & Bros., 1911.

Taylor, F. W. *The Principles of Scientific Management* (New York) Harper & Bros. First published 1911; reprinted edn 1913.

Tillett, A. et al., eds. *Management Thinkers* (London) Penguin Books, 1970.

The Times, 23 Nov. 1974.

The Times, 22 Nov. 1975.

Trotter, W. *Instincts of the Herd in Peace and War* (London) T. Fisher Unwin, 1916.

Vernon, R. V. and Mansergh, N. *Advisory Bodies: A Study of their Uses in Relation to Central Government 1919–1939* (London) G. Allen & Unwin, 1940.

Vickers, Sir G. *The Art of Judgment: A Study of Policy-Making* (London) Methuen. First published 1965; paperback edn 1968.

Wade, H. W. R. *Administrative Law* (London) Oxford University Press. Second edn 1967.

Waldo, D. *The Administrative State* (New York) Ronald Press, 1948.

Waldo, D. *The Study of Public Administration* (New York) Doubleday, 1955.

Webb, S. and B. *A Constitution for the Socialist Commonwealth of Great Britain* (London) Longmans, 1920.

Webb, S. and B. *Methods of Social Study* (London) Longmans, 1932.

Webb, B. *Our Partnership*, ed. by B. Drake and M. I. Cole (London) Longmans, 1948.

Weber, M. 'The presuppositions and causes of bureaucracy', reprinted in *Reader in Bureaucracy* ed. by R. K. Merton (New York) The Free Press, 1952.

Welch, H. J. and Myers, C. S. *Ten Years of Industrial Psychology* (London) Pitman, 1932.

White, L. D. *Introduction to the Study of Public Administration*, (New York) Macmillan, 1926.

White, L. D. 'The meaning of principles in public administration' in *The Frontiers of Public Administration*, ed. by J. M. Gaus et al. (Chicago) University of Chicago Press, 1936.

Willis, J. *The Parliamentary Powers of English Government Departments* (Cambridge, Mass.) Harvard University Press, 1933.

Willoughby, W. F. *Principles of Public Administration* (Washington) The Brookings Institution, 1927.

Willoughby, W. F. 'The science of public administration' in *Essays in Political Science in Honor of Westel Woodbury Willoughby* (Baltimore) Johns Hopkins Press, 1937.

Wilson, W. *Congressional Government: A Study in American Politics* (Boston) Houghton Mifflin, 1885; edn 1925.

Wilson, W. 'The study of administration', published as an essay in 1887 and reprinted in *Public Administration and Policy*, ed. by P. Woll (New York) Harper and Row, 1966.

Wise, E. F. 'The Civil Service in its relation to industry and commerce', in *The Civil Servant and His Profession* (London) Pitman, 1920.

Wood, D. 'The Ministers' men invade Whitehall', *The Times*, 10 June 1974.

Young, H. 'The invasion of Whitehall' *The Sunday Times*, 21 Apr. 1974.
'An escape from the machine' *The Times*, 24 Apr. 1973.

Government publications

Administrative Management in the Government of the United States: *Report of the President's Committee on Administrative Management* (Washington) US Government Printing Office, January 1937.

Administrative Management in the United States: Studies on Administrative Management No. 5, *The Exercise of Rule-Making Power* by J. Hart (Washington) US Government Printing Office, 1937.

Committee on Ministers' Powers Report (London) HMSO Cmd 4060 April 1932; reprinted edn 1972.

Department of Health and Social Security, *Management Arrangements for the Reorganised National Health Service* (London) HMSO, 1972.

Industrial Fatigue Research Board, Report No. 14 *Time and Motion Study* General Series No. 5, by E. Farmer (London) HMSO, 1923.

Industrial Fatigue Research Board, Report No. 26, *On the Extent and Effects of Variety in Repetitive Work* (London) HMSO, 1924.

Ministry of Munitions, Health of Munition Workers Committee Interim Report, *Industrial Efficiency and Fatigue* (London) HMSO Cd 8511, 1917.

Ministry of Munitions, Health of Munition Workers Committee Handbook, *The Health of the Munition Worker* (London) HMSO, 1917.

Ministry of Munitions, Health of Munition Workers Committee, Memorandum No. 1, *Sunday Labour* (London) HMSO Cd 8132.

Ministry of Munitions, Health of Munition Workers Committee, Memorandum No. 2, *Welfare Supervision* (London) HMSO Cd 8151.

Ministry of Munitions. Health of Munition Workers Committee, Memorandum No. 3, *Industrial Canteens* (London) HMSO Cd 8133.

Ministry of Munitions. Health of Munition Workers Committee, Memorandum No. 4, *Employment of Women* (London) HMSO Cd 8185.

Ministry of Munitions. Health of Munition Workers Committee, Memorandum No. 5, *Hours of Work* (London) HMSO Cd 8186.

Ministry of Munitions. Health of Munition Workers Committee, Memorandum No. 6, *Canteen Construction and Equipment: Appendix to No. 3.* (London) HMSO Cd 8199.

Ministry of Munitions. Health of Munition Workers Committee, Memorandum No. 7, *Industrial Fatigue and its Causes* (London) HMSO Cd 8213.

Ministry of Munitions. Health of Munition Workers Committee, Memorandum No. 8, *Special Industrial Diseases* (London) HMSO Cd 8214.

Ministry of Munitions. Health of Munition Workers Committee, Memorandum No. 9, *Ventilation and Lighting of Munition Factories and Workshops* (London) HMSO Cd 8215.

Ministry of Munitions. Health of Munition Workers Committee, Memorandum No. 10, *Sickness and Injury* (London) HMSO Cd 8216.

Ministry of Munitions. Health of Munition Workers Committee, Memorandum No. 11, *Investigation of Workers' Food and Suggestions as to Dietary: Second Appendix to No. 3.* (London) HMSO Cd 8370.

Ministry of Munitions. Health of Munition Workers Committee Memorandum No. 12 *Statistical Information concerning Output in relation to Hours of Work* (London) HMSO Cd 8344.

Ministry of Munitions. Health of Munition Workers Committee, Memorandum No. 13, *Juvenile Employment* (London) HMSO Cd 8362.

Ministry of Munitions. Health of Munition Workers Committee, Memorandum No. 14, *Washing Facilities and Baths* (London) HMSO Cd 8387.

Ministry of Munitions. Health of Munition Workers Committee, Memorandum No. 15, *The Effect of Industrial Conditions upon Eyesight* (London) HMSO, Cd 8409.

Ministry of Munitions. Health of Munition Workers Committee, Memorandum No. 16, *Medical Certificates for Munition Workers* (London) HMSO Cd 8522.

Ministry of Munitions. Health of Munition Workers Committee, Memorandum No. 17, *Health and Welfare of Munition Workers outside the Factory* (this Memorandum remained unpublished).

Ministry of Munitions. Health of Munition Workers Committee, Memorandum No. 18, *Further Statistical Information concerning Output in Relation to Hours of Work, with special reference to the Influence of Sunday Labour* (London) HMSO Cd 8628.

Ministry of Munitions. Health of Munition Workers Committee, Memorandum No. 19, *Investigation of Workers' Food and Suggestions as to Dietary: Second Appendix to No. 3 Revised edn* (London) HMSO Cd 8798.

Ministry of Munitions. Health of Munition Workers Committee, Memorandum No. 20, *Weekly Hours of Employment: Supplementary to Memorandum No. 5* (London) HMSO Cd 8801.

Ministry of Reconstruction. *The Business of Government,* Reconstruction Pamphlets No. 38 (London) HMSO. Three parts, 1919.

Papers Relating to the President's Departmental Reorganization Program (Washington) US Printing Office, Feb. 1972.

Report of the Royal Commission on Standards of Conduct in Public Life 1974-1976 (London) HMSO Cmnd 6524, July 1976.

Report of the Royal Commission on the Civil Service 1929-31 (London) HMSO Cmd 3909, 1931.

Royal Commission on the Civil Service, Fourth Report of the Commissioners (London) HMSO Cd 7338, 1914. Majority Report.

Royal Commission on the Constitution, 1969-1973, Vol. II, *Memorandum of Dissent,* by Lord Crowther-Hunt and Professor A. T. Peacock (London) HMSO Cmnd 5460-1, 1973.

The Civil Service Vol. I Report of the Committee (Fulton) 1966-68 (London) HMSO Cmnd 3638, 1968.

White Paper, *The Reorganisation of Central Government* (London) HMSO Cmnd 4506, Oct. 1970.

Index

absolutism, 10
Adams, W. G. S., 21
administration,
  administrative man, 65
  attitudes towards, 6, 33
  definition of, 4, 60–1
  delays in, *see* bureaucracy; rule of
    the bureau
  effect of democracy on, 10
  ethical aims of, 24; *see also* ethical
    idealism; eithics of
    administration
  human element in, 2, 6, 20, 26, 80,
    111
  politics – administration
    dichotomy, *see* politics
  Prussian, 10
  schools of, 30–1, 240–1
  science of, *see* science of
    administration
  scientific principles of, *see*
    POSDCORB principles;
    SLOCUS principles
  study of, 7, 24–5, 72, 240–1
  theory of, 3, 29–30
administrative law, *see* bureaucracy;
    power of officials
Admiralty, *see* British Civil Service,
    departments of
adult education, 140, 161
Albrow, M., 201, 202–3n, 205n, 226n
Allen, C. K., 206n
altruism, 141, 155
American administrative thought and
    practice, 2–6, 26–7, 30, 70,
    111–12, 137, 238–9
  traditional doctrines, 1–3, 5–20,
    26–7, 29, 32, 100, 235–40
    see also business

administration; human
    relations theory; politics
    and administration,
    separation of; POSDCORB
    principles; public
    administration
American Federal Civil Service, 6–8,
    74, 85, 136, 215
  departments of, 80, 83
    Bureau of Budget, 85
    giant, 136
    Treasury, 80, 84
  merit system, 8, 34
  party influence, 33–4, 237
  spoils system, 8, 33–4
  training of civil servants, 236–7
  see also Pendleton Act;
    President's Committee on
    Administrative
    Management
American government, 19, 33–4, 49,
    136–7
  Cabinet, 8
  congressional, 53, 68, 83, 85
  constitution of US, 6–7, 34–5, 53,
    83
  differences between British and,
    6–10, 22, 33
  executive branch, 9, 34, 53, 71, 74,
    79–85, 136, 230
  institutions of, *see* political
    institutions
  judiciary, 9, 34, 67, 84
  legislative branch, 9, 34, 53, 202,
    215
  President (Chief Executive), 8–9,
    30, 34, 74, 77, 81–5, 136, 230
  separation of powers, 9, 23, 34,
    52–3, 68, 229